SAP® Governance, Risk, and Compliance

 PRESS

SAP PRESS is a joint initiative of SAP and Galileo Press. The know-how offered by SAP specialists combined with the expertise of the publishing house Galileo Press offers the reader expert books in the field. SAP PRESS features first-hand information and expert advice, and provides useful skills for professional decision-making.

SAP PRESS offers a variety of books on technical and business related topics for the SAP user. For further information, please visit our website: www.sap-press.com.

Shivesh Sharma
Optimize Your SAP ERP Financials Implementation
2008, 696 pp.
978-1-59229-160-1

Manish Patel
Discover SAP ERP Financials
2008, 544 pp.
978-1-59229-184-7

Aylin Korkmaz
Financial Reporting with SAP
2008, 672 pp.
978-1-59229-179-3

Paul Theobald
Migrate Successfully to the New SAP GL
2007, 104 pp.
1-978-159229-166-3

Sabine Schöler, Olaf Zink

SAP® Governance, Risk, and Compliance

Galileo Press

Bonn • Boston

ISBN 978-1-59229-191-5

© 2009 by Galileo Press Inc., Boston (MA)

1st Edition 2009

German Edition first published 2008 by Galileo Press, Bonn, Germany.

Galileo Press is named after the Italian physicist, mathematician and philosopher Galileo Galilei (1564–1642). He is known as one of the founders of modern science and an advocate of our contemporary, heliocentric worldview. His words *Eppur si muove* (And yet it moves) have become legendary. The Galileo Press logo depicts Jupiter orbited by the four Galilean moons, which were discovered by Galileo in 1610.

Editor   Eva Tripp
English Edition Editor   Stephen Solomon
Translation   Lemoine International, Inc., Salt Lake City UT
Copyeditor   Julie McNamee
Cover Design   Jill Winitzer/Nadine Kohl
Photo Credit   Getty Images/Joel Sartore
Layout Design   Vera Brauner
Production   Kelly O'Callaghan
Typesetting   Publishers' Design and Production Services, Inc.
Printed and bound in Canada

Contents at a Glance

Contents

Introduction

A cursory glance at the daily papers shows that corporate governance, compliance, and risk management are highly topical issues. Even global enterprises such as Siemens and Volkswagen are finding it difficult to deal with increasingly insistent allegations of bribery and violation of compliance regulations. Even though, within enterprises, guidelines are usually in effect that specify external and internal compliance requirements, these enterprises often simply don't have the best IT tools that would enable them to integrate preventive measures, in particular, into their daily operations. The aim of such measures is to stop critical, unanticipated situations from occurring in the first place, if at all possible.

Target Audience

This book deals with all of the processes and components of the SAP solutions for governance, risk, and compliance (SAP solutions for GRC). Focusing on Process Control, Access Control and Risk Management, it presents application scenarios and configuration options for GRC. Each chapter first looks at the underlying business aspects of its topic and then uses several practical examples to illustrate the application and configuration of the software.

This book is targeted primarily at those people responsible for GRC within enterprises who want to become familiar with the scope of the SAP solutions for GRC software on the basis of typical application scenarios. The book also provides decision-makers in enterprises and IT departments, such as project leaders and project team members, with a useful overview of the subject that includes many ideas on how to use SAP solutions for GRC software in practice.

Target audience

The content of this book, including the screenshots, is based on the following releases:

Release status

11

- ▸ SAP GRC Process Control: Release 2.5
- ▸ SAP GRC Access Control: Release 5.2
- ▸ SAP GRC Risk Management: Release 2.0

Moreover, in the interest of being as up to date as possible, we've incorporated all of the functional additions and changes that were made right up to the time of printing.

Structure of the Book

This book is divided into the following chapters:

Overview **Chapter 1**, Overview of SAP Solutions for Governance, Risk, and Compliance, gives you an overall view of the general business problems associated with governance, risk, and compliance, and presents the range of SAP solutions to these problems. We also introduce you to a sample company that we'll use in typical application scenarios throughout the book.

SAP GRC Process **Chapter 2**, SAP GRC Process Control, deals with the SAP application for
Control process control. SAP GRC Process Control provides a risk-based procedure for creating a control framework and for indicating the most effective and powerful controls for business processes and cross-enterprise IT systems. In this chapter, we demonstrate how you can build and maintain in your system the required cross-enterprise data structures (organization, controls, risks, etc.) to ensure that you're in compliance with legal regulations. We use the example of a control design assessment to help you understand the corresponding maintenance dialogs. This chapter also shows you how to use automatic tests as well as manual ones. SAP GRC Process Control makes it unnecessary to integrate different applications for documentation, assessment and checks, remediation, and continual monitoring. Because SAP GRC Process Control is a packaged solution, all you have to do, for some areas of system configuration, is to activate SAP standard functions or various services once. Lastly, we describe the main configuration activities.

Chapter 3, SAP GRC Access Control, deals with the SAP application for comprehensive cross-enterprise access controls. SAP GRC Access Control enables you to define roles on a cross-enterprise level in a coordinated manner and to correctly execute and monitor the separation of functions. SAP GRC Access Control also provides you with functions for managing role definitions at a cross-enterprise level, for role provision and for authorized "superusers." This chapter explains the following main application scenarios:

- ▶ Risk analysis and remediation
- ▶ Enterprise role management
- ▶ Compliant user provisioning
- ▶ Superuser privilege management

Furthermore, it goes on to describe the essential configuration steps.

Chapter 4, SAP GRC Risk Management, shows how you can use the application to identify and document risks, and how these risks can be monitored and reduced by means of an effective internal control system. In this chapter, you'll learn, among other things, how to identify the relevant phases of the risk management process and how to implement the overall process across organizational and departmental boundaries throughout the enterprise. Besides the maintenance of the central organizational hierarchy, this chapter also describes in detail how to maintain and manage the required risks and activities catalogs. You'll also learn how to document activities and risks and how to carry out a risk analysis both with and without a risk management response option. SAP GRC Risk Management thus provides a generic framework of risk management methods for processes in all business areas. This enables you to identify and proactively monitor the risks, such as the financial, legal, and operational risks, of new business areas.

In this chapter, you'll also learn to what extent relevant users in all levels of the enterprise can use the available reports, dashboards, and so on to obtain transparent information about the current risk profile. Finally, you'll see that in many customizing activities, you only have to activate standard SAP functions or various services once. This chapter also makes specific recommendations in relation to configuration.

SAP GRC Global
Trade Services

Chapter 5, SAP GRC Global Trade Services – This chapter provides you an overview of the business scenarios for managing the requirements of cross-border goods trade. This involves compliance with legal control for import and export, sanctioned party lists, and local and regional requirements. The business scenarios are divided into three areas: compliance management, customs management, and management of financial risks and opportunities.

SAP Environment,
Health & Safety

Chapter 6, SAP Environment, Health & Safety – An Overview, gives you a brief introduction to the range of functions offered by this application. These functions include, in particular, business scenarios for environmental protection, occupational health, safety and industrial hygiene, and safety.

Chapter 7, An Outlook Ahead and a Product Roadmap, provides an overview of SAP's go-to-market strategy and a look at the SAP solutions for GRC product roadmap.

Acknowledgements

In comparison with other SAP products, the SAP product offering for IT-based support of governance, risk, and compliance in enterprises is still in its infancy. Knowledge of the newest and most up-to-date functions of the individual modules was required to properly formulate and present these components in this book. We would certainly never have been able to attain this level of knowledge without the help and insight of many colleagues. In particular, thanks are due to the SAP solutions for GRC product group team. We would also like to thank those colleagues who contributed their expert know-how to the text by carefully proofreading it and making valuable suggestions: Frank Rambo, Andreas Offermann, and Angela Wahl-Knoblauch.

Sincere thanks are also due to Eva Tripp at SAP PRESS, who supported us all the way, from the initial idea for this book project right up to the printing stage.

Sabine Schöler and **Olaf Zink**

Caution is the parent of safety. (Proverb)

1 Overview of SAP Solutions for Governance, Risk, and Compliance

In this chapter, we use a comprehensive practical example to describe external and internal compliance requirements. First, we acquaint you with our fictitious sample company. Then, using a sample set of problems as a basis, we give you an overview of the SAP product portfolio for governance, risk, and compliance.

1.1 Sample Company

In this section, we introduce you to our company, *Energy Without Plug (EWP)*. The company's business goal is to develop and sell energy supply solutions that obtain their energy from fuel cells.

Introducing the sample company

Fuel cells require oxygen and hydrogen, which react chemically with each other to create electricity and heat. A by-product of this process is water. The fuel cells developed by EWP are integrated into electricity supply systems, such as generators, and are a mobile and network-independent method of electricity generation.

EWP was founded six years ago by Thomas Schmidt and Andreas Schwarz, who are also the managing directors. Thanks to the company's success in the market, the company now has more than 100 employees. Its Procurement department organizes the acquisition of the fuel cell components from various suppliers. The job of the Production department is to assemble and further develop the fuel cells. The mass production of the components takes place in a plant in Switzerland, and the final assembly of the devices is done in the Netherlands. The Sales department is responsible for finding new application areas and for increasing sales of the existing solutions. Because it intends to enter promising markets in Europe, the United States, and Africa, EWP has also opened sales offices in these regions. In addition to these departments, the company has an accountant, an administrator, and an IT team. The following org chart illustrates the overall organizational structure of the company (see Figure 1.1).

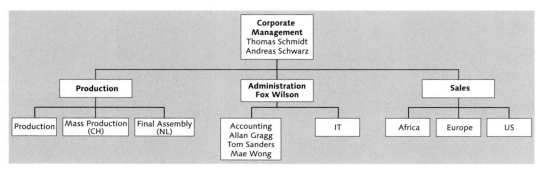

Figure 1.1   Org Chart of the Sample Company

The IT challenge

EWP has been a user of SAP for one year and has implemented additional functions of the SAP ERP portfolio. However, Thomas Schmidt and Andreas Schwarz are looking for additional IT support. They want satisfactory answers to the following questions:

▶ How can we gain an understanding of what business processes affect what figures in our company? What are our options for setting up internal controls?

▶ How can we overcome the risk of employee fraud? How can we protect our data and know-how from unauthorized access?

▶ How can we systematically identify and manage business risks?

▶ How can we ensure that we don't violate any embargo regulations? Are we handling our customs processing properly?

▶ How can we safely transport our procured goods and finished products?

Because Schmidt and Schwarz are committed SAP customers, they first ask SAP whether the SAP product portfolio contains a solution package that will answer their questions. And they aren't disappointed; they find out about the products that come under the heading of SAP solutions for governance, risk, and compliance (SAP GRC).

1.2   Motivation and Goals of the GRC Project

Noncompliance with regulations is simply not an option. From the viewpoint of EWP, it doesn't matter whether these are legal regulations or internal company guidelines. EWP's goal is to adhere to each individual regulation as closely as possible. EWP intends to cover the entire range of GRC by making individual investments. At the same time, it wants to minimize its investment in individual measures as much as possible.

But what does SAP mean by governance, risk, and compliance (see Figure 1.2)?

What is GRC?

▶ Governance management implements the strategic direction that leads to the enterprise's goals.

▶ Risk management assesses the business areas that are at risk and evaluates the possible effects of the risks.

▶ Compliance comprises the daily measures that are required to circumvent the identified risks to minimize as much as possible—and with an appropriate investment of time and resources—the potential damage to the enterprise.

Based on this definition, governance management, risk management, and compliance may appear to have little to do with each other. There is uncertainty on a company-wide level in EWP about how and to what degree the requirements are supposed to be implemented in the individual departments, on the country level, and throughout the group.

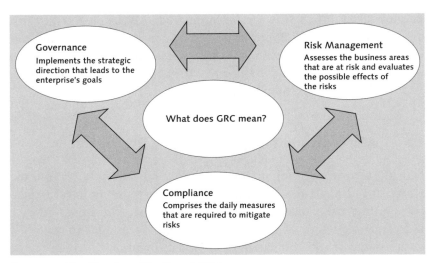

Figure 1.2 The Meaning of the Term "GRC"

Integrating GRC

However, the goal of the SAP solution for GRC is to support an integrated GRC framework. Until now, the managing directors of EWP didn't know that it's possible to get support for a holistic GRC framework. Nor are the benefits of an integrated GRC framework immediately obvious to them. So why is a holistic GRC framework desirable?

Fragmentation of GRC in enterprises

Let's consider the situation of companies who have implemented individual solutions rather than a uniform GRC framework (see Figure 1.3).

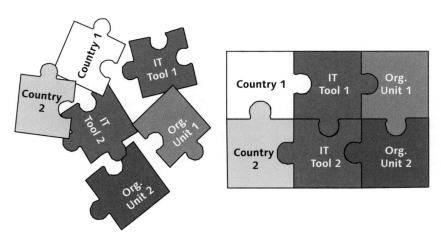

Figure 1.3 Typical Standalone Solutions in a GRC Implementation

In most cases, the requirements are implemented on the departmental level. If there are various implementation options, differences between each department and the other entities in the enterprise are inevitable.

The following scenario occurred at EWP. If devices belong to a new application area, a pilot application has to be tested and approved in advance. In the Africa sales area, fuel cells were sold to provide energy for water pumps in Kenya.

Example

Even though this was the first application scenario involving water pumps in the history of EWP, the sales representative in Africa decided to sell 100 fuel cells straight off, without first implementing a pilot application. When this omission was noticed at headquarters, it was too late; the contract had already been signed with the customer. As a result, the delivery period for the 100 units had to be prolonged, as the pilot phase had to be carried out before production of the order. This was because the management of EWP insisted that the pilot phase be implemented, even if this meant inconveniencing the customer. To minimize the risk of all 100 fuel cell units breaking down, a single unit first had to be inspected to establish how suitable the fuel cells were for supplying energy to water pumps in the local climate and other environmental conditions. In the pilot phase, the production team found that to function properly in the climatic conditions that the fuel cell would be exposed to when in use with water pumps, additional protective measures and more powerful cooling aggregates would be required. This led to higher production costs, which considerably reduced overall profit. However, because no further measures or developments were required to ensure the long-term functioning of the cells after the successful pilot phase, the financial losses were not excessive. The inconvenience caused to the customer by the delayed delivery was also minimized after the long-term reliability of the systems became obvious. Nonetheless, the sales representative's commission was proportionally reduced in line with the increased production costs.

If the central requirements are not known in the individual departments, or if the departments have a lot of discretion in the matter, this causes the requirements to be implemented inconsistently. As a result, it becomes increasingly difficult to predict risks, there is a lack of transparency, and work may be duplicated.

Inconsistent implementation of requirements

In many enterprises, different systems are used to map legal and internal company requirements. The following scenario occurred at EWP. Customs processing at EWP is done mainly on a manual basis. In the past, the final assembly warehouse in the Netherlands handled shipping. The relevant tasks were thus "bundled" in a single party. However, final assembly warehouses were then set up in the United States and Africa. In one case, a shipment to Libya had to be stopped at the last minute because the sales staff and employees in Africa who were handling the shipment locally were unaware of the consequences that making a shipment to Libya could have on business relationships with customers in other countries. The shipment was canceled (and again, the sales representative's commission was cut accordingly).

Having no system support, or non-centralized system support, leads to a situation where employees in different locations use different methods and work procedures. Also, in this kind of situation, risks and important business data are reported on according to the individual user's preferences. This in turn makes it a very complex matter to merge data from the individual areas. Individual solutions themselves can be used for piecemeal reporting only, which gives only a limited perspective on the risks.

Country-specific regulations

Globally active companies also have to deal with the requirement to fulfill country-specific regulations. Even though EWP isn't listed on the New York Stock Exchange, the company aims to comply with SOX.

Sarbanes-Oxley Act

The *Sarbanes-Oxley Act* (SOX) has been in force in the United States since 2002 in an effort to prevent financial accounting scandals. It is binding for all companies that are publicly listed in the United States. SOX aims also to monitor business processes and improve audit ability. As you might guess, support from IT applications plays a major role.

EWP believes it can only enhance the value of the company to voluntarily comply with country-specific regulations. Thus, if the company expands to Japan in the next few years, the intention is to comply with *Japanese SOX* as well, which is valid from 2008.

A uniform GRC framework would enable EWP to monitor the implementation of the various regional regulations and to consolidate its results on a global level in the future.

The bigger a company is, the higher the number of departments and divisions that have to deal with different requirements in terms of GRC. Examples of these different departments are Finance, Health and Safety, Global Trade, and Dangerous Goods Transport. The challenges are to ensure that all entities reach the same goals, the measures involved are unified, and the status is transparent.

GRC-relevant reports

The following scenario occurred at EWP. A global company guideline in the Finance area specifies that employees who create an order may not themselves initiate the payment of the corresponding invoice. For the first two months of the African subsidiary's existence, it had just one employee. When authorizations were set up in the system, this employee was granted all of the authorizations required to run the daily business of the subsidiary. In other words, from the IT viewpoint, the segregation of duties specified by headquarters was not implemented. Employees from Germany were integrated into the approval processes as a supporting measure on a short-term basis. Now, the African subsidiary employs 10 people, and the specified segregation of duties needs to be implemented within the company.

Example

The examples described previously show the consequences of using a standalone approach for GRC requirements.

The holistic approach made possible by a GRC framework helps to prevent duplicate work. Compliance tasks can be systematically integrated into daily operations. Also, results are more transparent and predictable. The outcome of all this is that management can make business decisions on the basis of a systematic risk analysis. This enables the company to achieve a competitive advantage that in turn enhances investor confidence.

Benefits of an integrated GRC approach

The GRC maturity model can be used to make this quite general description of benefits more concrete. The aim of the GRC maturity model is to pinpoint the current location of an enterprise and to create a realistic roadmap for implementing a GRC framework. The model has four phases (see Figure 1.4).

GRC maturity model

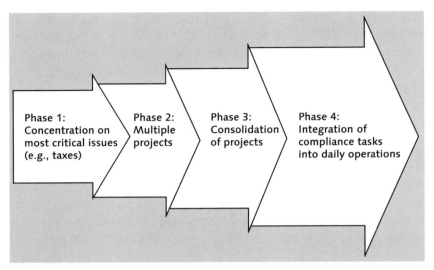

Figure 1.4 Maturity Model

Phase 1   In the first phase, enterprises concentrate on the most obvious and most critical compliance issues. This includes the fulfillment of external requirements. Financial statements have to satisfy the requirements of the financial authorities; tax declarations must be based on legal specifications; and export and import transactions have to be processed in accordance with embargo lists and customs regulations. This phase usually applies to small companies whose main focus is on daily operations. The main issues are business processing, the necessary financing, and customer satisfaction. Another characteristic of this phase is that there is little or no investment in tools and guidelines to satisfy GRC requirements.

Phase 2   In the second phase, a range of GRC projects is set up in the enterprise to implement legal and regional requirements. This includes company-specific requirements that need to be fulfilled to manage flexible business models. These initiatives are usually tactical in nature; in other words, they are set up where there is a specific need to manage compliance tasks.

In many cases, management is uncertain in this phase about whether the high number of compliance tasks can be implemented to the required quality level and with the required transparency of results. Different teams work on compliance tasks on an as-needed basis. The measures are set up in such a way that it's possible to react to requirements at short notice. Compliance tasks in this phase are not merged in any systematic or goal-oriented way. Because there is no central guiding instance, duplicate work is a possibility in this phase.

The uncertainty on the part of management usually means that a "stock-taking" process has to be carried out. What compliance requirements have to be fulfilled? What initiatives have been set up to fulfill these requirements? The answers to these questions provide management with an initial overview of the risks. Also, an overview of ongoing initiatives and the teams involved can be used to calculate the costs of compliance activities.

In the third phase, the standalone solutions are merged and consolidated. An enterprise-wide GRC framework is set up. Individual departments are identified that could be suitable as pilots for the step-by-step, enterprise-wide implementation of the GRC framework. After the pilot has been successfully completed, the implementation is rolled out throughout the enterprise until the final result of a uniform GRC framework is achieved. The status of the compliance activities and the risks to the enterprise can be reported on and consolidated as the final outcome of this phase.

Phase 3

The fourth phase is characterized by the integration of GRC tasks into daily operations. This integration process is largely automatic, thanks to the use of ERP software and the appropriate GRC applications that are based on them. This automation gives management an overview of all of the business processes and projects that are used or set up to carry out the GRC tasks. All organizational levels of the enterprise are involved in this phase. Consistent terminology and metrics are essential for good communication in this phase.

Phase 4

General empirical data shows that it takes between two and five years for an organization to progress through the individual phases and to reach the *operational excellence* maturity level in phase four.

EWP pinpoints its location on the borderline between phases two and three. It has set up various GRC projects, but management has no over-view of who is doing what, and when — the kind of overview that would help the company fulfill internal and external guidelines. Therefore, the company has to accept the possibility of duplicate work and, in particular, a lack of transparency regarding GRC activities. Managing directors Schmidt and Schwarz decide to respond to this situation. First, a "stock-taking" process is carried out of all external and internal guidelines. All GRC projects and tasks are listed, and at the same time, the directors research the SAP solutions for GRC.

SAP GRC solutions   The SAP GRC solutions offering are designed to build on and, if required, to extend the GRC-specific function modules of existing business processes. It takes into account that individual business processes consist of several individual steps. The business processes usually extend beyond departmental boundaries, and their technical support comes from different applications and systems.

The SAP GRC solutions portfolio enables companies to create a GRC framework within their organizations. This portfolio currently consists of the components described next (see Figure 1.5).

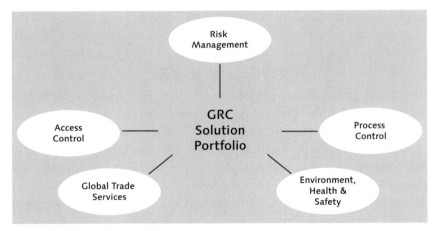

Figure 1.5   GRC Solution Offering

SAP GRC Access Control   *SAP GRC Access Control* ensures that employees perform only those tasks that are specified by a systematic segregation of duty. This is achieved by means of a system of restricted IT authorizations. SAP GRC Access Control uses functions to support a process in which only those system authorizations are assigned that don't jeopardize the secure operation of the processes, throughout all phases of the IT lifecycle (planning, implementation and testing, and operations with monitoring). This component takes into account the fact that new hires, terminations, and job changes within the enterprise are part of daily operations.

SAP GRC Process Control provides companies with an overview of the controls within their business processes on a company-wide level. It allows automatic and manual controls to be set up, which can be monitored, tested, evaluated, and, if required, transferred back to a noncritical stage by means of counter-measures.

SAP GRC Process Control

SAP GRC Risk Management is used to represent the negative effects in legal or financial terms of potential business deals. This component supports companies in identifying risks. It thus enables the affected company departments to identify and evaluate risks, and, if possible, to take measures to prevent or minimize these risks. An analysis of the degree of effectiveness of any such measures is also part of the functional scope of this component.

SAP GRC Risk Management

SAP GRC Global Trade Services supports the business processes and requirements involved in cross-border goods trade. This support includes compliance with the many different legal regulations and mapping of the customs processes that apply to procurement and sales. It also provides functions that help companies take advantage of benefits in global trade while minimizing any financial risks.

SAP GRC Global Trade Services

SAP Environment, Health & Safety (SAP EH&S) supports the requirements that companies have to fulfill in terms of the environment and social responsibility. This component includes functions for ensuring chemical safety, compliance with product-specific environmental regulations, and compliance with environmental protection, health, and industrial hygiene and safety regulations.

SAP Environment, Health & Safety

We'll look in more detail at each individual component in the following chapters.

The more laws and restrictions there are, the poorer people become. The more rules and regulations, the more thieves and robbers. (Lev Kopelev)

2   SAP GRC Process Control

In this chapter, you'll first learn the objectives of SAP GRC Process Control. You can use the application to introduce uniform automated control tests in procurement, sales order processing, and financial reporting across all departments and business areas.

We'll then illustrate in detail how you can set up and maintain the necessary organizational structure for adhering to legal requirements in the system. After we've uploaded or documented the organizational hierarchy, controls, control objectives, risks, sub-processes, and processes generally using an initial data upload, we'll describe how you can assign the relevant central processes to the particular organizations. You'll also learn how to assign users to their roles and how to create and plan a survey for example for a control design assessment. You'll learn about the necessary system steps or corresponding maintenance dialog using the example of a control design assessment.

You see how to use automatic tests in addition to manual tests. You'll be able to define rules or access a total of 200 predefined control rules for automatically testing or monitoring controls. Finally, you'll learn that you can use the provided analysis dashboards and reports to display the current status and relevant results for the different assessments and various monitoring activities very easily and, at the same time, very clearly at any time. This will enable you to analyze and assess the current situation of the company very quickly.

The system configuration of SAP GRC Process Control contains 13 sub areas in total. Mainly standard SAP functions or different services are activated once for some of these areas only. If required, you can define customer-specific data fields in the *User-Defined Fields* area. The *Administration Programs* area in particular makes functions available for managing and monitoring SAP GRC Process Control-specific workflows for system operation. Because SAP GRC Process Control is a packaged solution, the actual Customizing activities primarily take place in the *Attributes*, *Assessment*, and *Test* areas only.

2.1 Objectives of SAP GRC Process Control

Risk-based approach
SAP GRC Process Control takes a risk-based approach. In addition to identifying the most efficient controls for a corporation, the application enables you to set up and operationally use an effective control environment.

Sarbanes-Oxley Act, Section 404
The control documentation of SAP GRC Process Control guarantees company-wide and a uniform control management and thereby contributes to fulfilling the key requirements of Section 404 of the Sarbanes-Oxley Act. This control documentation approach as well as other functions of SAP GRC Process Control means that separate applications for documentation, tests, problem solving, and monitoring controls are a scenario of the past. With SAP GRC Process Control, you no longer have to retrospectively integrate separate sub-applications expensively in terms of costs and personnel required.

Employees can act in accordance with rules and regulations
Employees are also supported in such a way when operationally using SAP GRC Process Control and implementing effective controls that they can act in accordance with rules and regulations. Companies can also ensure that they implement legal requirements on time and effectively. This contributes not least to a significantly more cost-efficient business optimization of business processes.

Automatically testing or monitoring controls
You can also use SAP GRC Process Control to implement controls for risks based on control monitoring, self-assessments, and manual tests. In other words, you can use SAP GRC Process Control to assess the control design and tests and evaluate the effectiveness of the internal control system, another key requirement of Section 404 of SOX. You'll also be able to introduce standard automated control tests, for example, in procurement, sales order processing, and financial reporting across all depart-

ments and business areas. In particular, this will considerably reduce the monitoring and resource effort required for manual control testing to some extent. The automated monitoring functions of SAP GRC Process Control enable an effective alignment to the COBIT framework.

The standard SAP workflow functions which are used for SAP GRC Process Control includes sending manual control test tasks automatically to the employees responsible. Furthermore, the data model of the application enables you to provide and attach detailed test instructions and approved test templates, according to which manual control test tasks are to be performed. You can therefore reduce possible errors to a minimum during manual control tests. You can use functions for creating and sending surveys to perform self-assessments for controls very easily and flexibly at the level of individual units. These survey functions you can also use for the sign-off process in accordance with Section 302 of SOX .

Sarbanes-Oxley Act, Section 302

You can use a global heat map to display violations of control regulations, resulting risks, and the priority of remediation measures. Managers and the people responsible for the internal control system will therefore be able to recognize quickly and easily where the need for action is required. They will also be able to prioritize documented corrective measures and thereby prevent high process risks. An automatic corrective measure is generated in SAP GRC Process Control for each exceptional case. Employees and managers responsible can be notified immediately using exception handling. This approach means that risks can be quickly contained, prevented, or diminished by correspondingly initiating remediation measures.

Current status can be quickly analyzed and assessed

2.2 SAP GRC Process Control – Application

SAP GRC Process Control has seven functional areas in terms of content: *My Home, Compliance Structure, Evaluation Setup, Evaluation Results, Certification, Reporting Center,* and *User Access.*

Figure 2.1 shows that **My Home** has four detail functions. You can use the **Work Inbox** to display the complete list of your workflow tasks. In the **My Processes** area, you can access and maintain processes, sub-processes, and controls that you are authorized to access. You use **Reports**

My Home

and **Analytics** or the **Analytics Dashboard** link to access analytic reports that are based on test and assessment results for adhering to legal requirements. You use the **My Entity-Level Controls** link to access and maintain management controls you are authorized to access.

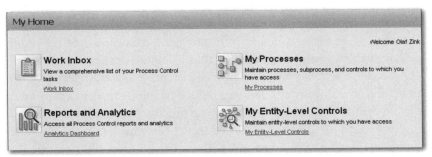

Figure 2.1 My Home

The *Compliance Structure* menu area encompasses five detail functions. Figure 2.2 shows that you can set up and manage the organization structure of the company under **Organizations**. You also assign sub-processes and management controls (entity-levels) at organization level. You can also identify the organizational unit as a Shared Services Provider and thereby release the corresponding sub-processes and controls.

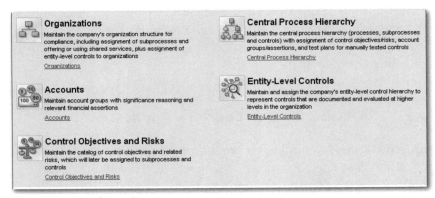

Figure 2.2 Compliance Structure

Compliance Structure

In the **Accounts** application area, you can maintain accounts and account groups with significance reasoning and relevant financial assertions. You use the **Control Objectives and Risks** function to define and manage the catalog of control objectives and relevant risks throughout the company and subsequently assign it to sub-processes and controls.

You can maintain and manage processes, sub-processes, and controls within the **Central Process Hierarchy** area. Here you can also assign control objectives/risks, account groups/assertions, and test plans for manually tested controls. You can use the **Entity-Level Controls** function to set up, assign, and maintain the entity-level controls or management controls of a company.

The *Evaluation Setup* menu area covers six detail applications (see Figure 2.3). In the **Assessment Surveys** area, you can document, store, and reuse questions in a Questions Library. You can use the Survey Library to create and store surveys easily with the help of the Questions Library for assessments relating to the control design, sub-process design and management controls, and self assessments. You can also use the survey function for the sign-off process.

Evaluation Setup

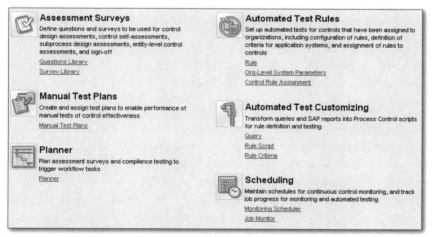

Figure 2.3 Application Area for Assessments and Tests

You can create and assign **Manual Test Plans**, which are used for performing manual tests for control effectiveness, using the function of the same name.

With the function in the **Planner** area, you plan the tests and assessment surveys, which are used to adhere to legal requirements, for a certain period of time and therefore trigger the sending of the corresponding workflow tasks.

You define rules for automatically testing controls using the **Automated Test Rules** function. You use the **Rule** navigation link to go directly to the rule configuration. You define the rule criteria for the system parameters of the target systems using the **Org-Level System Parameters** function. You use the **Control Rule Assignment** navigation link to assign rules to selected controls.

You can use the **Automated Test Customizing** application area to include queries and standard SAP reports in at least a semi-automated[1] way in the existing infrastructure for automated testing using the **Query**, **Rule Script**, and **Rule Criteria** functions.

You use the functions in the **Scheduling** area to initiate relevant control monitoring activities using the **Monitoring Scheduler** navigation link. You can also use the **Job Monitor** function to monitor whether the execution of a report or query has already been completed in the target system. In addition, in the *Results* column in the job monitor, you can display the confirmed monitoring results in detail from the relevant target system.

Evaluation Results
The *Evaluation Results* menu area consists of three detail applications. You can use the *My Tasks* function to display all your assessment, test, issues and remediation tasks. You can also perform the corresponding assessments from here.

In the *Monitoring* functional area, you can evaluate the workflow tasks assigned to the relevant user, which aren't used for adhering to legal requirements, for control monitoring. You can also display and process issues that are still open and track and maintain your own remediation measures in relation to control monitoring. The results of control monitoring aren't incorporated into the Analytics Dashboard reports and, consequently, are therefore not available to external auditors.

You can use the *Compliance* application area to evaluate the workflow tasks assigned to the relevant user for tests and assessments that are

---

1 Semi-automated because these reports and queries can be managed and scheduled in the corresponding target systems from SAP GRC Process Control. In this scenario, however, you currently still have to perform the necessary analyses and evaluations of the results manually.

used for adhering to legal or compliance requirements. You can also display and process issues that are still open and track and manage your own remediation measures. The assessment results are incorporated into the Analytics Dashboard reports and are therefore available to external auditors.

The *Certification* menu area contains the sign-off monitor and the planner. You can use the *Sign-off Monitor* function to monitor the sign-off status for the assigned areas of responsibility. This supports a swift implementation of the sign-off process in the company. You use the *Planner* function to plan and trigger the corresponding workflow tasks for the organizations that are subject to sign-off.

Certification

Figure 2.4 shows that the *Reporting Center* menu area has six reporting areas consisting of **Structure and Setup**, **Roles and Authorizations**, **Evaluation**, **Monitoring**, **Audit and Analysis**, and **Certification**. Each of these reporting areas contains several different evaluation reports. A total of 29 standard evaluation reports are available in the Reporting Center.

Reporting Center

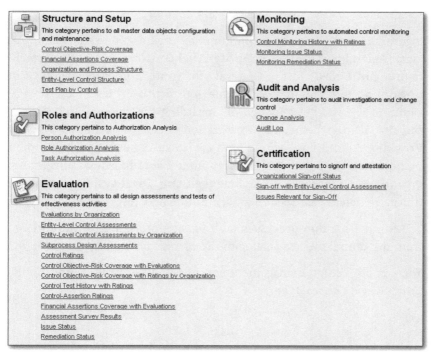

Figure 2.4 Reporting Center

User access

The last menu area, *User Access*, has two functional areas consisting of *Roles* and *Delegation*. You can use the *Roles and Their Tasks* navigation link to maintain the role assignments that control user access to application data and functions. In addition, you can use the *Successor/Remove* function to maintain a user's corresponding successor when the user leaves the company. You use the *Delegation* function to delegate your own access to applications and the corresponding task list to someone else. You can also store a substitute for a limited time frame here.

2.2.1   Organizational Structure

Creating an organization

You can set up and maintain the organizational structure of the company using the *Organizations* function. You can also identify an organizational unit as a Shared Services Provider. You set up and manage the organizational structure of the company using the **Compliance Structure • Organizations • Create or Open** menu path. You use this menu path to go to *Display Mode* first; then you can only switch to *Change Mode* for a previously selected organization by clicking the *Open* button. You then select *Create* to create a new organizational unit.

The General tab

Figure 2.5 shows that the definition of an organization can contain five tabs: **General, Subprocesses, Entity-Level Controls, Roles,** and **Attachments and Links.** On the **General** tab, you can maintain a long text description in addition to the name and identify whether the organization is to be subject to sign-off regarding the sign-off process. You can also define whether the organization is to act as a **Shared Services Provider.** In addition, you always create an organization based on a particular period of time. If you want to use automated controls for the organization, you must also maintain an **Org. Level System Parameter** (for more details, see Section 2.2.6, "Automated Tests").

The Subprocesses tab

You can use the **Sub-processes** tab to assign processes or subprocesses from the central process catalog to the corresponding organization.

The Entity-Level Controls tab

You can also assign management controls to an organization using the **Entity-Level Controls** tab.

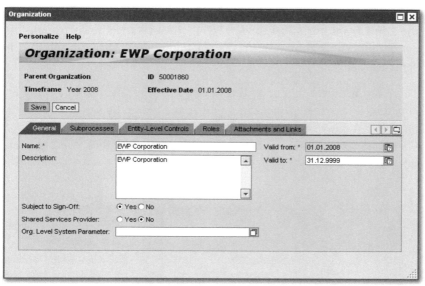

Figure 2.5 Defining an Organization

Figure 2.6 shows that the **Roles** tab displays which role (here, **Internal Control Manager**) has already been assigned to which person (here, **Thomas Schmidt**) for the relevant organization. However, the **Roles** tab does not contain a maintenance dialog because roles are assigned in the *User Access* menu area using *Roles and Their Tasks* functions.

The Roles tab

Role	Person	User
Audit Manager		
Automated Controls Specialist		
CEO/CFO		
Internal Control Manager	Thomas Schmidt	TSCHMIDT
Internal Auditor		

Figure 2.6 Roles Tab

You can use the **Attachments and Links** tab to upload and store documents and URL links for the organization.

The Attachments and Links tab

The Organizational Hierarchy task

To create, change, and maintain an organizational unit, you must assign the *Edit Organizational Hierarchy* (EDIT-HIER) task to the corresponding user. This task is contained in the *Internal Control Manager* role in the standard delivery.

Flexible organizational hierarchy

There are no restrictions for the structure of the organizational hierarchy, which means that you can organize the hierarchy setup completely flexibly with any number of hierarchy levels. In addition to the defined EWP organizational hierarchy, Figure 2.7 shows whether the organizations are subject to sign-off.

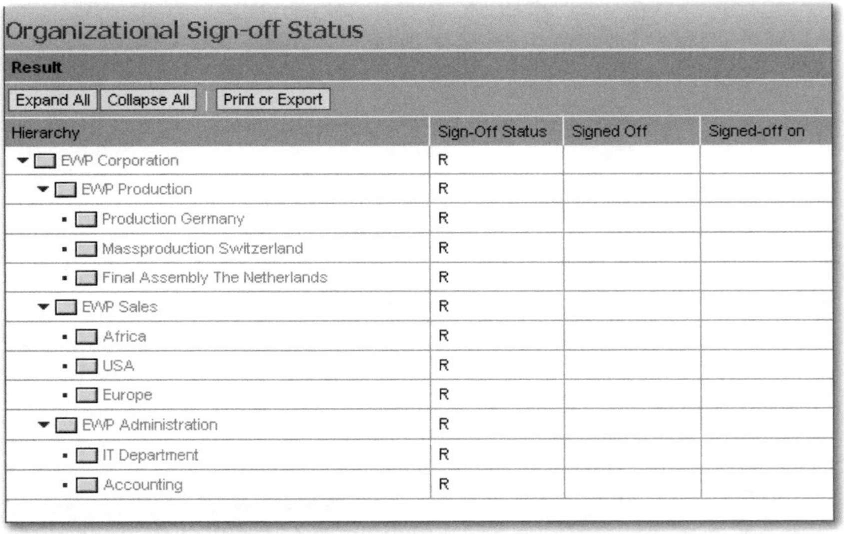

Organizational Sign-off Status

Result

Expand All | Collapse All | Print or Export

Hierarchy	Sign-Off Status	Signed Off	Signed-off on
EWP Corporation	R		
EWP Production	R		
Production Germany	R		
Massproduction Switzerland	R		
Final Assembly The Netherlands	R		
EWP Sales	R		
Africa	R		
USA	R		
Europe	R		
EWP Administration	R		
IT Department	R		
Accounting	R		

Figure 2.7 EWP Organizational Hierarchy

Time-dependent master data definition

In this chapter, we've already briefly mentioned that you always create an organization based on a particular period of time. This concept of time-dependent definition is used for all master data in SAP GRC Process Control. You can therefore display master data, as shown in Figure 2.8, for different periods of time and also track corresponding master data changes.

Central master data

However, we differentiate between two types of master data for SAP GRC Process Control master data. The central master data, or master data valid throughout the company, refers to the organizational structure, account groups, process catalog (processes, sub-processes, and controls), control objectives and risks catalog, and management controls.

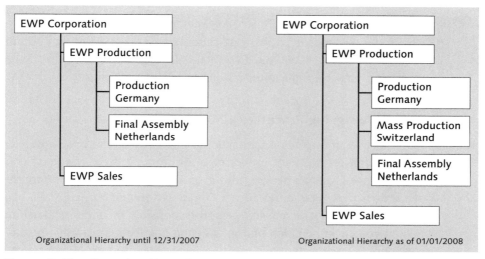

Figure 2.8 Time-Dependent Master Data

The organization-specific or local master data, in contrast, relates to the relevant organization and is therefore not valid throughout the company. Local master data can only be organization-specific processes or controls. Transactional data in SAP GRC Process Control results from the assessments and tests performed.

Local master data

However, you generally structure the organizational hierarchy as you would for all other central master data, using the *structure* functions in the SAP ERP backend system. For this reason, you usually upload all central master data into SAP GRC Process Control automatically using the MDUG (*Master Data Upload Generator*) data upload tool. MDUG uses the application functions relevant for the structure as a central data interface.

Central master data structure using MDUG

> **Note**
>
> You can download the MDUG tool free from the SAP Developer Networks (SDN) website.

Excel template generated in a few seconds

You can also use the MDUG tool to generate an Excel template very easily in a few seconds to populate all central master data. After the content of the template has been filled correctly, the data can usually already be uploaded into the application system within a few minutes.

2.2.2 Assigning Processes at Organization Level

Creating an organization

After you've set up the organizational hierarchy of the company, you must assign the relevant processes or Subprocesses for the particular organization. You can perform this assignment by selecting the **Compliance Structure • Organizations • Organizations** menu path, or it can be carried out by the relevant person responsible for the organization. When you click the **Open** button, a dialog box for maintaining the corresponding organization opens for a selected organization. Now navigate to the **Subprocesses** tab. The **Assign Subprocess** button should subsequently be available, as shown in Figure 2.9.

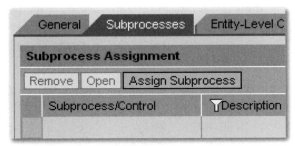

Figure 2.9 Assign Subprocess Button

Assign sub-process

Now select the corresponding process for the chosen *Accounting* EWP organization from the **Subprocesses** tab. Click the **Assign Subprocess** button now so that the maintenance dialog shown in Figure 2.10 is displayed in another dialog box.

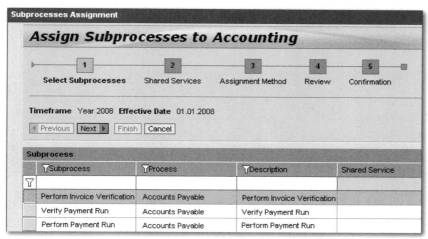

Figure 2.10 Selecting a Subprocess

> **Example**
>
> For the assignment example described on the following pages, we assume that the content of the master data of, in particular, controls, control objectives, and risks, was already linked to the subprocesses and processes using an initial data upload. We also assume that the relevant people responsible for the organizations were already assigned to the organizations. In the next chapter, we describe how you can assign people to roles.
>
> If you upload the central master data into the application system using an upload template created by the MDUG data upload tool, the contents of the structure of the central master data are linked automatically.

Data content is linked automatically

Selecting the subprocesses is the first step in the actual process assignment procedure. The **Perform Invoice Verification** subprocess is now selected and highlighted from the **Accounts Payable** process for the relevant organization. You can then click the **Next** button to go to the next stage of the assignment process.

Selecting a subprocess

Figure 2.11 shows that the next step in the assignment process now is to select the assignment method. The assignment method determines how the centrally linked process catalog data (process, subprocess, control objectives, risks, and controls) are transferred or assigned for the relevant organization. If you select the **Copy** assignment method, the organization (the *Accounting* EWP organization in the example) will be

Copying a subprocess

able to adapt or add new central subprocesses and controls at the local, organization-specific level.

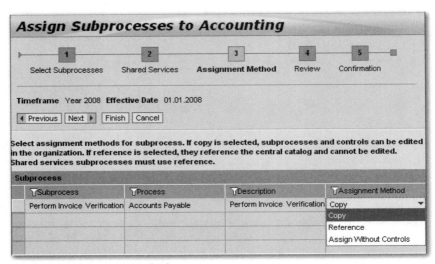

Figure 2.11 Assignment Method

Referencing a subprocess

If you select **Reference** as the assignment method, the subprocesses and controls will relate to the central process catalog, and changes can't be made at the local, organization-specific level.

In addition, you can't add any new subprocesses and controls locally with this assignment method. If you identify an organization as a Shared Services Provider, however, you must always reference the subprocesses.

Assigning a sub-process without controls

If, however, you select the **Assign Without Controls** assignment method, only the central subprocesses (including the control objectives and risks) are assigned without the controls for the organization. This means that you must add new organization-specific controls for the relevant organization at the local level.

Figure 2.12 shows that the control and subprocess were assigned to the *Accounting* EWP organization using the copy method. You can now use the **Finish** button to end the assignment process directly or use the **Submit** button to subsequently review or adapt the central control master data (see Figure 2.13).

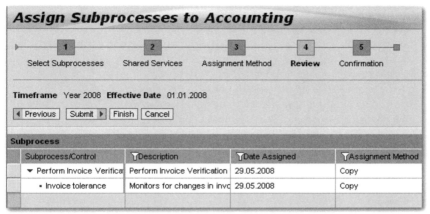

Figure 2.12   Reviewing an Assigned Subprocess

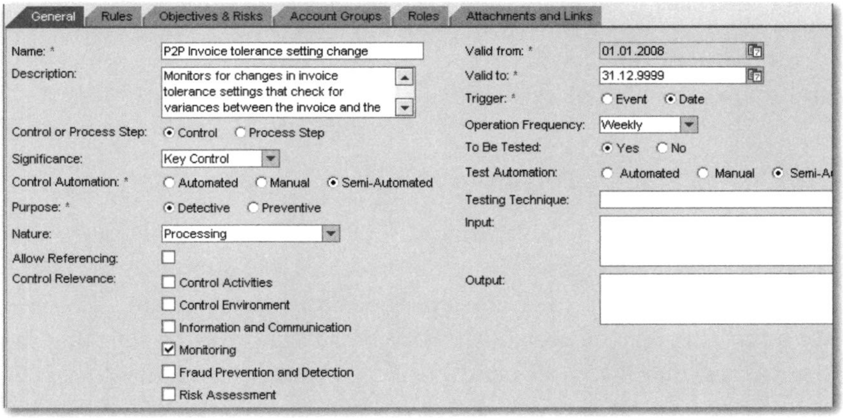

Figure 2.13   Control Master Data Sheet

In the assignment example just described, you selected a review of the assigned control master data using the corresponding button. In this case, however, an organization-specific adjustment of the central control data isn't necessary at the local level after you've successfully assigned the process. You can therefore complete the entire assignment process by clicking the *Save* button, followed by the *Finish* button.

> **Note**
>
> You can't influence the selection list of assignment methods displayed earlier in Figure 2.11 using Customizing options. If a company takes a strict top-down approach for its internal control system, it would be preferable if only the **Reference** assignment method could be selected in this case. At the moment, only a unique statement can be enforced for users trough guidance in this case or a corresponding system modification can be made.

You assign processes and subprocesses to an organization using the *Assign Subprocess to Organization* task (ASGN-PRORG) with the *Organization Owner* role provided by default.

In short, we've linked the content of the relevant organizations to their corresponding processes and subprocesses, and so on, in this chapter. This step, which facilitates important aspects of documentation requirements in accordance with SOX, generally only occurs once and merely has to be performed again if new organizational structures, processes, and so on are added or existing ones are changed.

2.2.3 Assigning a Person to a Role

Roles and their tasks

After you've set up the organizational hierarchy and assigned the organization owners and corresponding processes and subprocesses to the relevant organization, the next step involves assigning persons or corresponding users to the previously linked data structures by selecting the **User Access • Roles • Roles and Their Tasks** path (see Figure 2.14).

Assigning a Person to a Role

Figure 2.14 shows that two selection options (**Corporate and Organization** and **Process Hierarchy**) are available after you click the **Assign Person to Roles** button. In a previous step, the persons responsible were already assigned at the corporate and organization level using the **Corporate and Organization** option. From Figure 2.15, we can see that **Thomas Schmidt** has been assigned for the **Internal Control Manager** role at corporate level. You could also store another person at corporate level for the Audit-Manager role in accordance with the roles provided by default. However, this person could also be Thomas Schmidt again. In such a case, the role tasks are combined, and the assigned person can execute all activities of all assigned roles.

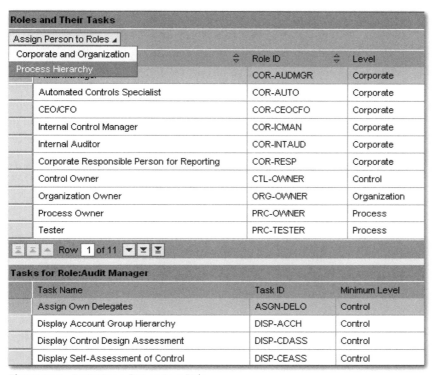

Roles and Their Tasks

	Role	Role ID	Level
	Assign Person to Roles ⊿		
	Corporate and Organization		
	Process Hierarchy	COR-AUDMGR	Corporate
	Automated Controls Specialist	COR-AUTO	Corporate
	CEO/CFO	COR-CEOCFO	Corporate
	Internal Control Manager	COR-ICMAN	Corporate
	Internal Auditor	COR-INTAUD	Corporate
	Corporate Responsible Person for Reporting	COR-RESP	Corporate
	Control Owner	CTL-OWNER	Control
	Organization Owner	ORG-OWNER	Organization
	Process Owner	PRC-OWNER	Process
	Tester	PRC-TESTER	Process

Row 1 of 11

Tasks for Role:Audit Manager

	Task Name	Task ID	Minimum Level
	Assign Own Delegates	ASGN-DELO	Control
	Display Account Group Hierarchy	DISP-ACCH	Control
	Display Control Design Assessment	DISP-CDASS	Control
	Display Self-Assessment of Control	DISP-CEASS	Control

Figure 2.14 Assigning a Person to a Role

Roles and Their Tasks

Assignments

Show All ▼ Copy Action ⊿

	Level	Object	Parent	Audit Manager	Internal Control Manager
	Corporate	EWP Corporation			Thomas Schmidt
	Organization	EWP Production	EWP Corporation		
		EWP Sales			
		EWP Administration			
		Production Germany	EWP Production		
		Massproduction Switzerland			
		Final Assembly The Netherlands			
		Africa	EWP Sales		
		USA			
		Europe			

Figure 2.15 Roles and Their Tasks

The Internal Control Manager selects the **Process Hierarchy** option by choosing the **User Access • Roles • Roles and Their Tasks** menu path and clicking the **Assign Persons to Roles** button. The Internal Control Manager can now use the *Assign Roles for Subprocess and Lower-Level Controls* (ASGN-RLPRC) in his assigned role bundle to assign the responsible person to the relevant subprocesses and lower-level controls. After you select the **Process Hierarchy** option, a dialog box like the one shown in Figure 2.16 appears.

Selecting roles and filters

It's clear that you can first select the role level and filter in the displayed dialog box. Depending on the present situation of the company, in this process you can store the persons to be assigned by role level (process, subprocess, control) individually or also simultaneously in a maintenance dialog. Because the EWP Corporation still has straightforward company structures, you can select all three role levels and not set a filter for a certain organization. When you click the **Next** button, the maintenance screen shown in Figure 2.17 is subsequently displayed.

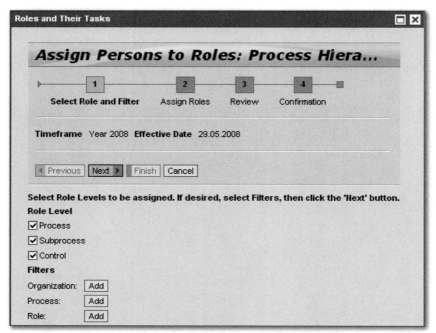

Figure 2.16 Assigning Persons to Roles: Process Hierarchy

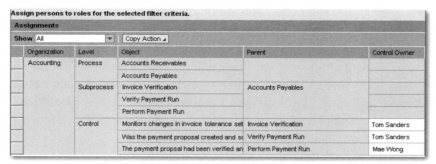

Figure 2.17 Assigning Persons to Roles at All Role Levels

The ready-for-input column fields for maintaining the **Control Owner** are displayed on the right-hand side of Figure 2.17. Because you previously selected all three role levels, another column for maintaining the Subprocess and Process Owner is displayed in each case on this dialog screen (further to the right and not displayed in Figure 2.17). Depending on the Customizing activity, you can select the Define whether review is required option and store a reviewer or validator in an additional column. The Customizing settings define whether the *Reviewer* column here is ready for input and therefore specifies whether a particular assessment or test must also be reviewed in each case by a different user.

Assigning roles

Because Thomas Schmidt, as the Internal Control Manager, has the *Assign roles for subprocess and lower-level controls* task in his assigned role bundle, he now assigns the corresponding process, subprocess, and control owners (e.g., Tom Sanders and Mae Wong) for the EWP corporation. You can use the **Next** button to subsequently display the dialog box shown in Figure 2.18.

Figure 2.18 Assigning Persons to Roles – Review

Review

After the Assign Roles step, the next step involves performing a technical review of the stored persons using the **Finish** button. If you've assigned persons who at this point aren't known as users in SAP GRC Process Control, a corresponding error message will be displayed during the review phase. However, if the review step is processed successfully, the **Assign Persons to Roles** assignment process is completed, and the **Confirmation** status is displayed.

2.2.4 Creating and Planning a Survey

Question Library

To enable you to create a survey using SAP GRC Process Control, you must first create a Question Library for the particular surveys using the **Evaluation Setup • Assessment Surveys • Question Library** path. Figure 2.19 shows that a couple of questions for all question categories have already been defined for the EWP corporation. You must define the answer type (*Evaluation, Yes/No/NA*, or *Text*) for the question's definition. For the *Yes/No/NA* and *Evaluation* answer types, you can also determine whether a comment is required for the answer.

Uploading new questions

You can also use the **Actions** button and select the *Copy* option to copy new questions from the existing Question Library, and use the *Upload* option to also upload new questions to the central Question Library.

Question Library

Create	Open	Delete		Actions ◢	
	Category		Question		
▽	All ▼				
	Control Design		The Control Design does consider the Control Objectives?		
	Control Design		Since the previous Assessment the Control Owner was changed?		
	Control Design		The Control Design needs to be changed due to legal requirements?		
	Control Design		The Control had been changed since the previous Assessment?		
	Subprocess Design		Since the previous Assessment the Subprocess was changed?		
	Subprocess Design		Since the previous Assessment the Subprocess Owner did change?		
	Self-assessment		The described control activities can be performed effectively?		
	Subprocess Design		Did the Subprocess Design change since the last Assessment?		
	Entity-level Control		The employees of the IT department understand and acknowledge their resp		
	Entity-level Control		The EWP employees are aware that a Code of Conduct does exist?		
	Entity-level Control		For the EWP Corporation a Code of Conduct exist?		
	Sign-off		For the area I am responsible the Sign-off can be performed		

Figure 2.19 Question Library for the Survey

After you've set up a Question Library for the required survey categories, you can define and manage surveys using the **Assessment Setup • Evaluation Surveys • Survey Library** menu path. You can use the **Create** button to create a new survey, and the **Copy** button to copy an already existing survey with its assigned questions. You can adapt the existing questions of the copied survey here during the copy process using the **Add** and **Delete** functions.

Survey Library

Figure 2.20 shows the **Create Survey** dialog box, which is displayed in another dialog box when you select the *Create* button. In addition to the survey category, you must define the name or title for a new survey. You should also identify the survey as active for later operational use and include the relevant questions in the survey using the **Add** button.

Creating a survey

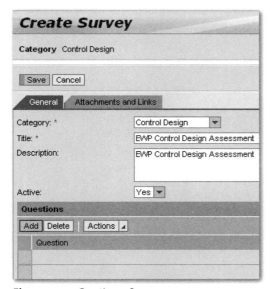

Figure 2.20 Creating a Survey

After you click the **Add** button shown in Figure 2.20, the **Add Questions** dialog box displayed in Figure 2.21 appears. You can now add the relevant questions for the survey from the Question Library you previously set up. You can display existing questions relating to the control design only using the corresponding filter function. If you want to include a question in the survey, you must select this question and then click the

Adding questions

OK button. You can then add the next relevant question, or several questions simultaneously, to the survey using the **Add** button.

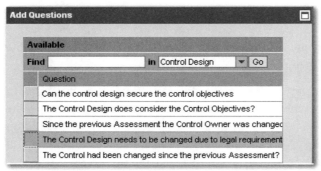

Figure 2.21 Adding Questions

Figure 2.22 shows that four questions of the **Control Design** category were added from the Question Library into the **EWP Control Design Assessment**. You must then use the **Save** button to save the new survey into the Survey Library.

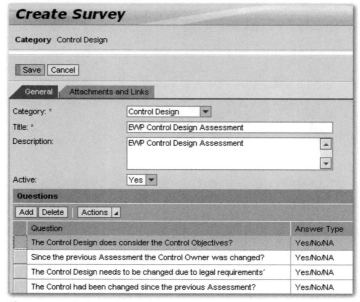

Figure 2.22 Saving a Survey

In the preceding example, you created a survey for a *control design assessment*. You can also create and subsequently plan surveys in the same way for a *process design assessment*, *self-assessments*, *entity-level control assessments*, and *sign-off*.

After you've created a survey for the EWP using control design, you can use a plan to schedule the corresponding survey under the **Evaluation Setup • Planner • Planner** menu path. This enables you to initiate the corresponding workflow tasks for the survey in relation to assessments or tests. You use the *Create* button to create a new plan and use the *Copy* button to copy an already existing plan with the corresponding selection parameters. The *Open* button enables you to revise a copied plan.

To create a plan, you must first select the relevant **Plan Activity**, such as **Perform Control Design Assessment**, for example, and assign the corresponding **Survey**. Figure 2.23 shows that, in addition to selecting a **Period** and the corresponding **Year** in the **Enter Plan Details** phase, you must also maintain the **Start Date** and **Due Date** for the relevant plan or survey. You can use the **Next** button to display the maintenance dialog of the Select Organizations phase.

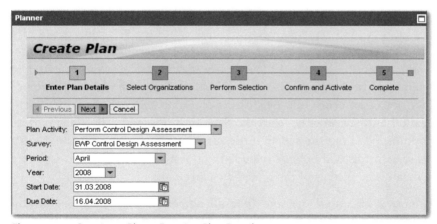

Figure 2.23 Creating a Plan – Entering Plan Details

In the **Select Organizations** phase, you must assign at least one organization to the plan in each case. You can assign several organizations to a plan by selecting a higher-level organization. For example, you could

Creating a plan

Entering plan details

Selecting organizations

plan the highest organization, the EWP Corporation, for the corresponding survey here. Following the planning in this case, all control owners in the relevant EWP organizations would receive workflow tasks for this control design survey. After you assign the Accounting EWP organization, you can use the Next button to display the dialog box shown in Figure 2.24.

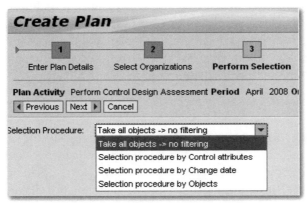

Figure 2.24 Creating a Plan – Performing a Selection

Performing a selection

Figure 2.24 shows how you can determine the different selection procedures in the **Perform Selection** phase. With the **Selection procedure by Control attributes** option, you can use the *Significance, Control Automation, Test Automation,* and *Frequency of Process* selection parameters to define the scope of the survey or the controls for the planning. You use the **Selection procedure by Objects** option to select controls by organization and subprocess. With the **Selection procedure by Change date** option, you limit the scope of the survey using the change date. In this case, controls will only be included in the survey planning if they were actually changed as of the selected change date.

Confirming and activating

Figure 2.25 shows that the **Take all objects → no filtering** selection procedure was used in the planning for the Accounting EWP organization. The plan was created for the **April** period and the year **2008** and it only selected five controls for an organization. You must now specify the **Plan Name** on the maintenance screen of the *Confirm and Activate* phase. You can then use the **Activate Plan** button to finish and automatically schedule the plan.

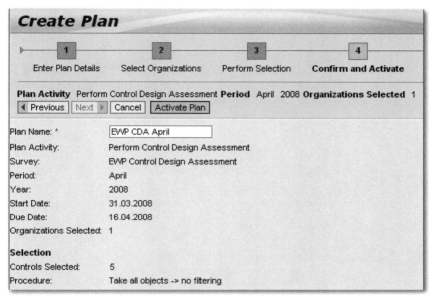

Figure 2.25 Creating a Plan – Confirming and Activating

Figure 2.26 shows that the plan you activated still has the **Planning** status. You can update the screen display using the Update navigation link (available in the lower-right area of the screen – not shown in the figure). If the survey planning has reached the **Completed** status, the relevant workflow survey tasks have been made available to the corresponding persons responsible for the Accounting EWP organization.

Plan Name	Plan Activity	Organizations	Period	Year	Status
EWP ToE 2007	Perform Test of Effectiveness	1	Year	2007	Completed
EWP ToE 2008	Perform Test of Effectiveness	1	Year	2008	Completed
EWP CDA 2007	Perform Control Design Assessment	1	Year	2007	Completed
EWP CDA March	Perform Control Design Assessment	1	March	2008	Completed
EWP CDA April	Perform Control Design Assessment	1	April	2008	Planning

Figure 2.26 Planner

You can always
reuse a survey you
create

> **Note**
>
> For a new time frame during planning, you can always reuse a survey you created in SAP GRC Process Control, without having to make any changes (see Figure 2.27). In addition, you can use the existing copy function to create a new survey and copy new plans quickly and easily using plans that already exist.

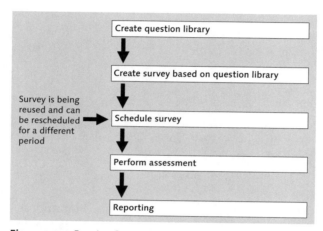

Figure 2.27 Reusing Surveys

In SAP GRC Process Control, you define and manage questions and surveys using the Internal Control Manager role with the technical COR-ICMAN role ID provided by default.

We can conclude that creating and using the different types of surveys in SAP GRC Process Control assesses whether internal controls work as planned in regular operation in accordance with the control definition and whether they are also effective.

2.2.5   Performing Control Design Assessments

Performing Control
Design Assessment

To perform a control design assessment, you (as the SAP GRC Process Control user) must first select the **My Home • Work Inbox • Work Inbox** menu path to check whether corresponding workflow tasks (**Perform Control Design Assessment**) exist in the inbox. You may first have to update the work inbox using the corresponding navigation link.

It's clear from Figure 2.28 that there are at least three **Perform Control Design Assessment** workflow tasks in the work inbox of EWP employee, Tom Sanders. By double-clicking one of the workflow tasks, you can go to the corresponding maintenance screen for the control design assessment (see Figure 2.29).

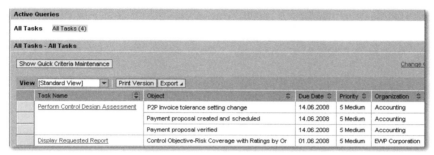

Figure 2.28 My Home – Work Inbox

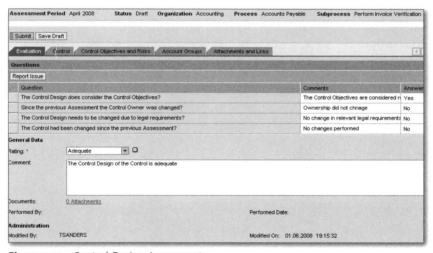

Figure 2.29 Control Design Assessment

The control owner now answers the questions about the control design according to the relevant answer type of the question and, if required, also notes an additional comment for each question. Relevant context information (assessment period, status, organization, etc.) about the relevant controls are displayed in a bar in the upper screen area and you can also display additional detail information on the corresponding **Control, Account Groups,** and **Control Objectives and Risks tabs.**

Control owner answers survey

Rating

Because the control definition was not changed since the preceding assessment, and the control design takes into account the corresponding control objectives, the control design rating is classified as adequate. You can use the *Submit* button to complete the assessment. As a result, this workflow task will also no longer be displayed in the work inbox. The control status is set from *Draft* to *Completed*, which means that you can't make any more changes to the assessment data. However, the corresponding workflow task still remains in the work inbox if you merely buffer the assessment data using the **Save Draft** button. This means that you'll be able to resume and, if necessary, change the assessment at a later stage.

Logging a person and a performed date

The **Administration** data area (see lower area in Figure 2.29) also displays which person has changed or performed the assessment. The last change date and date when the assessment was performed are also logged.

Reporting an issue

However, if there are significant deficiencies or deviations in the control design rating, the corresponding workflow task can only be forwarded when you've reported an issue using the **Report Issue** button (see also Figure 2.29).

Starting remediation

The control owner, Tom Sanders, reports the issue and assigns **Mae Wong** as the issue owner (see Figure 2.30). Mae Wong now receives the Start Control Design Remediation workflow task in her work inbox and subsequently initiates the remediation.

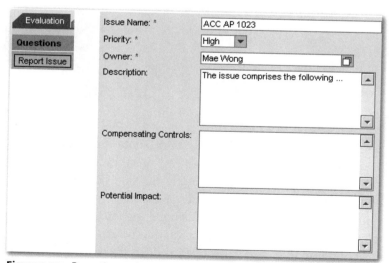

Figure 2.30 Reporting an Issue

If an unwanted assessment occurs, or a threshold is exceeded during automatic testing or automatic control monitoring, the corresponding issue is reported automatically.[2] The automatically assigned issue owner can therefore initiate issue remediation immediately.

Automatic issue reporting

When you've reported an issue and started remediation, you can use different activities or persons as the remediation owner to remove the issue. If the issue has been remediated, a workflow task is triggered automatically and requires a new test or control assessment.

New test/ assessment

2.2.6 Automatic Tests

You can use two test procedures in SAP GRC Process Control. Manual tests, which you use for performing control effectiveness and can be created using the **Evaluation Setup • Manual Test Plans • Manual Test Plans** menu path, and automatic tests, for which you can define rules for automatically testing and monitoring controls using the **Evaluation Setup • Rules for Automatic Tests • Rule** path (see Figure 2.31).

Rules for automatic tests

Configuration controls

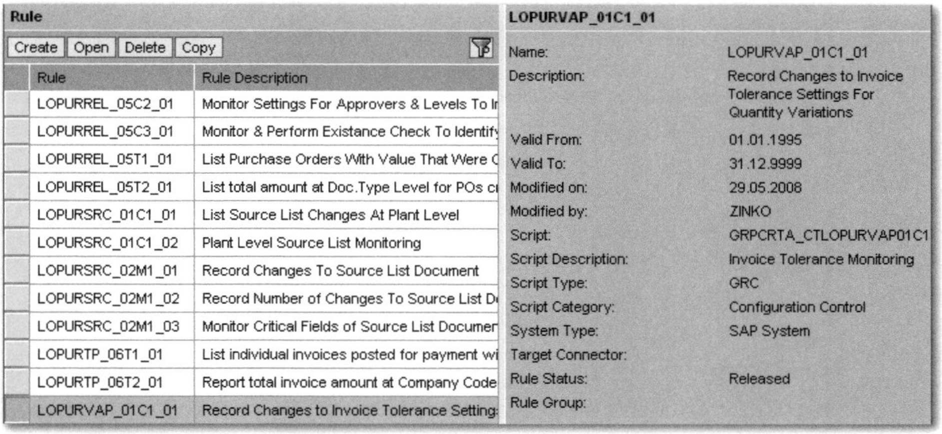

Figure 2.31 Rules for Automatic Testing

---

2 Currently, you still have to analyze and evaluate the confirmed results manually for standard SAP and ABAP Query reports that were identified in SAP GRC Process Control as controls for fulfilling legal requirements. However, issues can be reported automatically for the approximately 200 predefined automatic controls.

You can use the **Rule** navigation link to go directly to the rule definition in the *Evaluation Setup* menu area. You then use the **Open** button to go to the detail maintenance of a rule (see Figure 2.32).

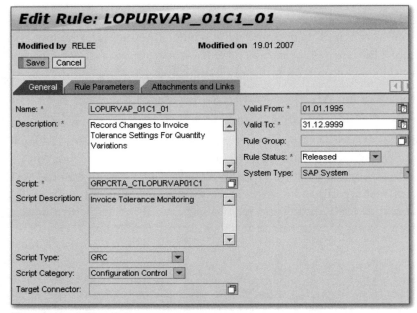

Figure 2.32 Editing Rules

Figure 2.32 shows the definition details of an automatic monitoring rule that you can use to record changes to invoice tolerance settings for quantity variations. The **LOPURVAP_01C1_01** rule has been predefined for a configuration control and monitors possible changes to Customizing settings in relation to the invoice tolerance parameters stored there. A **Script Type**, **Script Category**, **Script**, and **System Type** (here, **SAP System**) are also assigned to the rule. You must also set the **Rule Status** to **Released** for operational use. You can use the **Rule Parameters** tab to maintain the relevant rule criteria and corresponding tolerance values for the rule.

Automatic controls

Figure 2.33 illustrates the dependencies of different objects or system fields described previously regarding the rule definition. In addition, Figure 2.33 shows that you must ultimately assign a rule with specific rule parameters to a control in each case. Depending on the intended use, the control is executed automatically within the planning (compliance tests) or scheduling (monitoring control tests) function in accordance with the specified periodicity and can therefore be identified as an *automatic control*. As indicated in Figure 2.33, however, you can also assign a rule with different rule parameters, rule criteria, and so on, to different or same controls.

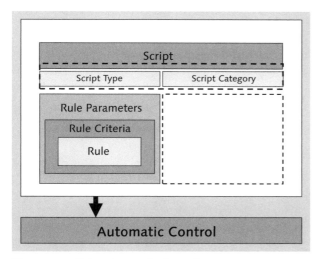

Figure 2.33 Rule – Automatic Control

You can maintain the relevant rule criteria and corresponding tolerance values for the rule on the **Rule Parameters** tab (see Figure 2.34). You can use the **Add** button to select and add other rule criteria from a selection list in accordance with the script assigned to the rule. The **Changes** analysis type is assigned for the **TOLERANCE_KEY** rule criterion. This means that each Customizing change of invoice verification tolerance values in this case is automatically recorded as an issue with a **Medium** deficiency value. You can also select an absolute or procedural tolerance value for the analysis type. In this case, you can define for which frequency of occurrence or case number a deficiency issue is to be reported.

Rule parameters, rule criteria

You can store up to two different analysis types for one rule parameter within the rule criteria. However, the **Filter** analysis type (see also Figure 2.34) must always be available at least once.

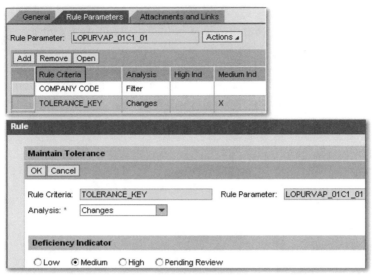

Figure 2.34 Rule Parameters, Rule Criteria, Rules

Assigning the rule to the control You can use the **Evaluation Setup • Rules for Automatic Tests • Assigning the Control Rule** menu path and the **Assign Rules To Selected Control** button to assign a rule to a specific control (see Figure 2.35).

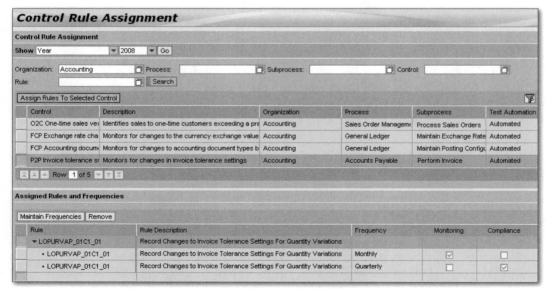

Figure 2.35 Assigning the Rule to the Selected Control

You can then use the **Maintain Frequencies** button to determine the frequency or execution periodicity.

You must also define whether the automatic control is only to be used for adhering to legal requirements (compliance test) or simply for automated threshold monitoring (monitoring control test).

Compliance and monitoring control test

You can use the **Query, Rule Script, and Rule Criteria** functions from the **Evaluation Setup • Rules for Automatic Tests • Customizing for Automatic Tests** application menu to integrate queries and standard SAP reports at least semi-automatically into the existing SAP GRC Process Control infrastructure for automatic testing. This is semi-automatic because you can manage and execute or plan these programs and reports in the corresponding target systems from SAP GRC Process Control. In this scenario, however, you still have to perform the necessary analysis and the evaluation of confirmed reports manually for standard SAP and ABAP Query reports.

Queries and standard SAP reports

You can use the function under the **Evaluation Setup • Planner • Planner** path to plan assessment surveys, manual tests, and so on for adhering to legal requirements for a certain period of time. The planning triggers the sending of corresponding workflow tasks for the assessment surveys and manual tests in SAP GRC Process Control.

Automatic controls and monitoring

 You can use the functions in the **Evaluation Setup • Scheduling • Scheduling** path for scheduling primarily relating to the automatic monitoring of threshold values, transactions, and Customizing changes.

For SAP GRC Process Control, approximately 200 predefined automatic control rules are already available for SAP ERP applications from Oracle, PeopleSoft, and SAP. A total of approximately 70 automatic control rules for SAP GRC Process Control are predefined for a corresponding SAP ERP target application (see also Figure 2.36).

Predefined automatic control rules

	Customizing	Transaction	= 70
FI	10	8	18
P2P	14	8	22
SD	12	14	26
IT	4		4

Figure 2.36 SAP Transaction and Configuration Controls

> **Note**
>
> Automatic testing in SAP GRC Process Control relates to testing the effectiveness of master data changes or of specific transactions and possible changes of certain Customizing settings.

Reducing manual control tests

Predefined automatic control rules for SAP GRC Process Control mean that standard automated control tests can be implemented in areas such as procurement, sales order processing, and financial reporting across all departments and business areas. As a result, to some extent, you'll be able to reduce the amount of monitoring and resources required for manual control testing in particular. The automated monitoring functions of SAP GRC Process Control also enable an effective alignment to the COBIT framework.

Figure 2.37 illustrates the necessary activities, including the required Customizing activities, for using SAP GRC Process Control functions operationally for automatic testing and monitoring.

The assessment results used for adhering to legal requirements are incorporated into the Analytics Dashboard reports. You can also evaluate these using the reports under the **Reporting Center • Evaluation** menu path. You can use the standard reports under the **Reporting Center • Monitoring** menu path to analyze the monitoring results that aren't used to adhere to legal requirements.

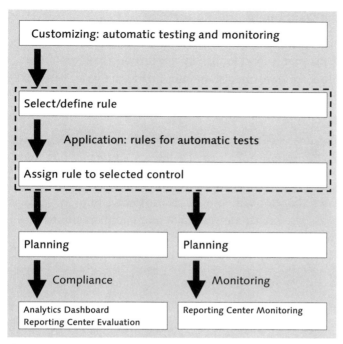

Figure 2.37 Necessary Steps for Automatic Testing

Thomas Schmidt, as Internal Control Manager, decides that the monitoring control described in Section 2.2.5, "Performing Control Design Assessment," and previously executed manually, is to be monitored automatically in the future for the Accounting EWP organization using the LOPURVAP_01C1_01 rule. This will considerably reduce the amount of manual monitoring and resources required to monitor corresponding Customizing changes relating to tolerance values for invoice verification.

Manual control will be executed automatically in future

To enable other cost-saving options to be used in the long term, Schmidt also decides to use additional automatic controls for the Accounting EWP organization. Because approximately 70 automatic control rules altogether were predefined for SAP GRC Process Control for SAP ERP target applications, an analysis is now to be carried out to see which other controls can be automated in the future.

Other cost-saving options

2.2.7 Analysis Dashboard and Reports

Analysis Dashboard and reports

In SAP GRC Process Control, you can use the *My Home, Evaluation Results,* and *Reporting Center* menu areas to display the current status and relevant results for the different assessments and monitoring activities very easily and clearly. This allows you to analyze and assess the current corporate situation quickly.

The Evaluation Results menu area consists of the three areas of **My Tasks, Monitoring, and Compliance**. You can use the **My Tasks** function to display all of your own assessment, test, issue, and remediation tasks.

Monitoring

Figure 2.38 shows that you can use the **Monitoring** function area to display and process issues that are still open and maintain and track the corresponding remediation measures related to control monitoring.

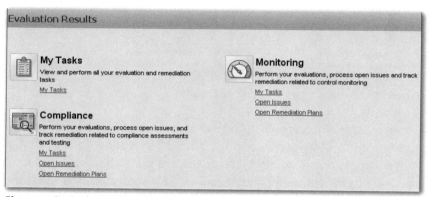

Figure 2.38 Evaluation Results

Compliance

You can use the **Compliance** application area to display and process open issues for tests and assessments (used for adhering to legal requirements), and track and manage your own remediation measures. Unlike the control monitoring results, the assessment results are incorporated into the Analytics Dashboard reports here and are therefore also available to external auditors for further evaluation.

Analytics Dashboard

As the SAP GRC Process Control user, you can use the *Analytics Dashboard* function in the **My Home • Reports and Analyses • Analytics Dashboard** application menu to access Analytic Dashboards that are based on test and assessment results for adhering to legal requirements.

Thomas Schmidt wants to get a current overview of the whole EWP corporation for testing the effectiveness of controls. For this reason, he first looks at the *Control Effectiveness Test* dashboard in the Analytics Dashboard shown in Figure 2.39. Because Schmidt was assigned the role of Internal Control Manager, and this role was defined in relation to the corporate level, he can access all corporate test data for the control effectiveness for further analyses and evaluations.

Control Effectiveness Test

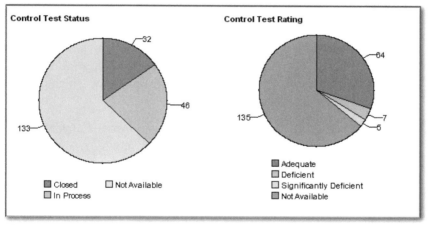

Figure 2.39 Control Test Status and Assessment

In addition to the *Control Effectiveness Test* overview, the *Survey Assessment Overview* dashboard is also available in the Analytics Dashboard. You can also use this overview to effortlessly obtain a current overview of the results for assessment surveys. However, Schmidt subsequently wants to get a current overview of existing issues for the whole EWP corporation and therefore now looks at the *Issue Overview* dashboard in the Analytics Dashboard shown in Figure 2.40.

Effortless overview of current results

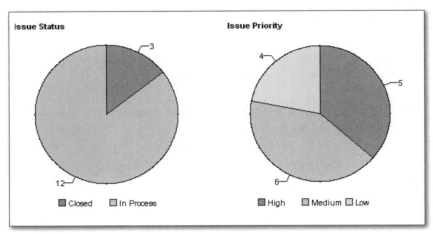

Figure 2.40 Issues

The *Issue Overview* dashboard from Figure 2.40 shows that 15 issues are currently recorded for the EWP corporation, three of which have already been closed again, however. The overview on the right relating to the issue priority also shows that 5 issues were identified with a high priority when the issues were reported.

Extended dashboards
Schmidt also looks at the *Remediation Plan* overview and *Sign-off* dashboard in each case in the Analytics Dashboard shown in Figure 2.41. Currently, three remediation measures are closed and nine remediation plans are in process.

> **Note**
>
> You can go to a detail view for all graphic dashboard overviews in the Analytics Dashboard by double-clicking (partial) graphic segments. In the remediation overview, for example, this enables you to identify who reported the issue or who the remediation agent is. At the same time, all master data (organization, process, control, etc.) is also displayed for the relevant issue.

Reporting Center
You also have another option with the *Reporting Center* menu area to obtain a current overview of the numerous activities and results in SAP GRC Process Control. There are 29 standard evaluation reports available in this menu area for a range of different purposes. You can analyze monitoring results using the standard reports under the **Reporting Center • Monitoring** menu path.

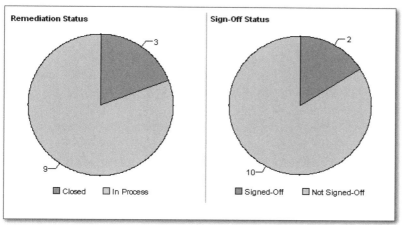

Figure 2.41 Remediation and Sign-Off Status

You evaluate assessment results, which are used to adhere to legal requirements, using the **Reporting Center • Evaluation** menu path. Figure 2.42 shows the **Control Ratings** report from the *Evaluation* area. The three different icons in the column on the right illustrate the corresponding control assessments.

Assessment results

Control Ratings

Results

Print or Export

Organization ⇕	Process ⇕	Subprocess ⇕	Control ⇕	Control Design
Accounting	Accounts Payable	Perform Invoice Verification	P2P Invoice tolerance setting change	☑
Accounting	General Ledger	Maintain Exchange Rates	FCP Exchange rate changes	☑
Accounting	Accounts Payable	Payment Run	Payment proposal created and scheduled	⊕
Accounting	Asset Management	AM Asset depreciation posting	AM Review of new capitalized assets	☑
Accounting	Asset Management	AM Asset master data creation	AM Author chges to asset master data	🛑
Accounting	General Ledger	Maintain Exchange Rates	FCP Exchange rate changes	☑
Accounting	General Ledger	Accounting document changes	FCP Accounting document changes - qty	☑
Accounting	Sales Order Management	Maintain Posting Configurations	O2C One-time sales versus all sales	☑
Accounting	Accounts Payable	Payment Run	Payment proposal verified	☑

Figure 2.42 Control Design Assessments

> **Note**
>
> By double-clicking one of these icons (green checkmark, yellow warning icon, red stop sign), you can go to the relevant detail overview of the control assessment. You therefore don't have to execute another report to receive corresponding context information about the control.

Issue status

You can also evaluate issues using a tabular report in the **Reporting Center • Evaluation • Issue Status** menu path. Figure 2.43 shows that 15 issues are currently recorded for the EWP corporation, although three of these issues have already been closed again. We already illustrated this situation in the Analytics Dashboard in Figure 2.40. In the overview in Figure 2.43, the issue type is also displayed in a column to indicate whether the issue relates to a control design assessment and so on.

Issue Status

Results

Print or Export

Reported by	Issue Type	Issue Status	Issue Priority
WF-BATCH		In Process	Low
WF-BATCH		In Process	Medium
WF-BATCH		In Process	Medium
MWONG	ISSUE_CAT/CD	Validated	High
TSANDERS		In Process	Medium
MWONG		Closed	Medium
MWONG		Closed	High
TSANDERS		Draft	Low
MWONG		In Process	Low
TSCHMIDT		In Process	High
MWONG		In Process	Medium
TSANDERS		In Process	Medium
MWONG		Submitted	High
TSANDERS		In Process	Low
ASCHWARZ	ISSUE_CAT/CO	Closed	Medium

Figure 2.43 Issue Statuses

Reporting selection criteria

A wide range of selection criteria is available for all reports in the *Reporting Center* area to restrict the required data selection. For example, you can use a period of time (period, year), master data (organization, process, control), and three assessment levels to make a selection. You can also specify that only results of a control design and/or self-assessment survey, and so on, are to be selected and displayed. When selecting a report, you can also determine whether you want a report to be executed immediately or sent to the work inbox by work item (refer to the lowest workflow task in Figure 2.28). Sending reports by work item improves the performance of the system.

Figure 2.44 shows that you can adapt all reports on a personalized basis in the *Reporting Center* menu area using the available **Personalize fields** navigation link. For example, you can remove existing column fields from the report display and add other available fields.

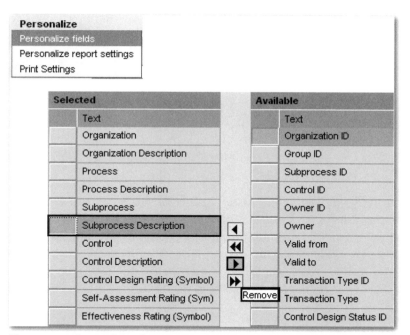

Figure 2.44 Personalizing Reports

The reporting functions presented in this chapter reveal that you can easily and clearly display the current status and relevant results for different assessments and monitoring activities in SAP GRC Process Control using a range of reports and dashboards. This helps the Internal Control

Personalizing reports

Manager and management analyze and assess the current corporate situation quickly.

The reporting results differentiate between whether the control tests are used for adhering to legal requirements and therefore represent a *compliance test* or are simply used for automated threshold monitoring and therefore represent a *monitoring control test*.

Depending on which role the user has, for example, a control owner or organization owner, only the data of the user's assigned area of responsibility is made available to the user.

In particular, the analysis functions (dashboards) of SAP GRC Process Control contribute to assessing the effectiveness of controls, remediation measures, and so on, and help to keep you informed at all times. The Analytics Dashboard reports are also available without restriction to external auditors for analysis and evaluation purposes.

2.3 SAP GRC Process Control – System Configuration

The system configuration of SAP GRC Process Control contains 13 sub-areas in total. For some of these areas, such as *General*, *Workflow*, *Cases*, *NWBC Settings*, and *Event-based Monitoring*, standard SAP functions or different services are mainly only activated once.

If necessary, you can define customer-specific fields in the *User-Defined Fields* area. The *Administration Programs* area provides particular functions for managing and monitoring SAP GRC Process Control-specific workflows for system operation. In other words, the actual Customizing activities mainly only take place in the *Attributes* and *Assessment and Test* areas, and, to a limited extent, in the *Structure* area.

In the *Attributes* area, you can create specific roles for GRC Process Control and assign corresponding task bundles to these new roles. The *Assessment and Test* area, in addition to defining a few other attributes and setting system switches for automatic testing and monitoring in particular, comprises the necessary activities for configuring and registering required connectors. The configuration effort in this area depends linearly on the number of systems connected to SAP GRC Process Control and the number of automatic controls or control rules used.

You can use the *Structure* area to set up the central master data structures, create organization-specific objects and perform different assignments. The underlying functions for the structure are also used here as a central data interface for the MDUG data upload tool.

The *General* Customizing area under the **SAP GRC Process Control • General** menu path enables you to activate *Business Configuration Sets (BC Sets)* and log changes to tables. In the *Set Up Transport Connection* Customizing activity, you can implement the settings for transporting the objects that are created when the structural setup is established.

SAP GRC Process Control • General

SAP also makes specialized contents or attribute characteristic values available for GRC Process Control with *BC Sets.* You can initially activate the 15 BC Sets provided in the standard SAP delivery and, in a second step, then change the corporate requirements accordingly, provided that these have characteristic values that you can change as you wish.

Business Configuration (BC) Sets

You can use the *Record Table Change* function to log changes made to control and Customizing tables. You should only activate logging for Production and Customizing clients because an activation results in twice as many database updates. In addition, the database memory load also increases considerably. For the reasons mentioned, we recommend that you don't use this Customizing function for application tables. SAP GRC Process Control is therefore generally operated in a separate system (such as Human Capital Management) for table logging.

Recording table changes

In the *Set Up Transport Connection* Customizing activity, you can implement the settings for transporting the objects that are created when the structural setup is established. If you want to set up the hierarchy data in the web application for SAP GRC Process Control and not in the Expert Mode, it's essential that you deactivate the automatic transport connection by entering "X" beside the CORR abbreviation (for more information, see Section 4.4.1, "Risk Management Menu," in Chapter 4).

Setting up a transport connection

> **Note**
>
> Because the objects for the hierarchy setup and organizational structure have master data characteristics, we recommend that you deactivate the automatic transport connection. In fact, this is absolutely necessary if the structure or hierarchy is to be set up in the web application. You must enter "X" in the *Value abbr.* field beside the CORR abbreviation for this purpose.

2.3.1 Role Editing

Role editing

The **Role Editing** activity is the first Customizing activity in the **Attributes (SAP GRC Process Control • Attributes• Role Editing)** area. You can create specific roles for GRC Process Control here and assign corresponding tasks to these new roles. Figure 2.45 shows that SAP provides a set of sample roles by BC Set.

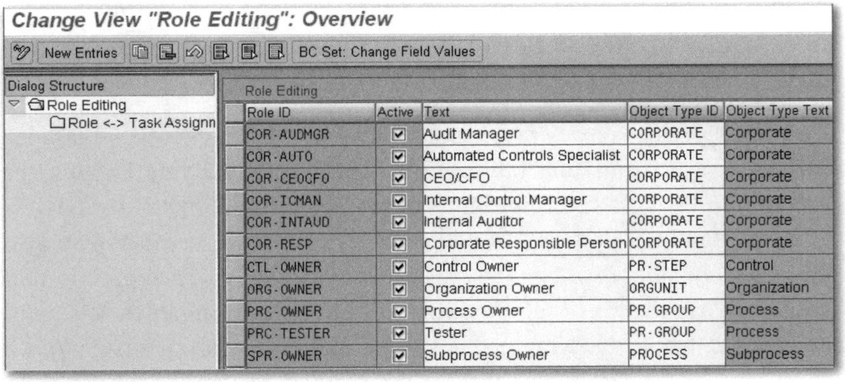

Role ID	Active	Text	Object Type ID	Object Type Text
COR-AUDMGR	☑	Audit Manager	CORPORATE	Corporate
COR-AUTO	☑	Automated Controls Specialist	CORPORATE	Corporate
COR-CEOCFO	☑	CEO/CFO	CORPORATE	Corporate
COR-ICMAN	☑	Internal Control Manager	CORPORATE	Corporate
COR-INTAUD	☑	Internal Auditor	CORPORATE	Corporate
COR-RESP	☑	Corporate Responsible Person	CORPORATE	Corporate
CTL-OWNER	☑	Control Owner	PR-STEP	Control
ORG-OWNER	☑	Organization Owner	ORGUNIT	Organization
PRC-OWNER	☑	Process Owner	PR-GROUP	Process
PRC-TESTER	☑	Tester	PR-GROUP	Process
SPR-OWNER	☑	Subprocess Owner	PROCESS	Subprocess

Figure 2.45 SAP GRC Process Control Sample Roles by BC Set

When you create a role, you must specify or select the **Role ID**, a name, and the **Object Type ID** level. The selection of the **Object Type ID** level (e.g., corporate) determines the authorization or task bundle for that role. The Internal Control Manager role is authorized to execute tasks that concern the whole corporation. Alternatively, you can also maintain the roles using the GRC Process Control web application.

From Figure 2.46, however, you can see that the tasks provided by SAP can't be changed because there is no maintenance dialog. You can therefore simply arrange the task bundle assigned to a role (by object type level) on a customer-specific basis. If you want a role to only have display functions, you'll only assign display tasks (prefix **DISP**) to the role accordingly.

Customer-specific task bundle for each role

Display View "Role <-> Task Assignment": Overview

Dialog Structure		
▽ ☐ Role Editing		
🗁 Role <-> Task Assignn		

Role ID   ORG-OWNER 🔾

Text   Organization Owner

Role <-> Task Assignment

Task ID	Text
ASGN-DELO	Assign Own Delegates
ASGN-MC20U	Assign Entity-Level Controls to Organization
ASGN-PRORG	Assign Subprocess to Organization
ASGN-REPLO	Assign Replacement at Organization Level
DISP-ACCH	Display Account Group Hierarchy
DISP-CDASS	Display Control Design Assessment
DISP-CEASS	Display Self-Assessment of Control
DISP-CHGAN	Display Change Analysis Report
DISP-CPCAT	Display Central Process Catalog
DISP-GENCA	Display General Control Attributes
DISP-HIER	Display Organizational Hierarchy
DISP-LOAUD	Display Audit Log Report for Local Objects
DISP-MC20U	Display Entity-Level Controls at Organization Level

Figure 2.46   Tasks Can't Be Changed

In the next *Edit Attribute Values* activity, which you'll find using the **SAP GRC Process Control • Attributes • Edit Attribute Values** menu path, you can define values for attributes such as controls or risks. You can define attributes with fixed (can't be changed) values that you can define as you wish and, in turn, depend on other attributes. You can use the values fixed here in the corresponding help function in GRC Process Control. If you don't store any attribute values here, the selection lists for the input help will remain empty, or technical key entries will be available. Figure 2.47 shows that the attribute values are provided through BC Sets that you nevertheless first have to activate.

Editing attribute values

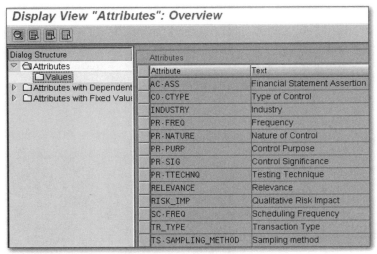

Figure 2.47 Attribute Values Delivered by Default by SAP

Freely definable attribute values Figure 2.48 shows that you can define and change the **Type of Control** attribute as you wish in relation to the number of entries and characteristic values.

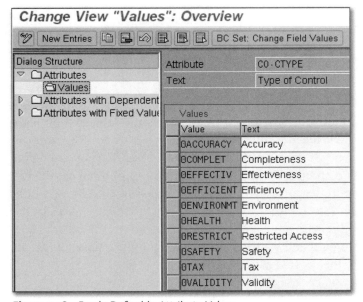

Figure 2.48 Freely Definable Attribute Values

In the last *Edit Frequency Periods* Customizing activity within the *Attributes* area, under **SAP GRC Process Control · Attributes · Edit Frequency Periods,** you can define specific periods for required frequencies (*Monthly, Annually, Semi-Annually,* etc.) for the *Scheduling Frequency* attribute. Sample data is also made available in a BC Set with this activity.

Editing frequency periods

2.3.2 Workflow

For GRC Process Control, you must maintain the **SAP GRC Process Control · Workflow · Perform Automatic Workflow Customizing** activity without errors under the *Maintain Runtime Environment* access node. You can optionally configure the other nodes of this Customizing activity. However, only the highest *Maintain Runtime Environment* node must be supplied with a green checkmark (the indicator for an error-free configuration).

Performing automatic workflow Customizing

When you select the *Maintain Runtime Environment* access node and then use the icon for performing the automatic workflow Customizing, the system automatically implements all required settings.

Maintaining a runtime environment

After the successful automatic workflow configuration, you should use the *Plan Background Job for Missed Deadline* node (**SAP GRC Process Control · Workflow · Perform Automatic Workflow Customizing · Plan Background Job for Missed Deadline**) to plan the corresponding background job with an interval of 20 minutes until the next schedule check.

Planning a background job for a missed deadline

> **Caution**
>
> Authorization for the SAP_ALL authorization profile is absolutely necessary for the automatic workflow configuration. To meet today's security requirements in a development system, you could also apply the Firefighter function of SAP GRC Access Control to use a corresponding user with the required authorization profile for automatic workflow Customizing.

After you complete the automatic workflow Customizing, under the **SAP GRC Process Control · Workflow · Perform Task-Specific Customizing** path, you should now implement all required settings for adjusting the standard tasks and workflow samples provided.

Performing task-specific Customizing

Assigning agents   You must specify the possible agents for each task here because only these assigned agents will be allowed to start workflows. If GRC Process Control standard tasks and workflow samples should be assigned not just to one certain user, we recommend that you define all dialog standard tasks (not background tasks) and workflow samples as **General Task** under **Assign Agents,** as shown in Figure 2.49 and Figure 2.50. You can also assign an organizational unit, job, or position to a task or workflow as a possible agent, which means that no changes will be necessary in the workflow component when personnel changes occur in the organizational structure.

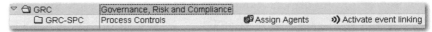

Figure 2.49 "Assign Agents" Navigation

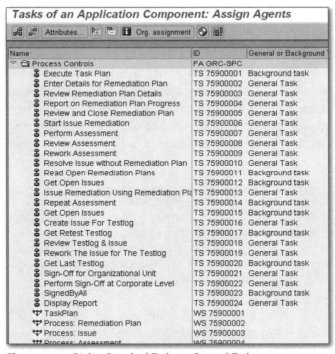

Figure 2.50 Dialog Standard Tasks as General Task

Tasks or workflows can be started as a response to events that were generated by application functions. In this case, specific events are agreed upon as triggering events of the task or workflow. For this reason, you must activate the corresponding linkages by subsequently using the **Activate Event Linkage** navigation link under **SAP GRC Process Control · Workflow · Perform Task-Specific Customizing**, as shown in Figure 2.51.

Activating event linkage

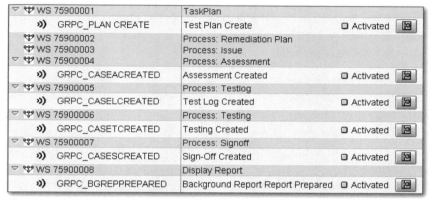

Figure 2.51 Activating an Event Linkage

After you successfully activate the event linkage, you can use the **SAP GRC Process Control · Workflow · Event Queue Administration** path in the Implementation Guide (IMG) to perform specific definitions for improving performance when processing workflows (see Figure 2.52).

Event queue administration

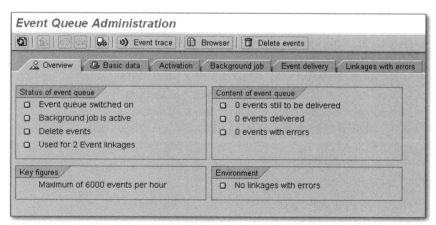

Figure 2.52 Event Queue Administration

Generating workflows involves using many dialog processes, which can lead to a very high system load if you have a large number of events. To avoid a too high load, you can write events for defined event linkages in the event queue.

The Overview tab
Figure 2.52 shows that the active configuration settings and information about the current status of the event queue are displayed on the **Overview** tab. In the **Key figures** area, you see how many events can be processed per hour based on the settings on the **Background job** tab. The system shown in Figure 2.52 can currently process a maximum of 6,000 workflow events per hour.

The Basic data tab
You should store a user as an administrator on the **Basic data** tab (this and the following tab is not shown in detail within figure 2.52). The administrator you enter here is notified if there is a workflow with errors, for example, or if another *event receiver* has errors. You should also enter a value for confirming workflows or event receivers with errors. We recommend that you use the *Deactivate* Linkage selection option here. You can define a specific setting for each event linkage. If you haven't implemented any specific configuration for an event linkage, the default setting will be used.

The Activation tab
On the **Activation** tab, you should check the *Activate Event Queue* checkbox. Furthermore, you should use the *Event Linkages* button to check whether the event linkage is to be activated for the object types and events listed in Figure 2.53. We recommend activating the event queue if many workflows occur or are generated regularly. However, if only a few workflows are generated, processing will be quicker if you don't activate the event queue for the relevant object types.

> **Note**
>
> Because a high number of workflows are usually generated for the GRPC_CA-SEA and GRPC_CASET object types, SAP recommends that you activate the event queue for these two object types at least.

The Background job tab
On the **Background job** tab, you should now adjust the entries for **Number of events per read access** and **Time interval between two read accesses** to the system capacity of the system used. A background job reads the event queue regularly in accordance with the details stored

in the **Time interval between two read accesses** field. The workflow events found in this case are made available to the corresponding event receivers. For the **Number of events per read access** field, the value recommended by SAP is approximately 12 read accesses per minute, whereby 12 workflows per minute are sent for each work process (see Figure 2.54). For 10 available work processes, for example, this means that 120 workflows are sent per minute.

Object Type	Event	Recipient Type
GRPC_BGREP	PREPARED	WS75900008
GRPC_CASEA	CREATED	WS75900004
GRPC_CASEL	CREATED	WS75900005
GRPC_CASES	CREATED	WS75900007
GRPC_CASET	CREATED	WS75900006
GRPC_PLAN	CREATE	WS75900001

Figure 2.53 Possible Object Types and Events for Activating Event Linkage

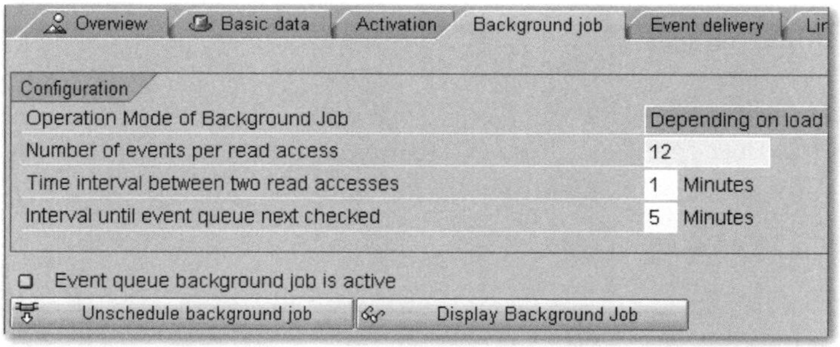

Figure 2.54 Background Job

By choosing the **Display Background Job** button, you can also use Transaction SM37 or SM37C, if necessary, and monitor the logs of executed jobs.

Finally, on the **Event delivery** tab, you should define how you want the event receiver to be started. Figure 2.55 shows that the Processing of events can run sequentially or in parallel on a specified server group. The **Start of receivers** process can occur synchronously or asynchronously. Currently, only the synchronous start of receivers is supported for parallel processing.

The Event delivery tab

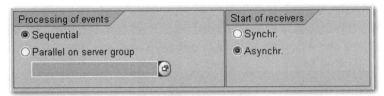

Figure 2.55 Sequential Processing of Events with Asynchronous Start of Receivers

Sequential processing with asynchronous start

The type of delivery recommended by SAP is the sequential processing of events with an asynchronous start of receivers. You can use sequential processing of events with a synchronous start in a quality assurance system for test purposes, for example. Using parallel processing of events with a synchronous start means that you can distribute the system load on a particular server group. In this case, the event is delivered to the application servers assigned to this server group. If you don't enter a server group when you select parallel processing with a synchronous start, the parallel execution will occur on all application servers.

Changing event type linkage for GRPC* object type

You should use the **SAP GRC Process Control** · **Workflow** · **Change Event Start Linkage for GRPC* Object Type** path to change the event start linkage for the delivered object type for the *Change Event Start Linkage for GRPC* Object Type* Customizing activity. Select a line with the **GRPC_CASE*** object type in each case as shown in Figure 2.56, and use the Detail button to navigate to the maintenance dialog for the event start linkage.

Event Type Linkages					
Object Category	ObjectType	Event	Receiver Type	Type linkage	Enable event
BOR Object Typ	APPOINTMNT	REPLY_RECEIVED	WS74500790	☐	☐
BOR Object Typ	BUSISB001	INITIATED	WS50100024	☐	☐
BOR Object Typ	GRPC_BGREP	PREPARED	WS75900008	☑	☐
BOR Object Typ	GRPC_CASEA	CREATED	WS75900004	☑	☑
BOR Object Typ	GRPC_CASEL	CREATED	WS75900005	☑	☐
BOR Object Typ	GRPC_CASES	CREATED	WS75900007	☑	☐
BOR Object Typ	GRPC_CASET	CREATED	WS75900006	☑	☑
BOR Object Typ	GRPC_PLAN	CREATE	WS75900001	☑	☐
BOR Object Typ	IDOC	PROCESSSTATEREA	TS30200090	☐	☐
BOR Object Typ	IDOCALEAUD	INPUTERROROCCUR	TS00407904	☐	☐
BOR Object Typ	IDOCALFW	INPUTERROROCCUR	TS00200353	☐	☐

Figure 2.56 Changing Event Start Linkages for GRPC* Object Type

You can now deactivate the *linkage* in the maintenance dialog of the event start linkage. To do this, you should either remove the **Linkage Activated** checkmark or (as shown in Figure 2.57) enter the "GRPCW_ EVENT_CHECK_FB" function module in the **Check Function Module** field.

Removing activated linkages

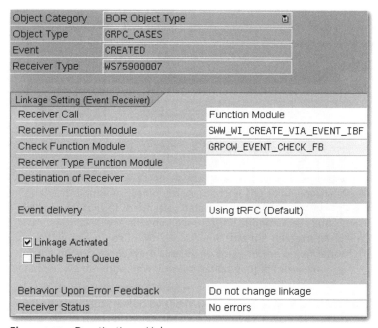

Figure 2.57   Deactivating a Linkage

To increase the performance of the workflow processing in GRC Process Control, you should register the logical RFC target in the qRFC monitor. This involves entering the logical RFC target used by the workflow into the **Destination** field, as shown in Figure 2.58, using the **SAP GRC Process Control • Workflow • Register Workflow System in qRFC Monitor** menu path. You use the **Registration** button to register the logical RFC target in the qRFC outbound queue.

Registering a workflow system in the qRFC monitor

The entry in the **Max. Conn.** field determines how many connections the queue can open or how many dialog processes can be saved. In the **Max. Runtime** field, you define how many processing seconds are to be assigned to a target if several targets are in the queue. If there is a preferred target, you can increase the default value (60 seconds) for this target. You should not enter anything in the **W/o tRFC** field.

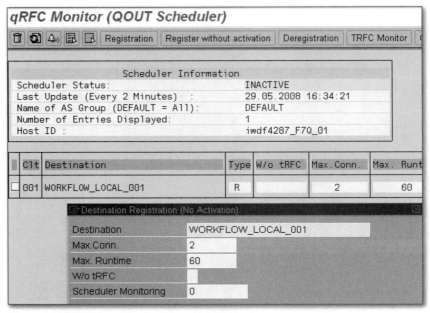

Figure 2.58 RFC Target Registration in qRFC Monitor

Transferring work
items to successors

You can schedule the *Transfer work items to successor* program using the **SAP GRC Process Control • Workflow • Transfer Work Items to Successor** menu path. If required, the "GRPC_REPLACEMENT_MASS_ACTI-VATE" program transfers the workflow tasks or work items of previous GRC Process Control users to the corresponding successors in this case.

Setting up
reminders and
escalations

You maintain reminders and escalations using the **SAP GRC Process Control • Workflow • Set Up Reminders and Escalations** path. You can configure reminders for automatic review and monitoring functions and escalations for overdue control designs, control and process assessments, manual tests, and so on. Reminders and escalations in this case can be sent to process owners, test owners or specific role owners, to mention a few.

> **Note**
>
> Due to the required technical knowledge of workflows, a detailed description for configuring reminders and escalations is beyond the scope of this book. You normally have to entrust the corresponding configuration of reminders and escalations to an SAP workflow specialist. At this point, however, we should mention that development authorization and authorization for maintaining workflows are necessary for the corresponding configuration.

You should store a user as an alternative recipient for the Customizing activity under the **SAP GRC Process Control · Workflow · Define Alternative Recipient for Work Items** path. This user receives the work items, for which the system did not determine a recipient. The alternative recipient should also have administration authorization and be able to determine the relevant correct recipient.

Defining alternative recipients for work items

You can subsequently use the **SAP GRC Process Control · Workflow · Configure Personal Worklist for GRC PC Access** path with the IMG to assign the role type first and then define the query. You can then assign the query role and specify the category.

Personal worklist

You can use the *Assign Role Type* activity to link the application and the POWL (Personal Object Worklist) type (GRPC_INBOX in each case) with a particular role. However, to be able to link all roles with the personal worklist, you must leave the *Role* field empty in the corresponding Customizing maintenance table.

Assigning role types

If you created default queries using Transaction POWL_QUERY, you use the Define Query IMG activity to activate them for a certain user, or the Assign Query Role activity to activate them for a particular user group or complete application.

Defining queries

In the Define Category activity, you can create default categories to assign default queries to categories. If you don't assign any categories here, a default assignment will be created for a Without Category Assignment user query.

Defining categories

If required, you can then use the IMG under **SAP GRC Process Control · Workflow · Configure SAPconnect** to set up the *SAPconnect* communication interface. To send external e-mails through the SAP system, you implement the settings in accordance with the Customizing documentation.

Configuring SAPconnect

> **Note**
>
> For the *SAPconnect* communication interface, we recommend that you only send acknowledgements of receipt when testing the e-mail function. In the live system, however, you should deactivate the option for acknowledgements of receipt.

Scheduling jobs for sending e-mail

You can use the **SAP GRC Process Control** • **Workflow** • **Schedule Job for Sending E-Mail** Customizing activity to schedule a specific program. This program checks whether new work items exist, and determines the e-mail address of the recipients. SAP provides default text for the corresponding notification, and this is stored in the "GRPC_NOTIF_INBOX" dialog text. You can create your own dialog text with Transaction SE61 and store it as an option for the "GRPC_WF_NOTIFICATION" program.

Checking Customizing for Case Management

You can use the **SAP GRC Process Control** • **Cases** • **Check Customizing for Case Management** IMG activity to check now whether the configuration for *Case Management* delivered with SAP GRC Process Control was transferred to the current client without errors, technically speaking.

Figure 2.59 shows that the Customizing configuration for Case Management does not contain any errors because all traffic lights are green. If there are errors, a red light is displayed and you can double-click to subsequently go to the corresponding Customizing activity. You can use the *Customizing Cross-System Viewer* button (Transaction SCU0) to compare the Customizing settings in the current client with those in the delivery client. In addition, SAP Note 753547 describes how you can transfer the delivered settings from the delivery client to the current client again.

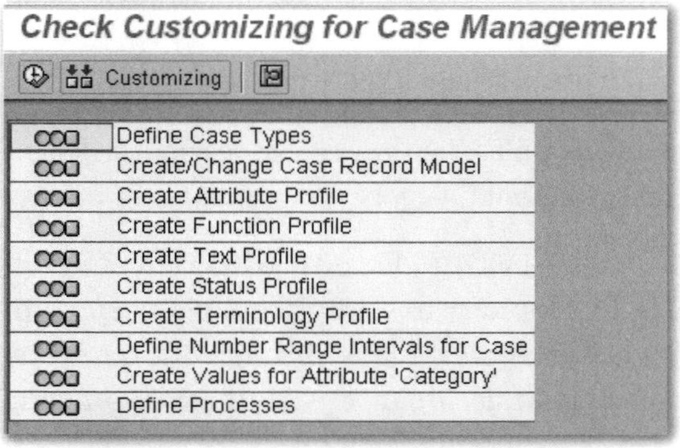

Figure 2.59 Case Management Configuration Contains No Errors

In the next **SAP GRC Process Control • Cases • Define Number Range for Cases** IMG activity, you simply maintain the number range for the case. When you create or save a case, an internal system number is automatically assigned to this case. We recommend that you define at least another number range interval in each case because number range 01 in SAP GRC Process Control is used by all available case types.

Defining number ranges for cases

With the Create Index for Case Attribute Table IMG activity, you can use the **SAP GRC Process Control • Cases • Create Index for Case Attribute Table** menu path to improve the performance for the case attribute database table. Use the ABAP Dictionary maintenance dialog to create a *nonunique index* here for the *Client* and *External Reference* fields of the "SCMG_T_CASE_ATTR" case attribute table, and then activate the index.

Creating indexes for case attribute tables

You can use the IMG to schedule the "GRPC_CLOSING_BACKGROUND" program under the **SAP GRC Process Control • Cases • Copy Cases to New Period after Sign-Off** path. If a sign-off is performed for an organizational unit in SAP GRC Process Control, the program copies all cases that are still open (e.g., remediation measures that have not yet been completed) to a new period and also resets the workflows.

Copying cases to a new period after sign-off

If required, you can also schedule the **SAP GRC Process Control • Cases • Copy Documents to New Period After Transfer** activity to a new period after you've successfully transferred open tasks. After you transfer a task that is still open, the relevant documents for this task, which were created during assessments or tests for issues or remediation plans, are also transferred to the new period with this activity.

Copying documents to a new period after transfer

SAP GRC Process Control provides four selection procedures for the scheduling function in the application. However, you can use the **SAP GRC Process Control • Planning and Scheduling • Maintain Selection Procedure** activity, if necessary, to set up an object selection adapted on a customer-specific basis for the scheduling function.

Maintaining selection procedures

2.3.3   Structure

You can use the Additionally Supported Languages IMG activity with the **SAP GRC Process Control • Structure • Additionally Supported Lan-**

Additionally supported languages

guages menu path to define other languages that you can use to display the application interface. Because each language is assigned a **Sequence** indicator (see Figure 2.60), you can also change the sequence of the languages. The **Sequence** indicator here determines which language is selected for the application if the logon language isn't available.

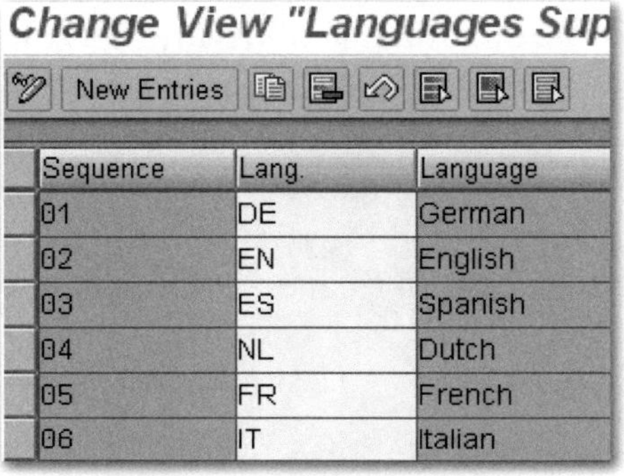

Sequence	Lang.	Language
01	DE	German
02	EN	English
03	ES	Spanish
04	NL	Dutch
05	FR	French
06	IT	Italian

Figure 2.60 Languages Supported in SAP GRC Process Control

If you want to use the subsequent **Set Up Structure: Expert Mode** IMG activity with additional languages, you must maintain the additional language support.

Cleaning up HR data

After SAP GRC Process Control is delivered and installed, it still contains some superfluous table entries in Table HRP1000 in particular. You should delete these entries on all accounts in two steps using the **SAP GRC Process Control • Structure • Clean Up HR Data** Customizing activity.

Table HRP1000

Note

If you don't delete the entries delivered in Table HRP1000, the validity data and names for the delivered objects in particular could overlap with the new structural objects created and consequently cause data inconsistencies.

After you've successfully deleted the data of the superfluous table entries, you should reset the number ranges using the next Define Number Ranges for Master Data Objects IMG activity.

However, you only need to define other number ranges using the **SAP GRC Process Control • Structure • Define Number Ranges for Master Data Objects** IMG activity if a separate number range is to be used in your corporation for individual or all SAP GRC Process Control objects. Figure 2.61 shows that "**$$$$**" is the default number range.

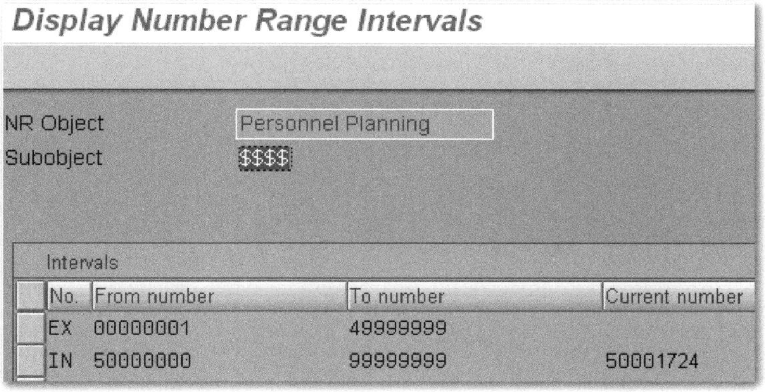

Defining number ranges for master data objects

Display Number Range Intervals

NR Object	Personnel Planning
Subobject	$$$$

Intervals

	No.	From number	To number	Current number
	EX	00000001	49999999	
	IN	50000000	99999999	50001724

Figure 2.61 Default $$$$ Number Range

> **Note**
>
> Because Organization Management functions (BC-BMT-OM) are used for the structure of internal controls, you maintain the number ranges for SAP GRC Process Control in the **Personnel Planning** number range object (see Figure 2.61).

With the IMG under **SAP GRC Process Control • Structure • Set Up Structure: Expert Mode**, the power user (COR-ICMAN role ID) in particular should set up the central structures, create organization-specific objects, and perform different assignments.

Setting up structures: Expert mode

One of the things you should use expert mode for is to create the first two nodes of the organizational hierarchy. You can define an organization in change mode first using the **Edit • Create Organizational Unit** menu path (see Figure 2.62). With the selected top node organization, you can now use the **Create** button to create another organization node under the selected organization. Because you've now created a top node and lower-level organization node, SAP GRC Process Control recognizes the top node as the highest corporation level.

Highest corporation level

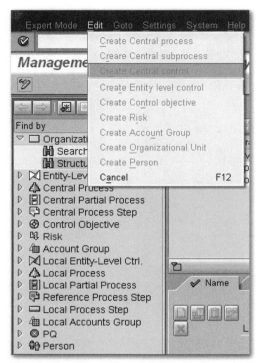

Figure 2.62 Expert Mode for Defining Central Objects

ASGN-RLORG task

To enable you to assign roles at corporation level as a user in SAP GRC Process Control, the ASGN-RLORG task must be assigned to you. In the BC Set roles provided, this task is assigned to the Internal Control Manager with the COR-ICMAN role ID. In this context, note that the corresponding access role can only be assigned to *one* user at corporation level using the IMG.

The organizations you previously created are now available in the web application for SAP GRC Process Control. You can now also use the web application to define additional organizations as lower-level nodes for the organizations already created.

Organization-specific objects

Also note that no SAP GRC Process Control-specific flow logic or automatic context linkages are available in expert mode when you create objects. Technically speaking, in expert mode, all organization-specific objects are perceived as individual objects that you must create and connect to central objects.[3] The advantage of Web applications is that many organization-specific objects are created automatically when you assign them to the organization.

If you discover errors relating to data consistency, the expert mode functions are beneficial because they enable you to call all objects and their connections individually.

In the **SAP GRC Process Control · Structure · Select Organizational Hierarchy as relevant for PC** IMG activity, if necessary you can now define which of the organizational hierarchies you stored for SAP GRC Process Control is actually relevant. All organizational hierarchies are displayed by default because there is no entry in this Customizing table in the default settings provided.

Selecting relevant organizational hierarchies

You can then use the IMG to activate the Shared Objects Memory function for central data structures under **SAP GRC Process Control · Structure · Shared Objects Memory · Activate Shared Objects Memory**. This can improve system performance when you call data in the web application. If you activate this function for the central organizational hierarchy, the system loads the data for the corresponding period into the buffer when a user calls data. If another user then requests the organization hierarchy data for the same period, the data is loaded from the buffer and not from the database. However, if the requested period does not match the buffer period exactly, the data is read directly from the database and presented to the user.

Activating shared objects memory

If you activate the Shared Objects Memory for the central structures and catalogs, a separate area instance is created for each individual period. However, you should only activate the shared objects memory if your users generally call data with read access.

You can use the **SAP GRC Process Control · Structure · Shared Objects Memory · Monitor Active Areas** menu path for the Monitor Active Areas activity to monitor which area instances exist in which version in the system for SAP GRC Process Control.

Monitoring active areas

---

3 This does not apply for the initial master data upload using the MDUG tool. If the MDUG upload template is populated correctly, the uploaded data objects will also be linked with the central structures.

If an area with the prefix CL_GRPC_SHM* is displayed in the initial screen, this means that at least one user is accessing an object of the corresponding area. By double-clicking an area, you can display more details about the available area instances. Figure 2.63 shows that no user is currently accessing an SAP GRC Process Control object with the CL_GRPC_SHM* area in this system.

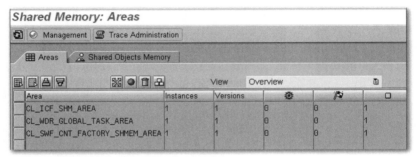

Figure 2.63 Monitoring Active Areas

SAP GRC Process Control • User-Defined Fields

Note

We won't describe in further detail the necessary activities under the **SAP GRC Process Control • User-Defined Fields** menu path for developing user-defined fields for SAP GRC Process Control.

If required, you can create data objects (domains, data elements, structures, etc.), for example, in the ABAP Dictionary in this IMG area. Furthermore, you can create new infotypes here and make them available for expert mode. You can also use an activity to upload functions for the new infotype, change the appearance of user-defined fields by implementing and activating Business Add-Ins (BAdIs), and define how you want user-defined fields to be included in an online report.

At this point, we won't discuss the development of user-defined fields for SAP GRC Process Control further. Due to the knowledge of ABAP development required, such a description is beyond the scope of this book. You must entrust the corresponding development of user-defined fields to an SAP ABAP expert. However, we should mention that the ABAP developer will need the S_DEVELOP authorization profile or an equivalent authorization for the corresponding development of user-defined fields.

Specifying names for ratings

In the Specify Names for Ratings IMG activity, you must store the names of the three (adequate, significant deviation, etc.) possible assessment or rating levels that you want to be used for assessments and tests. You use the **SAP GRC Process Control** • **Assessment and Test** • **Specify Names for Ratings** menu path for this purpose.

> **Note**
>
> There are three assessment options for SAP GRC Process Control because SAP traffic light functions are used in the application for display purposes. This means that the whole flow logic is based on three assessment levels. Although you can adjust the names of the three values on a customer-specific basis, modifying the flow logic to extend this table to four assessment options or restrict it to only two assessment options is a serious modification that we advise against on all accounts.

If necessary, to specify which evaluation results you actually want to be included in the problem report, you can use the Determine Controls at Entity Level: Necessity of Issue Report activity with the **SAP GRC Process Control** • **Assessment and Test** • **Determine Controls at Entity Level: Necessity of Issue Reports** path for assessing or testing controls at the organization level. For example, you can specify here that only controls with an inadequate or significant deficiency rating should be displayed in a report.

Determining controls at entity level

You can use the **SAP GRC Process Control** • **Assessment and Test** • **Define Summarization for Control Group Evaluation at Entity Level** path to determine how you want the assessments for management controls of subordinate levels to be summarized. For example, you can define whether the whole assessment for the lower-level node is to be determined by the worst assessment or by an average assessment.

Defining control group evaluations at entity level

You can then use the IMG under **SAP GRC Process Control** • **Assessment and Test** • **Specify Whether Review Is Required** to specify whether a particular assessment or test still also has to be reviewed or validated by another user. You can also decide whether the remediation plans also require validation in each case (see Figure 2.64).

Specifying whether a review is required

You can overwrite the settings implemented here when you assign processes to an organizational unit. If the validation details don't change, a validation indicator set in the central Customizing table (e.g., for the control design assessment) means that each (control design) assessment must be reviewed. However, you can't overwrite the defined validation indicator for assessments of management controls under any circumstances at a later stage.

Validation		
Indicator	Activate	Text
VALIDATION1	☑	Validation of Control Design Assessment
VALIDATION2	☑	Validation of Self-Assessment of Control
VALIDATION3	☑	Validation of Subprocess Design Assessment
VALIDATION4	☑	Validation of Entity Level Control Assessment
VALIDATION5	☑	Validation of Remediation Plan
VALIDATION6	☑	Validation of Manual Test of Control Effectiveness

Figure 2.64 Review or Validation Required?

Skipping review depending on evaluationNevertheless, you can now use the **SAP GRC Process Control • Assessment and Test • Skip Review Depending on Evaluation** Customizing path to specify that an additional review isn't required for certain assessments.

To explain this function, we assume that you've set the central validation indicator for the control design assessment in the preceding Customizing activity (refer to Figure 2.64). The result now of the activated setting shown in Figure 2.65 for an adequate control design assessment (green traffic light) is that an additional validation does not have to be performed in this case.

Skip Validation Depending on the Rating		
Indicator	Activate	Text
SKIP_VAL_ASCD_GREEN	☑	Skip Validation of Control Design Assessment If Rating Is Green
SKIP_VAL_ASCD_RED	☐	Skip Validation of Control Design Assessment If Rating Is Red
SKIP_VAL_ASCD_YELLOW	☐	Skip Validation of Control Design Assessment If Rating Is Yellow
SKIP_VAL_ASCE_GREEN	☐	Skip Validation of Control Efficiency Assessment If Rating Is Gree
SKIP_VAL_ASCE_RED	☐	Skip Validation of Control Efficiency Assessment If Rating Is Red
SKIP_VAL_ASCE_YELLOW	☐	Skip Validation of Control Efficiency Assessment If Rating Is Yello
SKIP_VAL_ASMC_GREEN	☐	Skip Validation of Management Control Assessment If Rating Is G
SKIP_VAL_ASMC_RED	☐	Skip Validation of Management Control Assessment If Rating Is R
SKIP_VAL_ASMC_YELLOW	☐	Skip Validation of Management Control Assessment If Rating Is Y
SKIP_VAL_ASPD_GREEN	☐	Skip Validation of Process Design Assessment If Rating Is Green
SKIP_VAL_ASPD_RED	☐	Skip Validation of Process Design Assessment If Rating Is Red
SKIP_VAL_ASPD_YELLOW	☐	Skip Validation of Process Design Assessment If Rating Is Yellow
SKIP_VAL_TECO_EXC	☐	Skip Validation of Control Effectiveness Test If There Are Except
SKIP_VAL_TECO_NO_EXC	☐	Skip Validation of Control Effectiveness Test If There Are No Exc

Figure 2.65 Skip Validation Depending on the Rating

2.3.4 Automatic Testing and Monitoring

To use the technical functions of SAP GRC Process Control operationally in the application for automatic testing and monitoring, you must first configure the corresponding RFC connectors. You can set up the RFC connectors using the **SAP GRC Process Control · Assessment and Test · Automatic Testing and Monitoring · Configure RFC Connectors** menu path. You can connect SAP GRC Process Control to other SAP and non-SAP systems in this case. After you technically configure the RFC connectors, you should also perform a connection test to see whether the RFC connection setup was successful.

Configuring RFC connectors

You can use the IMG under **SAP GRC Process Control · Assessment and Test · Automatic Testing and Monitoring · Maintain System Type** to store system types (SAP, Oracle, PeopleSoft, etc.), from which the source data for automatic testing and monitoring originates (see Figure 2.66).

Maintaining system types

System Type	
System Typ	Syetem Type Description
CC	Compliance Calibrator
LOCAL	Local System
MAPPQRY	Multiple Applications Query
ORACLE	Oracle
PSFT	PeopleSoft
SAP	SAP System

Figure 2.66 Maintaining System Types

You configure a connection to one or more internal/external systems using the **SAP GRC Process Control · Assessment and Test · Automatic Testing and Monitoring · Register Connectors** Customizing path. You can carry out the configuration using the definition of the target and source connector, as shown in Figure 2.67. The **Target Connector** here represents the connection definition that the GRC system uses for connecting to the other (target) systems. The **Source Connector** is the corresponding SAP GRC Process Control system. If there is more than one target connector for the source connector, you must define a **Default Target Connector**.

Registering connectors

Connector Setup			
System Type	Target Connector	Source Connector	Default Target Connector
SAP	QVD	F7Q	☑
SAP	TB F7K	TB F7Q	☐

Figure 2.67 Registering Connectors

Rule

In the *Rule* Customizing area, you can combine rules in rule groups and define rule deficiency descriptions using the **SAP GRC Process Control • Assessment and Test • Automatic Testing and Monitoring • Rule • Create Rule Group or Maintain Rule Deficiency Description** menu path. Rules are grouped for reporting purposes in this case. Rule deficiency definitions are used when rules are being processed. Resulting exceptions or deficiencies are rated based on the entries stored here. You can change rule deficiency descriptions and thereby take into account existing corporate policies. For example, you could automatically re-categorize a *Catastrophic* exception definition received from a target system to *Very Critical*.

Transporting master data

The Customizing entries in the Transport Master Data area under the **SAP GRC Process Control • Assessment and Test • Automatic Testing and Monitoring • Transport Master Data** path aren't connected to the automatic SAP Transport Management System. However, you generally need to transport these maintenance entries from one system to another. You can therefore use the four IMG activities in the *Transport Master Data* area to include the corresponding Customizing entries of system parameter objects for rule criteria, rule scripts, rule definitions, and organization levels, including their dependent object entries, into transport requests.

Open the relevant activity here and then navigate to the **Table View • Transport** menu option (see Figure 2.68). Now create a transport request, and select the objects to be transported. You must then include the selected objects in the transport request.

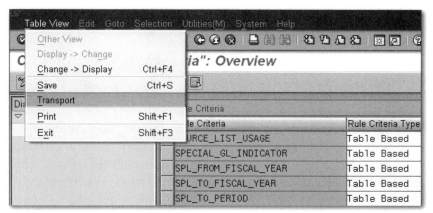

Figure 2.68 Transporting Selected Objects

Different Web Service definitions (with the GRPC* prefix) are provided for SAP GRC Process Control. You must register and publish the corresponding Web Services in the UDDI (Universal Description, Discovery, and Integration)directory using the Activate Inbound Web Service IMG activity by selecting the **SAP GRC Process Control • Assessment and Test • Automatic Testing and Monitoring • Web Services • Activate Inbound Web Services** path or using Transaction SICF as a business service.

Activating inbound
Web Services

Open the **SOAP Application for RFC-Compliant FMs** folder as shown in Figure 2.69, and then select the GRPC* Web Services to be published.

Web Service Administration for SOAP Runtime

SOAP Application/Service Definition/Variant/Web Service	Access Address
▷ 🗀 SOAP Application for RFC-Compliant FMs	
▷ 🗀 SOAP Application for XI Proxies	

Figure 2.69 UDDI Registration of Web Services

In the *UDDI Publications* area of the *Web Service ID* dialog box, you can enter the corresponding name of the UDDI registration and then publish the Web Service.

> **Note**
>
> You'll find more information about UDDI registration in the SAP Help Portal. Search for *UDDI* or *Maintaining UDDI Registries* there.

Configuring ports

As soon as you've configured an HTTP connection for outbound Web Service calls, you can configure a logical port using the **SAP GRC Process Control • Assessment and Test • Automatic Testing and Monitoring • Web Services • Configure Port** menu path or Transaction LPCONFIG. The logical port is specifically used for this outbound Web Service. After you define the logical port, you must register it as a connector for Web Services using the *Register Connectors* activity already described.

Registering connectors for Web Services

For integration with the Compliance Calibrator functions of SAP GRC Access Control, you need to set up two different Web Services and two logical ports in the *Register Connectors for Web Services* IMG activity. You can perform this configuration using the **SAP GRC Process Control • Assessment and Test • Automatic Testing and Monitoring • Compliance Calibrator Integration • Register Connectors for Web Services** path. You use the first Web Service to obtain a list of individual users with rule violations and the second Web Service to call detailed information about the rule violations. For both Web Services, you must configure logical ports that you then assign to the Compliance Calibrator connectors and that are also used for the necessary job scheduling.

2.3.5   Reporting

Creating indexes for tables for infotype 1001

If necessary, you can use the **SAP GRC Process Control • Reporting • Create Index for Table for Infotype 1001** menu path with the *Create Index for Table for Infotype 1001* IMG activity to improve the performance of the HRP1001 database table. Use the ABAP Dictionary maintenance dialog to create a *nonunique index* here for the *Subtype Client, Type of Linked Object, Plan Version, Plan Status, Linking of Object Type* and *Object ID*, and *End Date* fields and then activate the index.

Activating BAdIs for weighting a reporting line for aggregations

You can then use the *Activate BAdI for Weighting a Reporting Line for Aggregation* activity to activate a Business Add-In (BAdI) and, in doing so, define how the overall assessment is to be determined in hierarchical reports. You can use a BAdI to assign a greater weighting to individual reporting lines, for example. You define and activate a BAdI using the **SAP GRC Process Control • Reporting • Activate BAdI for Weighting a Reporting Line for Aggregation** path.

If the *Maintain Reporting Buffer* function is active in your application system, all data for all reporting types available at the corresponding time is determined and stored in the reporting buffer. If you now call a report in SAP GRC Process Control, the data is read from the buffer. In the IMG activity, of the things you can use the **SAP GRC Process Control • Reporting • Maintain Reporting Buffer** menu for is to establish that reporting buffers are generally to be used for reports.

Maintaining reporting buffers

After you've determined the selection criteria for the reporting buffer, you should activate the reporting buffer as shown in Figure 2.70. You should also determine the error handling if the reporting buffer does not contain any data. In the **Cleanup** area, you also specify how many old versions of a report are to be held in the reporting buffer and how long they are to be kept as backup copies.

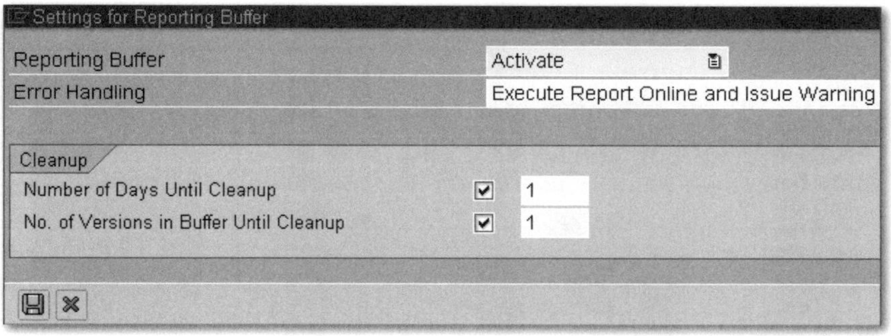

Reporting buffer cleanup

Figure 2.70   Creating a Reporting Buffer

You can then create the reporting buffer using the *Create Reporting Buffer* and *Create* buttons. You must also maintain the time frame and year because you can create a separate buffer for each time frame. You can also use this transaction to monitor the status of the reporting buffer (see Figure 2.71). The buffer should be regularly filled with new data using the corresponding *Fill Reporting Buffer* function.

Filling reporting buffers

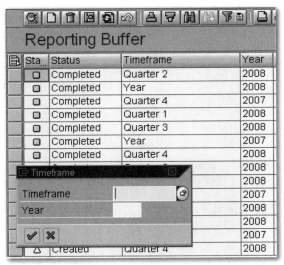

Figure 2.71 Maintenance and Status Monitoring of Reporting Buffer

Entering roles for determining the person responsible for an object

Several roles are relevant for a particular object for SAP GRC Process Control; therefore, several persons may also be responsible for an object. For this reason, you can store the role for each object type under **SAP GRC Process Control · Reporting · Enter Role to Determine Person Responsible for an Object** to determine which person responsible is displayed in the SAP GRC Process Control reports. If you don't enter anything here, the system will determine the object owners by default using the tasks entered in the *RESP_TASK* field and GRPCOBJTYPE table.

Activating alternative downloads of print reports

You can use the subsequent *Activate Alternative Download of Print Reports* activity if performance problems occur when you display print reports. In the IMG activity under the **SAP GRC Process Control · Reporting · Activate Alternative Download of Print Reports** path, you then specify that print reports are to be downloaded using a specific service for SAP GRC Process Control. The alternative service consequently downloads print reports more quickly in compressed form and with a certain data volume. The threshold for this data volume depends on the relevant hardware infrastructure. To use the alternative download of print reports, you must activate the HTTP/1.1 settings on the SAP server and in the web browser settings of the corresponding users.

You can use the *Define Column Fields for Reports Display* activity to extend or change the reporting columns in an SAP GRC Process Control report. A certain group of columns is identified as a field group here, and a predefined *field group* exists for each report. You can adapt field groups using the **SAP GRC Process Control • Reporting • Define Column Fields for Reporting Display** menu path. The field groups for SAP GRC Process Control reports are identified with the GRPC_REPORT* prefix. Each individual report is also assigned to a reporting type.

You can use the **SAP GRC Process Control • Reporting • Transfer Data to SAP BW** Customizing activity to call the IMG for transferring data into SAP BW or SAP NetWeaver BI. You can activate the supplied *DataSources for SAP GRC Process Control* there.

You can then use the **SAP GRC Process Control • Sign-off • Deactivate Issue Types for Sign-Off** path in the IMG activity to specify that certain issue types aren't to be taken into account for the sign-off .

Figure 2.72 shows that you can use this method to deactivate the sign-off for issues related to assessing the subprocess design. That is, the issues of this assessment would therefore no longer be contained in the list of issues that require a comment during sign-off. In the standard system, note that all issue types are taken into consideration for the sign-off.

Defining column fields for displaying reports

Transferring data to SAP NetWeaver BI

Deactivating issue types for sign-off

Case Type	Category	Sign-Off	Priority
G_AS	CD	Yes	Low
G_AS	CE	Yes	Low
G_AS	MC	Yes	Low
G_AS	PD	No	Low
G_TE	TE	Yes	Low

Figure 2.72 Deactivating Issue Types for Sign-Off

In the IMG under **SAP GRC Process Control • Sign-Off • Change Notice Text for Sign-Off**, you can now change the notice text that is displayed in the web application during sign-off.

Changing note text for sign-off

To transport the text change using Transaction SLXT, you must save it in a separate package in the SAP customer namespace. Select the **General text** document class, as shown in Figure 2.73, and enter "GRPCSIGNOFF_NOTE" in the **Name** field. By clicking the **Change** button, you now go to change mode and can change the notice text or enter new text.

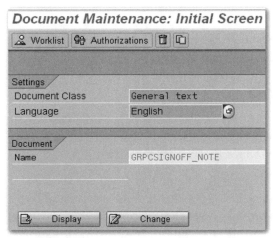

Figure 2.73 Changing Notice Text for Sign-Off

SAP GRC Process Control • Administration Programs

> **Note**
>
> We won't describe the activities under the **SAP GRC Process Control • Administration Programs** menu path in more detail because functions for managing and monitoring SAP GRC Process Control-specific workflows in particular are available here. You can use these functions as required in the live operation of SAP GRC Process Control. However, you should activate the GRPC application logs for remediation in SAP GRC Process Control because these are deactivated by default.
>
> If required, you can also use the consistency check of the validity periods to check whether the validity of lower-level objects is within the validity of higher-level objects.
>
> Programs are available in the Administration Programs area that you can use to check and, if necessary, repair work items with invalid objects; check Case Management Customizing; reorganize cases and workflows; and enable assessments or tests to be started ad-hoc. For more information, refer to the documentation of the individual programs.

You can use the *Analyze Application Log for Scheduling* function to call logs that the system has written during task scheduling.

For remediation in SAP GRC Process Control, you should activate the GRPC application log, which you can use to display and analyze API accesses or authorization logs. You can restrict the logs to certain criteria here, such as object, external number, time frame, and the user who created the log. Remember, however, that activating the GRPC application logs can affect the performance of the server.

SAP NetWeaver Business Client (NWBC) is the frontend web interface for SAP GRC Process Control. A specific NWBC configuration is required, which you can implement using the **SAP GRC Process Control • NWBC Settings • Set Up SAP NetWeaver Business Client** menu path. Also read SAP Note 1108563 for the configuration, and, in particular, use the path specified in this note for configuring NWBC.

Setting up SAP NetWeaver Business Client

You must set up number ranges for event-based monitoring by initializing the GRPC_EVENT and GRPC_ EVTLG number range objects using the **SAP GRC Process Control • Event-Based Monitoring • Set Up Number Range for Event Tables** path.

Setting up a number range for result tables

You can then use the **SAP GRC Process Control • Event-Based Monitoring • Set Up Evaluation Delay** menu path to delay the time for executing evaluation reports. In this case, however, the event queue should not be overloaded with reports waiting for execution. The current default value for delaying the execution of evaluations is 15 minutes.

Setting up evaluation delays

Before you can use the previously defined Web Services, you must release them for the SOAP runtime using the **SAP GRC Process Control • Event-Based Monitoring • Release Web Service** path.

Releasing Web Services

You can now use the **SAP GRC Process Control • Event-Based Monitoring • Test Web Service** IMG path to test the definitions of Web Services before operational use.

Testing Web Services

You'll subsequently require the ICF service (*International Communication Framework*) for all Web Services because it forms the access point for HTTP requests. You set up the ICF node for publishing the service, or you activate it (see Figure 2.74) using the **SAP GRC Process Control • Event-Based Monitoring • Set Up ICF for Service** menu path.

Setting up ICF for services

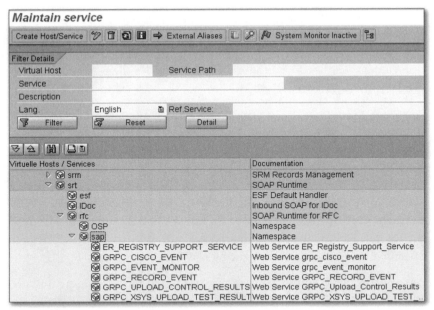

Figure 2.74 Maintaining Web Services

BAdI implementation for notification about rule violation

Finally, you can use the **SAP GRC Process Control • Event-Based Monitoring • BAdI Implementation for Notification About Rule Violation** path to implement a notification after a rule has been violated. Use GPC_EVENT_BASED for event-based error monitoring and GRPC_SCHEDULED_BASED for scheduled-based errors.

Two safety measures are better than one. (Cahier)

3   SAP GRC Access Control

SAP GRC Access Control provides a comprehensive range of functions to ensure that individual users within a corporation only receive the access rights they require for their daily work. As result related authorization risks will be detected, mitigated and prevented automatically. In this chapter, we describe the main application scenarios in detail and then present reporting options and configuration steps.

3.1   Overview of SAP GRC Access Control

How can we achieve complete compliance gradually in terms of the necessary separation of duties (SOD) in a corporation? How can we discover if user rights are being abused, and how do we avoid this in future? How can we reliably detect potential regulatory violations?? Using SAP GRC Access Control is the answer to these questions and therefore the solution for controlling access and authorizations in a corporation. SAP GRC Access Control consists of the following four business scenarios:

- ▶ **Risk Analysis and Remediation**
  Analyzes and remediates risks supporting an initial cleaning of the authorizations (Virsa Compliance Calibrator).

- ▶ **Enterprise Role Management**
  Manages enterprise roles during the design time of new roles (Virsa Role Expert).

- ▶ **Compliant User Provisioning**
  Performs compliant user provisioning so that no new violations are created with new user profiles (Virsa Access Enforcer).

▶ **Superuser Privilege Management**
Manages superuser privileges for emergency access (Virsa Firefighter).

3.1.1 Access Risk Analysis and Remediation

Analyzing user data

In the *Access Risk Analysis and Remediation* application area, compliance with specifications that affect the segregation of duties (SOD) in the enterprise is supported in real time. Security controls should be prevented from being violated. In this case, the authorization assignments are first read and then analyzed in the connected SAP ERP systems. Risks are evaluated, the reason is detected, and the root cause can easily be resolved.

Adhering to the segregation of duties

When you evaluate read assigned authorizations, you use a rule set for the SOD. For example, if one and the same employee can create a vendor master record, trigger a purchase order, and initiate payment after an invoice has been received, this is regarded as a high risk. This comprehensive authorization profile means that the employee can invent a fictitious vendor and use regular business transactions to transfer company funds to an account. This would make it very easy for an employee with criminal intent to defraud the company.

Managing risks throughout the enterprise

You can use SAP GRC Access Control throughout the enterprise to find, evaluate, and correct violations of the SOD. In addition to SAP ERP systems you can also check applications from Oracle, PeopleSoft, JD Edwards, and Hyperion.

3.1.2 Enterprise Role Management (Virsa Role Expert)

SAP GRC Access Control already supports you when you design roles in the enterprise. The testing and maintenance phase follows the standardized and centralized design phase of roles. SAP GRC Access Control covers roles for the following business processes in SAP:

▶ Human resources

▶ Procure to pay

▶ Order to cash

- ▶ Finance (general accounting, project systems, fixed assets)
- ▶ Basis, security, and system administration
- ▶ Materials management
- ▶ Advanced Planning and Optimization (APO)
- ▶ Supplier Relationship Management (SRM)
- ▶ Customer Relationship Management (CRM)

You can use SAP GRC Access Control to assign ownership for defining roles to business units. Role owners then define which activities and restrictions apply for the role. Therefore, they are subsequently also obliged to initiate approval processes for a role and use SAP GRC Access Control to store the history about changes made to roles. As another option, role owners can display the roles in which a certain transaction (e.g., triggering the payment run) was assigned. They can also compare different roles.

Defining auditable roles

3.1.3 Compliant User Provisioning (Virsa Access Enforcer)

As jobs and responsibilities change in the enterprise, so too must the associated change in system authorizations be organized. New employees join the enterprise, and others leave. Areas of responsibility are redefined, or others are shared. SAP GRC Access Control supports you with the *Compliant User Provisioning (Virsa Access Enforcer)* function area by making it easier to process assigning and changing privileges and, at the same time, prevent any possible segregations of duties from being violated.

If a job changes and, consequently, more comprehensive system access is also required, the employee makes this request himself by applying for the necessary profile through SAP GRC Access Control. The application triggers a workflow that is used to submit this change request to the employee's manager for approval.

Automatic workflow for approval

You can also use an interface (*HR Real Time Agent*) to connect SAP GRC Access Control to SAP ERP Human Capital Management (SAP ERP HCM). Changes in the employee master record are managed by *infotypes* in the SAP ERP HCM application. You can use them to see whether an

Integration with SAP ERP HCM

employee is leaving or joining the company, or whether his job profile has changed. The manager responsible is also displayed in the employee master record. You can use this interface to forward this HR-related information to SAP GRC Access Control and automatically notify the managers affected by the employee change. Notification occurs in the form of actions that are assigned to the managers or employees themselves. You'll learn more about using actions later in this chapter.

After you've requested the required authorization change, the possible effect is simulated. A check is carried out to see whether the rules set for the SOD will be violated if the request is approved.

SAP GRC Access Control enables the user to request the required authorization profiles without having to deal with the finer technical aspects in detail. The employee's manager can grant the access rights after he has used a simulation to assess the risk of the change. This reduces the workload of the IT department and means that it no longer has to discuss complex technical details of authorization profiles with the owners of the business units.

3.1.4 Superuser Privilege Management (Virsa Firefighter)

Assigning access rights in an emergency

In emergency situations, you can use SAP GRC Access Control to assign more access rights to end users than they normally require for their daily work. You do this by preparing a "Superuser" ID that is assigned to the user temporarily in an emergency.

All activities performed by the user under the "superuser" user ID are recorded and subsequently monitored and evaluated in detail.

3.1.5 Summary

Risk Analysis and Remediation

Figure 3.1 provides an overview of SAP GRC Access Control. The *Risk Analysis and Remediation* application area takes effect when you analyze the existing assignment of access rights for the first time after you've implemented SAP GRC Access Control. You also perform periodic checks of the SOD in the *Risk Analysis and Remediation* application area.

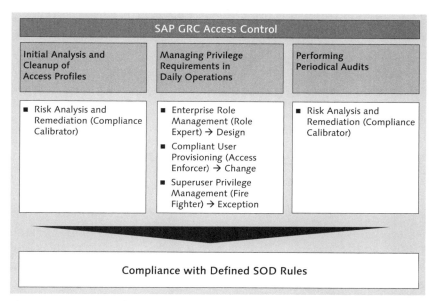

Figure 3.1 Overview of SAP GRC Access Control

To respond safely and with minimum risk to daily change requests for access rights, you use the other application areas of SAP GRC Access Control.

With Enterprise Role Management (Virsa Role Expert), you can already ensure that the required SOD is complied with when you design roles.

Enterprise Role Management

If additional access rights are requested for a user profile, there is a risk that, due to this additional assignment of the authorization, the individual user will contain access rights that are too comprehensive from the point of view of SOD. This situation never occurs with *Compliant User Provisioning (Virsa Access Enforcer)* because the change is checked for possible risks before it's finally approved.

Compliant User Provisioning

In exceptional cases, users have to perform necessary repairs or have to perform important transactions. So they need emergency access without violating segregation of duties. This exceptional case is mapped using the *Superuser Privilege Management (Virsa Firefighter)* application area.

Superuser Privilege Management

SAP GRC Access Control provides a comprehensive, cross-enterprise record of access controls that enables you to define coordinated roles throughout the enterprise and perform and monitor the SOD correctly. SAP GRC Access Control also provides enterprise-wide management in terms of defining and providing roles and of functions for privileged superusers.

3.2 Initial Analysis and Cleanup of Authorization Profiles

After we've successfully implemented SAP GRC Access Control for the EWP corporation, we first analyze the access rights assigned in the applications and IT systems. The objective is to find possible security and segregation of duties violations of errors in the authorizations assigned and any resulting risks for the enterprise.

3.2.1 Identifying Risks

The starting point for reviewing the situation is the management overview of the authorization assignments that violate the rules for the segregation of duties (SOD). You obtain the analysis results by selecting the **Informer • Management View • Risk Violations** function path. The analysis results in Figure 3.2 show that **59** users were analyzed. The result of this analysis is **233** cases where the rules for the SOD were violated.

Management View

The **Management View** also provides information about how the identified risks are distributed on the different business processes. For example, **67** risks were identified in the **Procure to Pay** process.

By double-clicking the lettering of the **PR** column (procure to pay) in the lower-right section of the screen, you receive a list of risks that have been identified for the procure to pay business process.

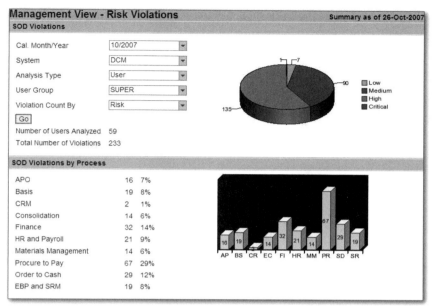

Figure 3.2 Management View of Identified Risks

The numbers in the column on the right (see Figure 3.3) indicate how often the risks in question have been found. In this case, the risks have been identified for one user respectively.

SOD Violations by Process Procure to Pay

System: DCM — Last Run on: 10/2007

Risk Description	Risk Level	No. of Violations
P001: Create fictitious vendor and initiate payment to the vendor	High	1
P002: Maintain a fictitious vendor and direct disbursements to it	High	1
P003: Create fictitious vendor invoice and initiate payment for it	High	1
P004: Purch unauthorized items and initiate payment by invoicing	High	1
P005: Purch unauth items and hide by not fully receiving order	High	1
P006: Hide inventory by not fully receiving order but invoicing	High	1
P007: Purch unauthorized items and enact payment for them	High	1
P008: Maintain a fictitious vendor and initiate purchase to vendor	High	1
P009: Receive services and release blocked invoice to offset recpt	Medium	1
P010: Maintain PO and release a previously blocked Invoice	Medium	1

Figure 3.3 Overview of Risks for Procure to Pay Business Process

However, what exactly the risks involve is interesting for further analysis. The **P003** risk specifies that the user can create fictitious vendor invoices and also release payment for them. When you double-click the **P003** risk ID, the **Risk Information** window opens (see Figure 3.4).

Critical combination of functions

The risk information provides details about which critical combination of functions the user can execute. These are **AP01 - AP Payments** and **AP02 - Process Vendor Invoices** in the case presented here. This violates the rule for the SOD because a user should only execute one business function.

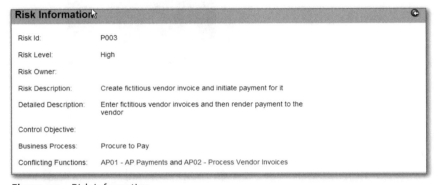

Figure 3.4 Risk Information

You can use the risk information to read the function conflicts at the business level. For the analysis, you don't need to know the technical details of the privilege concept.

Catalog of functions

SAP GRC Access Control has a catalog of functions that map the entire business processes of an enterprise. You can use the functions to bundle transactions and authorization objects. The bundling occurs in such a way that the rules for the SOD are complied with when you assign a function to a user.

If you want to check which transactions are assigned to the Process Vendor Invoices function, double-click the **AP02** function (Process Vendor Invoices).

There are 37 transactions assigned for the selected AP02 function (see Figure 3.5). Corresponding authorization objects are stored in these transactions (see Figure 3.6). You go to the list of authorization objects by selecting the **Permission** tab.

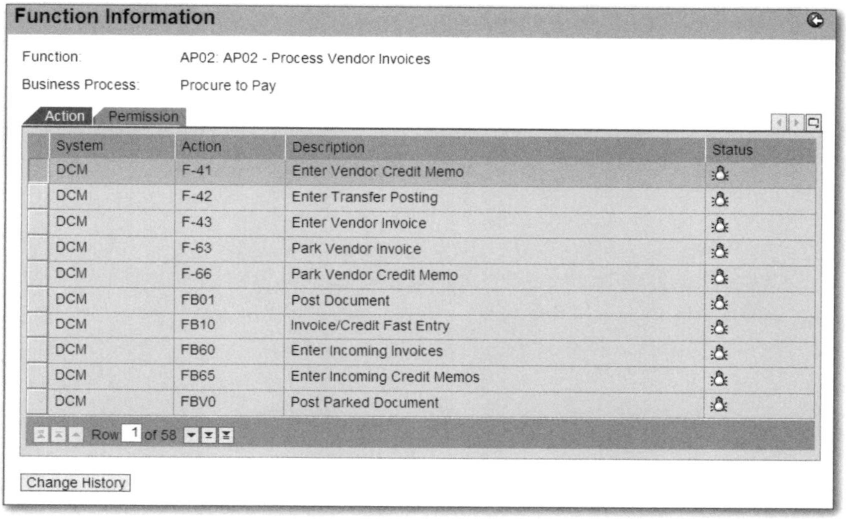

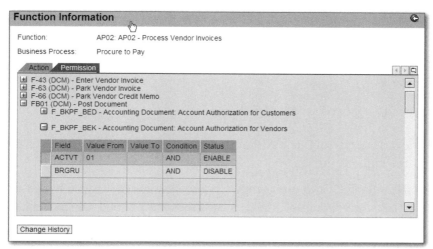

Figure 3.5 Function Information – List of Transactions

Figure 3.6 Function Information – List of Permission Objects

A catalog of risks, functions, and corresponding transactions and authentication objects is provided with SAP GRC Access Control. Possible com-

Risk rules

binations of authentication objects and transactions between two functions result in the list of risk rules (see Figure 3.7). SAP GRC Access Control provides over 100,000 risk rules, which, if they aren't observed, leads to a violation of the SOD and therefore represents a risk to the enterprise.

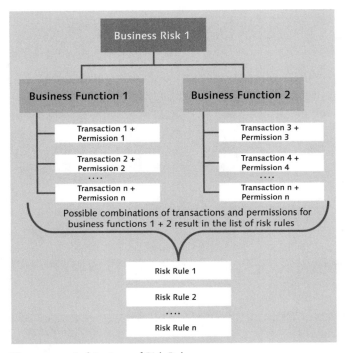

Figure 3.7 Architecture of Risk Rules

Rule architect You can use the rule architect to expand the list of risk rules in the course of the implementation.

Business applications of third-party vendors You can basically also connect ERP systems that aren't provided by SAP to SAP GRC Access Control. The data basis for functions and rules integrated into SAP GRC Access Control is also designed to read and evaluate permissions from business applications from Oracle, PeopleSoft, JD Edwards EnterpriseOne, and Hyperion. You can also connect your own applications (*legacy systems*) to SAP GRC Access Control. This approach enables you to check and improve compliance with the required SOD throughout the enterprise, even if an enterprise operates third-party business applications.

3.2.2 Cleaning Up Privilege Profiles

After the entire list of SOD violations has been made available, you must determine how to deal with this violation in each individual case.

According to the identified P003 risk, the accountant, Alan Gragg, has such extensive permissions that he could create fictitious vendor invoices and also release payment for them later (see Figure 3.8).

User Analysis at Permission Level - Detail Report

User Id: Alan Gragg (AGRAGG)   **User Group:** SUPER   **System:** All

Risk Description	Level	Permission Object	Field	Value	Role/Profile	System
P00300101: Create fictitious vendor invoice and initiate payment for it	High	Transaction Code Check at Transaction Start	Transaction Code	Post with Clearing (F-04)	&_SAP_ALL_15	DCM
P00300101: Create fictitious vendor invoice and initiate payment for it	High	Transaction Code Check at Transaction Start	Transaction Code	Post with Clearing (F-04)	SAP_NEW_30D	DCM
P00300101: Create fictitious vendor invoice and initiate payment for it	High	Transaction Code Check at Transaction Start	Transaction Code	Post with Clearing (F-04)	SAP_NEW_30E	DCM
P00300101: Create fictitious vendor invoice and initiate payment for it	High	Transaction Code Check at Transaction Start	Transaction Code	Enter Vendor Credit Memo (F-41)	&_SAP_ALL_15	DCM
P00300101: Create fictitious vendor invoice and initiate payment for it	High	Transaction Code Check at Transaction Start	Transaction Code	Enter Vendor Credit Memo (F-41)	SAP_NEW_30D	DCM
P00300101: Create fictitious vendor invoice and initiate payment for it	High	Transaction Code Check at Transaction Start	Transaction Code	Enter Vendor Credit Memo (F-41)	SAP_NEW_30E	DCM
P00300101: Create fictitious vendor invoice and initiate payment for it	High	F_BKPF_KOA: Accounting Document: Authorization for Account Types	ACTVT: Activity	Create or generate	&_SAP_ALL_4	DCM

Figure 3.8 User Analysis at Permission Level

You can call the detail report for the user analysis by choosing the **Informer • Risk Analysis • User Level** menu path. Select the *Detail* report format. This report displays the list of all violated risk rules at permission level.

If you intend to process each violation of SOD individually, double-click to go to the ID number in the screen where you can specify how the risk is to be handled.

You can use the following three options here (see Figure 3.9):

Options for handling risks

► **Mitigate the risk**
Reduce the risk for complying with access permission.

▶ **Remove access from the user**
Remove access permission from the user completely.

▶ **Delimit access for the user**
Temporarily limit access permission for the user.

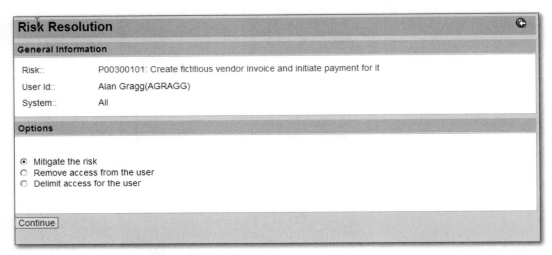

Figure 3.9 Risk Resolution

Mitigating the Risk for Complying with Access Permission

Mitigating the risk
You can create a control to mitigate the risk of comprehensive user permission for the enterprise. This can be so that a report is set up that performs a weekly check to see whether Alan Gragg (the user) has actually created a fictitious vendor and initiated a payment to the provider. A dual-control principle should also be established here. Tom Sanders, the second employee in Financial Accounting at EWP, has the task of checking the detailed payment run every month. If the report isn't requested by Tom Sanders every month through the payment run, the managing director, Andreas Schwarz, is notified of this via email.

Removing Access Permission from the User Completely

Removing access permission
In larger enterprises, users don't have an overview of which permissions have been granted to them over the years. The permissions are very

often no longer adapted to meet the requirements of the current job or were created too comprehensively from the beginning. If the job description doesn't require the comprehensive permission, you can avoid the risk in this case by removing the access permission completely. At EWP, this means that Alan Gragg will no longer be able to create vendors or start payment runs in the future. To remove this permission for Alan Gragg, a work order is sent by workflow to the IT department following the decision by management to ensure that the mitigation of the permission can be technically implemented.

Temporarily Limit Access Permission for the User (Delimit Access for the User)

Temporarily limiting the assignment of permissions for a user is a useful way of mitigating risks if a basic solution is found in this time frame. At EWP, the division of work between Alan Gragg and Tom Sanders will essentially change within two months. After two months, Tom Sanders will take over vendor maintenance worldwide, and Alan Gragg will be responsible for the payment run worldwide. The *Create a Vendor Master Record* and *Initiate Payment Run* functions will therefore no longer be assigned to only one person. A SOD to two people will be successfully implemented. Here, the order for the technical implementation is also sent by workflow to the IT department, following approval by management.

Delimiting access permission

Setting up the SOD for Alan Gragg and Tom Sanders may cause other SOD violations.

Prevention through simulation

To avoid issues here in advance, perform a simulation run before the actual technical implementation of the permission change by clicking the Simulate button when you call a report.

This enables you to simulate the assignment of other privileges to a user (see Figure 3.10), which means that you can rule out new risks from occurring for the entire enterprise by changing the privilege profile of individual employees.

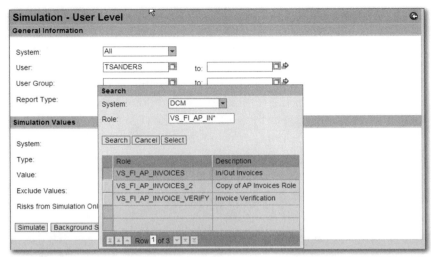

Figure 3.10 Simulation at User Level

For large enterprises, after you perform this analysis for the first time, you'll get a high number of SOD violations. Compliance owners in the enterprise often have to resolve more than a million SOD violations. It's unrealistic to process every single violation. To deal with this type of situation, we recommend that you proceed as follows.

First, check the role concept, and resolve the existing SOD violations there within the roles and composite roles. Then, check whether certain roles can be removed for users, to ensure that the SOD is complied with throughout the enterprise.

Critical activities by Superuser Privilege Management

If you can't remove permissions for a user due to the size of the department, you can use Superuser Privilege Management to set up a specific user ID for critical activities (e.g., end-of-quarter closing). The employee then can perform the end-of-quarter closing under this special user ID, however, all of the work that the employee performs using this user ID will also be recorded down to the last detail.

If the options described previously are impractical, you can retain the critical permission assignment in individual cases. In this situation, however, you should ensure that the risk associated with this will be mitigated as much as possible. This can be done, for example, by another employee periodically creating and signing off on corresponding audit reports.

3.2.3 Preparing Audits

You can also use the reporting functions for the first-time analysis to prepare subsequent audits. The objective here is to obtain a regular overview of which risks exist due to SOD violations.

Preparing audits using reports

3.2.4 Rule Architect

SAP GRC Access Control provides a comprehensive combination of functions and associated rules for the SOD. This combination covers the following business processes of different business applications:

Processes in the SAP System

Rule architect – processes in the SAP system

- ► Human Capital Management (SAP ERP HCM)
- ► Procure to pay
- ► Order to cash
- ► Financials
  - ► General accounting
  - ► Project system
  - ► Fixed assets
- ► Basis, security, system administration
- ► Advanced Planning and Optimization
- ► Supplier Relationship Management(SAP SRM)
- ► Customer Relationship Management (SAP CRM)
- ► Consolidation

Processes in an Oracle System

Rule architect – processes in the Oracle system

- ► Human resources
- ► Procure to pay
- ► Order to cash
- ► Finance

115

- General accounting
- Project systems
- Fixed assets
- System administration

Processes in a PeopleSoft System

- Human resources
- Procure to pay
- Order to cash
- Finance
  - General accounting
  - Fixed assets
  - System administration

Processes in a JD Edwards System

- Human resources/payroll
- Procure to pay
- Order to cash
- Finance
  - General accounting
  - Consolidation

Processes in a Hyperion System

- Custom rules

You use the rule architect to extend the combination of rules and functions provided by SAP GRC Access Control. This consequently means that you can adjust the rule set to enterprise-specific requirements and also implement industry-specific extensions.

You also often have to connect application systems, which were developed by customers, to SAP GRC Access Control. In this situation, you use the rule architect to create customized functions and rules for customer development and then include them in the overall analysis.

An important function in the rule architect is creating organization rules. You can use this function to store the organizational structure of the enterprise by mapping the company structure in detail. If an employee's privilege profile means that he can create fictitious vendor master records for a company and then allow a payment to this vendor, this is identified as a violation of SOD. However, the situation is different if the two functions *Create Vendor Master Record* and *Initiate Payment* affect different companies (different *company codes* in SAP terminology). The employee can create vendors within one company code and initiate the payment within another company code. Due to the organizational segregation of rules, this means that there is no longer a risk that the employee will transfer funds to a fictitious vendor.

Organization of enterprise

3.3   Defining and Managing Roles

The basic objective is to plan possible roles in an enterprise so far ahead that SOD violations will be ruled out when you implement the roles in privilege profiles. This enables you to prevent any possible errors or fraud from the outset.

Employees from IT and the business unit can use *SAP GRC Access Control Enterprise Role Management* to jointly work out the best possible role structure for the enterprise. Each role is checked to see whether it violates the rules that an enterprise has established for achieving SOD. Obviously, this check is performed before the roles are released for use in a live system.

3.3.1   Defining Roles

You can use SAP GRC Access Control to establish a standardized method for designing roles in the whole enterprise. A basic prerequisite for standardization is that you must follow the naming conventions for roles and profiles.

Standardized method for designing roles

For example, you can specify that there should be a role in the enterprise that is to bundle the activities for processing the vendor master record. This consists of the following tasks in detail:

- ▶ Creating the vendor master record
- ▶ Changing the vendor master record
- ▶ Locking the vendor master record
- ▶ Setting the deletion indicator for the vendor master record

You create a role for maintaining the vendor master record, which contains a description of the assigned activities (see Figure 3.11). You can access the transaction for creating roles from the **Role Management** • **Roles** • **Create** menu path.

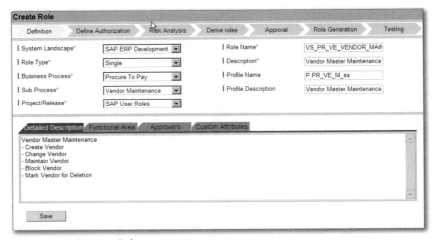

Figure 3.11 Creating Roles

3.3.2 Assigning Transactions and Authorizations to Roles

Also user-friendly for non-IT specialists Next, you define the transactions that you want to belong to the role. Employees of business units who don't have an IT background can also perform the implementation. The user selects the functional area, for example, *Procurement Department*. The assignment of the functional area to a role is used to categorize it.

To obtain details about the authorization data, click the corresponding button (see Figure 3.12). A list of the assigned functions is displayed (see Figure 3.13).

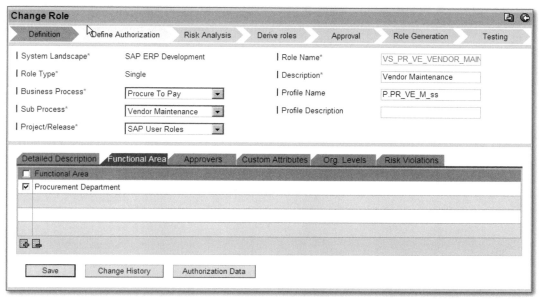

Figure 3.12 Selecting a Functional Area

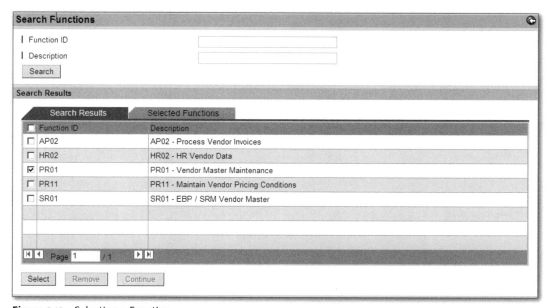

Figure 3.13 Selecting a Function

Selecting the **PR01** function **Vendor Master Maintenance**, for example, displays a list of the transactions you want to be bundled in the function (see Figures 3.13 and 3.14).

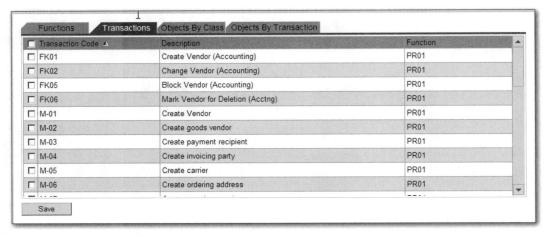

Figure 3.14 Assigning Transactions

If you only assign a single function to the role, the corresponding transactions will be "compatible" with each other, without there being any fear of the SOD being violated. At this point, however, you can also generally assign transactions that don't appear in the selection list to this functional area. Nevertheless, there is a risk here that adding transactions will violate the SOD, such as if you were to add Transaction F-43 (Enter Vendor Invoice) to this functional area.

3.3.3 Performing Risk Analysis

Designing and implementing without risks

After you've designed the role, you initiate the risk analysis for it (see Figure 3.15). Within risk analysis, you check whether assigning several functions or manually assigning transactions to a role would lead to the rules for the SOD being violated. *SAP GRC Access Control Rule Architect* is used as the basis here.

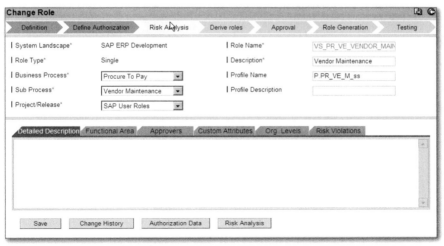

Figure 3.15 Starting Risk Analysis

In our example, the combination where vendor master records can be created with the initiation of payment to the vendor is listed as a risk. The reason for this is that Transaction F-43 (Enter Vendor Invoice) has been manually added to the PR01 function (Vendor Master Maintenance) (see Figure 3.16).

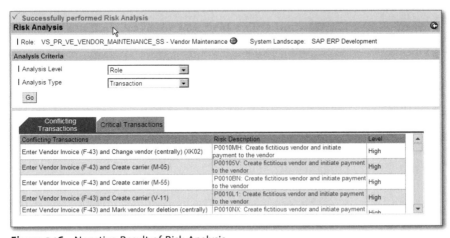

Figure 3.16 Negative Result of Risk Analysis

3.3.4   Activities for Avoiding Risks

You can only create secure roles

If possible, you should only create roles that won't violate the guidelines for SOD. If a risk arises during testing, you must clean up the roles as much as possible based on the assigned transaction codes until the risk no longer exists. In our example, the assignment of Transaction F-43 (Enter Vendor Invoice) to the PR01 function (Vendor Master Maintenance) has been deleted (see Figure 3.17). You often can't rule out every risk within the framework of defining roles. In this case, you need to mitigate each risk.

Performing the risk analysis after deleting the Transaction F-43 assignment yields a positive result this time.

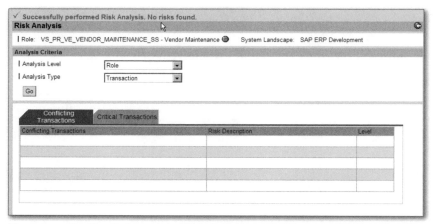

Figure 3.17   Positive Performance of Risk Analysis

3.3.5   Deriving Roles

Saving time by deriving roles

Roles that you create for a particular organizational unit can be reused for a different organizational unit. In Enterprise Role Management, you can use background jobs to load the organizational hierarchies that are created in the SAP backend system. This means that you can access the organizational hierarchy when you're defining roles. For large companies, the same rules for SOD apply worldwide for all purchasers. For example, the roles for the purchasing area in the United States can therefore be reused for Germany by simply specifying the corresponding company code change when deriving the role. In addition, roles that are assigned to a higher hierarchy level (company code) are derived at subordinate hierarchy levels (divisions). This means that all roles assigned to the company code can be transferred to the relevant divisions (see Figures 3.18 and 3.19).

Figure 3.18 Deriving Roles

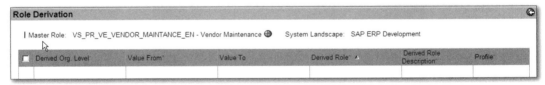

Figure 3.19 Deriving Roles According to Organizational Units

Because the organizational hierarchy can be accessed when roles are being derived, this saves role design teams a lot of time in creating and generating roles.

3.3.6 Approving Roles

Based on the result of the risk analysis, there is no reason not to actually use the role, so you can trigger a request for approval by clicking the corresponding field (see Figure 3.20).

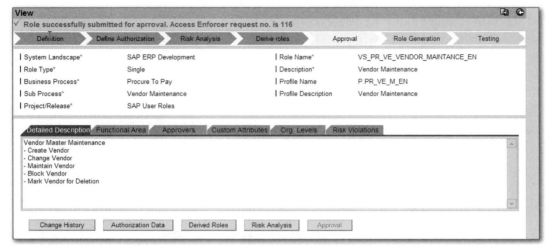

Figure 3.20 Role Successfully Sent for Approval

Audit-proof documentation of approval process You initially generate a request here, which you send by email to the person who must approve it. This email contains a link to the *Compliant User Provisioning* application area of SAP GRC Access Control. The list of open requests for approval is displayed for the approver (see Figure 3.21).

Request No. ▲	Request Type	Priority	Request Date
31	New Access	HIGH	05/04/2007
23	RE_ROLE_APPROVAL	RE_HIGH	05/02/2007
116	RE_ROLE_APPROVAL	RE_HIGH	01/13/2008

Requests For Approval
List Of Requests

Figure 3.21 List of Requests for Approval

The details of the request become available after the request for approval is selected. Based on this information, the approver can then **Approve**, **Reject**, or **Hold** the request (see Figure 3.22).

By formally approving the role using workflow and Compliance User Provisioning functions, the approver ensures that all details of the approval process for new or changed roles can also remain traceable. This information is also available for a subsequent check, if required.

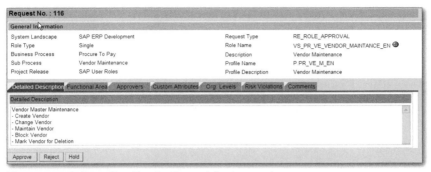

Figure 3.22   Information About a Request for Approval

3.3.7   Generating Roles

After a successful approval, a last step involves generating the role (see Figure 3.23). You do this simply by selecting the corresponding button. The result is that the role is automatically created in the assigned SAP backend system, and the relevant privilege profile is generated.

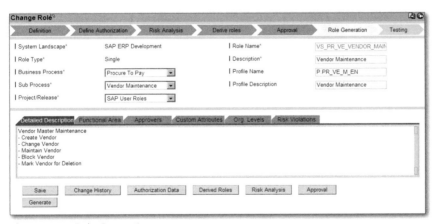

Figure 3.23   Role Generation

3.3.8   Mass Maintenance

The requirements for designing roles are subject to regular organizational changes in an enterprise. To simplify role maintenance, a transaction is also available that enables you to perform mass changes of roles.

3.4 Compliant User Provisioning

Compliant User Provisioning functions are used when users have to request new or changed access rights due to changed business circumstances.

These functions can be used to ensure that no new violations of the specified SOD occur when access rights are set up or changed. Implementing self-services means that the individual user can request changes. All individual steps are documented in the course of the individual review and approval steps. These must then (if required for a review) be submitted accordingly.

Enterprises today are often faced with the following issues:

▸ Owners in the business units aren't involved in the process of assigning access rights. The main reason for this is that information about access rights is generally written in such an IT-specific way that the business owner can't understand the contents.

▸ The approval process is performed manually. A greater number of IT employees are involved. The process from making the request, up until it's approved, is recorded in emails or table programs such as Microsoft Excel. Approval processes generally take too long. There is also the risk that nobody will review the risk of assigned authorizations and the consequences of possible changes anymore.

▸ Management in the enterprise will only be able to trace, with difficulty, who received what authorization, when and why. In particular, checks will barely provide an overview of the associated risks.

These issues are solved with SAP GRC Access Control. SAP GRC Access Control does the following:

▸ Enables you to request a new user account for a user or a change to the existing user account

▸ Automatically provides necessary information to the user in request form

▸ Accesses roles, which were devised for the enterprise in advance, when you make a request

▶ Directly sends email notification to the manager, who must approve the request

▶ Informs the manager if the master records of his employees changes in SAP ERP HCM

3.4.1 Requesting Self-Service Access Rights

Employees can use self-service functions to request access rights themselves. In our example, a new accounting employee, Mae Wong, has been hired in the United States.

The request form begins with identifying whether this is a new Access account, which functional area is affected, which systems the access right is required for, and what the general reason is for the request (see Figure 3.24).

Form to request access rights

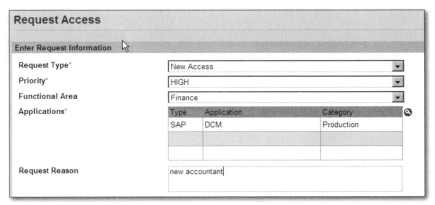

Figure 3.24 Request Form

The manager responsible is also identified. This automatic identification is possible because SAP GRC Access Control receives this information from the connected SAP ERP HCM application. The organizational unit that the employee is assigned to is also important information (e.g., which plant, division) (see Figure 3.25).

Automatically identifying the manager responsible

Figure 3.25 Other Details in the Request Form

3.4.2 Assigning Roles

Enterprise-specific role catalog

The next step involves assigning roles. This is done using a button; that is, the user has access to the enterprise-specific role catalog directly from the form used for making the request. In our example, the **In/Out Invoices** role is selected. By navigating through the individual buttons, the requestor can look at information such as detailed descriptions, functional areas, and so on, for the role (see Figure 3.26).

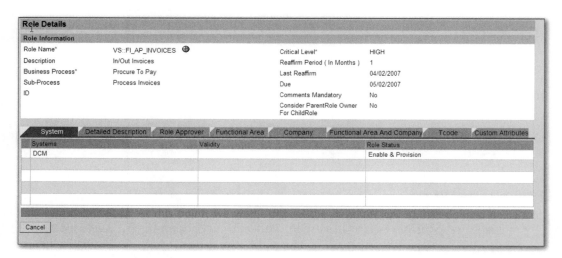

Figure 3.26 Role Details

By submitting the request, it's created and saved under an ID number (see Figure 3.27). The request is automatically sent to the manager who must approve it.

Workflow for controlling the approval process

You can design the workflow that controls this approval process as you wish. For example, you can create a multilevel approval process where the manager responsible doesn't necessarily have to assume the role of approver.

Figure 3.27 Request Successfully Created

3.4.3 Analyzing Risks and Approving Requests

In the next step, the manager, Fox Wilson, can review the request after receiving the notification. Additional details are displayed by double-clicking the request number (see Figure 3.28)

Request No. ▲	Request Type	Priority	Request Date
93	Change Account	HIGH	07/23/2007
86	New Access	HIGH	07/09/2007
39	New Access	HIGH	05/16/2007
25	New Access	HIGH	05/03/2007
120	New Access	HIGH	01/14/2008
117	New Access	HIGH	01/13/2008
110	Change Account	HIGH	11/01/2007

Figure 3.28 List of Requests for Approval

A risk analysis is carried out automatically. This involves checking whether the assigned functional areas will cause SOD to be violated. If there is a risk, this is identified by a red flag on the corresponding tab (see Figure 3.29).

Analyzing the risk before approving the request

Fox Wilson is of the opinion that the risk can be mitigated by evaluating corresponding monthly reports about Mae Wong's activities. To prove during a review that this risk has actually been mitigated, SAP GRC Access Control documents whether Mae Wong also regularly performs this activity. In particular, default reports provide a summary of the activities that were set up to mitigate risks and provide the reviewers with detailed information about whether mitigation was also practiced. Fox Wilson doesn't think it necessary to delimit the access rights; therefore, despite the risk identified, he decides to grant the access rights and initiates the approval (see Figure 3.30).

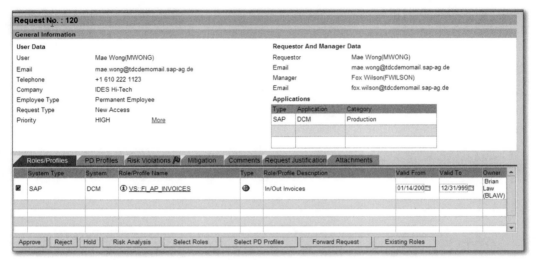

Figure 3.29 Overview of Request

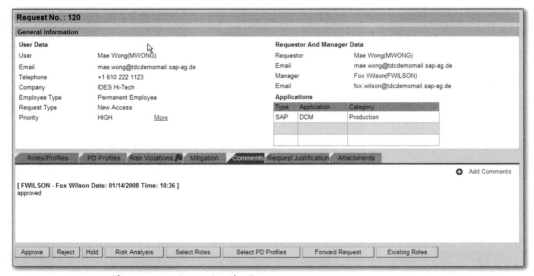

Figure 3.30 Approving the Request

3.4.4 Enterprise Application Systems

In addition to assigning access rights to SAP ERP applications, you can also request, analyze, and approve access rights for ERP systems from Oracle, PeopleSoft, and JD Edwards via SAP GRC Access Control. Users can consequently be offered a standard tool for managing authorization requests, even if ERP systems of different manufacturers are being used live in the enterprise.

Third-party business applications

3.4.5 Saving Request History

For the purpose of later reviews, there is a guarantee that the steps for making a request and also for approval are recorded in detail. Request history therefore provides information about who approved the request, which risk analysis was performed, and which reasons were stored in the system. In larger companies, it's useful to establish a multilevel approval process involving several people. In this case, the approval steps to be performed are subsequently also specifically documented in the system.

Documentation for audits

3.5 Superuser Privilege Management

The *Superuser Privilege Management* (Virsa Firefighter) Access Control application is used when, in exceptional cases, employees are allowed to execute transactions that aren't part of their normal job profile.

A superuser/privileged user ID is a special user ID that enables the employee to perform specific activities. Whenever the employee logs on using the privileged user ID, he must first specify the reason for using the user ID. All of the activities that the user will perform while logged on with the privileged user ID are then displayed.

Using the superuser ID only after specifying a reason

We strongly advise against using a privileged user ID that would be similar to the SAP_ALL privilege in terms of the scope of the privilege. Instead, we recommend that you set up a privileged user ID for each business application area. This will keep the scope of access rights and associated risks as small as possible.

Never use SAP_ALL

In our EWP corporation example, only Alan Gragg can change vendor master data. However, if Alan Gragg isn't available, Mae Wong can also perform changes to the vendor master data in special exceptional circumstances.

When Mae Wong logs on to the SAP system, she can access the privileged user IDs provided for her by selecting *Superuser Privilege Management* in the *SAP Easy Access* menu.

When the privileged user ID is selected, the system requires the user to specify the reason why the privileged user ID is needed. In this case, the specified reason is that the vendor address must be updated for the check run (see Figures 3.31 and 3.32).

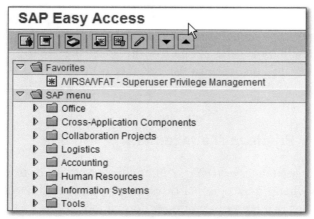

Figure 3.31 Accessing Superuser Privilege Management

After Mae Wong selects the preconfigured **Reason Codes** and specifies the actions she anticipates she will perform, the privileged user ID is activated. She consequently gains access to the menu that will enable her to perform the corresponding change to the vendor master data.

Notification about using superuser ID

The moment the *User menu for Firefighter Vendor Maintenance* appears, the controller of the privileged user ID is notified (see Figure 3.33). This role is performed by Fox Wilson at EWP. This privileged user ID is also locked for other users. This ensures that only one of all the users provided with these access rightscan work under this privileged user ID at a time, which guarantees that the activities performed under the privileged user ID can be uniquely assigned to one person. This uniqueness is necessary to ensure auditability.

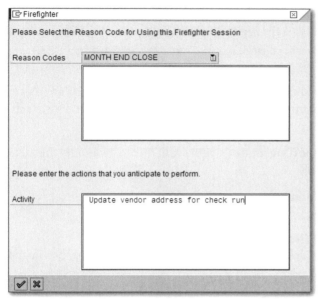

Figure 3.32 Reason for Using Privileged User ID

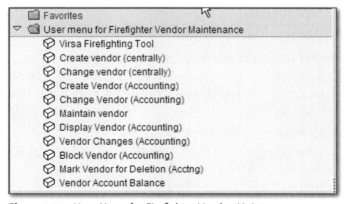

Figure 3.33 User Menu for Firefighter Vendor Maintenance

133

The *Superuser Privilege Management (Virsa Firefighter)* application now records all activities performed by the user of the privileged user ID. The following information is stored in this case:

▶ All activities of the user are categorized by transaction code and users.

▶ Changes are recorded in change documents (CDHDR table).

▶ Programs that were started using Transactions SA38 or SE38 are listed.

▶ Tables that were changed with Transactions SE16 or SM30 are listed. Changes to table entries are documented (if the change update is activated in the tables).

Comprehensive reporting options are available to evaluate the data accordingly:

▶ **Log Summary Report**
This report provides usage lists by privileged user ID.

▶ **Reason/Activity Report**
This report provides an overview of the reason why the privileged user ID was used.

▶ **Transaction Usage Report**
This report lists the transactions that have been executed during a session.

▶ **Log Report**
This report lists all details from a session.

▶ **Invalid Firefighter IDs, Controllers or Owners Report**
This report lists all expired, deleted, or locked user IDs. This is possible because the privileged user ID has a time window that specifies how long it's valid for.

▶ **SOD Conflicts in Firefighter Report**
This report specifies whether a privileged user has violated a SOD rule when performing his "special assignment."

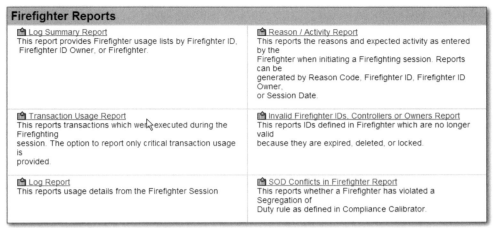

Firefighter Reports

📄 Log Summary Report This report provides Firefighter usage lists by Firefighter ID, Firefighter ID Owner, or Firefighter.	📄 Reason / Activity Report This reports the reasons and expected activity as entered by the Firefighter when initiating a Firefighting session. Reports can be generated by Reason Code, Firefighter ID, Firefighter ID Owner, or Session Date.
📄 Transaction Usage Report This reports transactions which were executed during the Firefighting session. The option to report only critical transaction usage is provided.	📄 Invalid Firefighter IDs, Controllers or Owners Report This reports IDs defined in Firefighter which are no longer valid because they are expired, deleted, or locked.
📄 Log Report This reports usage details from the Firefighter Session	📄 SOD Conflicts in Firefighter Report This reports whether a Firefighter has violated a Segregation of Duty rule as defined in Compliance Calibrator.

Figure 3.34 Reports for Privileged User

The reporting you call from the **Reports • User Reports** menu path is also used as the basis for reviews (see Figure 3.34). It therefore documents that customized privileged user IDs are merely assigned in exceptional situations also.

▶ Before activating the user IDs in the system, users must give a reason why they require the privileged user ID.

▶ As part of a dual-control principle, a "controller" is informed about the activation of the privileged user ID.

▶ Each activity performed by the user under the privileged user ID is documented and evaluated.

This means that you can plan and implement special permission assignments in advance. If necessary, you can assign permissions promptly and without interrupting ongoing business operations.

You can also use the scope of functions of the privileged user to mitigate risks when SOD is violated. The privilege profile is limited for the affected user. If the user then has to perform critical activities (e.g., end-of-quarter closing work), a corresponding exception user ID is made available for the user. All activities performed by the user under this user ID can therefore be logged and evaluated down to the last detail.

3.6   SAP GRC Access Control – Application and Configuration

This structure of this section is based on the following four application areas of SAP GRC Access Control:

▶ Risk Analysis and Remediation (Virsa Compliance Calibrator)

▶ Enterprise Role Management (Virsa Role Expert)

▶ Compliant User Provisioning (Virsa Access Enforcer)

▶ Superuser Privilege Management (Virsa Firefighter)

3.6.1   Application and Configuration of Risk Analysis and Remediation

You can use the *Risk Analysis and Remediation* application area to manage SOD in the whole enterprise. This includes defining risks for SOD, using controls to mitigate risks, and using alert messages. Comprehensive reporting is also provided. These options are reflected in the application menu (see Figure 3.35):

▶ **Informer**
Gives an overview about the reporting possibilities.

▶ **Rule Architect**
Defines and adapts rules for of relevant business processes SOD.

▶ **Mitigation**
Used to restrict or monitor identified risks for users, roles, and profiles.

▶ **Alert Monitor**
Provides an overview of critical situations, such as:

  ▶ Performing a critical transaction (e.g., deleting data in a database)

  ▶ Performing a transaction, which, in combination with other transactions, violates the rules for SOD

  ▶ A mitigation report was not initiated in the scheduled time interval.

▶ **Configuration**
Used to adapt the Compliance Calibrator to a changed system landscape, for example.

Figure 3.35 Menu Overview for the Application and Configuration of Risk Analysis and Remediation

Informer

In the *Informer* area, the user has access to reports that can be divided into the following groups (see Figure 3.36):

- ▶ **Management View**
- ▶ **Risk Analysis**
- ▶ **Audit Reports**
- ▶ **Security Reports**

The common feature of all reports in Management View is that you can navigate from the graphical overview to call additional detailed information by clicking. The detailed information will inform you about the identified risk as well as its description and weighting. You also have access to the risk history and can see which SOD violations form the basis of the risk.

Navigating to detailed information

In the next section, you'll learn more about the management views available.

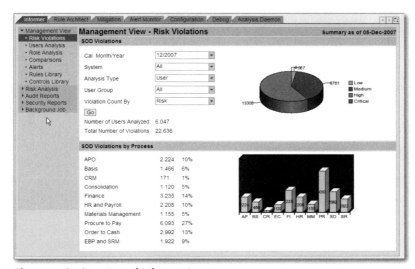

Figure 3.36 Overview of Informer Area

Management View
The **Risk Violations** management view, which you can access from the **Informer • Management View • Risk Violation** menu path, provides an overview of all SOD violations for all SAP ERP applications or one SAP ERP application to be selected (see Figure 3.37). Risks are displayed in the pie chart according to their weighting. The breakdown of identified risks is displayed by business process in the lower area.

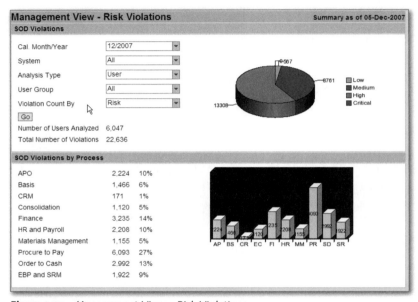

Figure 3.37 Management View – Risk Violations

Management View – User Analysis
The **User Analysis** management view, which you can access from the **Informer • Management View • User Analysis** menu path, displays the SOD violations for a specific user group in a specific system (see Figure 3.38). The pie chart provides an overview of how many users don't cause any violations, for how many users risk mitigation has been implemented, and for how many users a risk has been identified. By double-clicking one of the areas in the pie chart, you can access the detailed list of affected users.

In the lower part of the **Management View** for the **User Analysis**, you get an overview of how many critical actions can be performed by users in a system. You can also call the list of critical actions/transactions by double-clicking here.

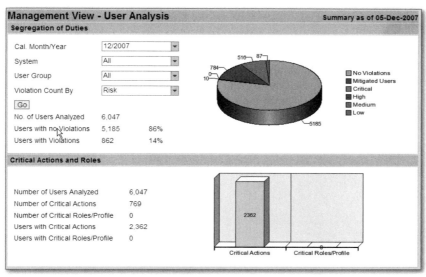

Figure 3.38 Management View – User Analysis

As is the case with the *User Analysis* management view, you can also evaluate the SOD violations (based on the defined roles in a system) for a key date (see Figure 3.39).

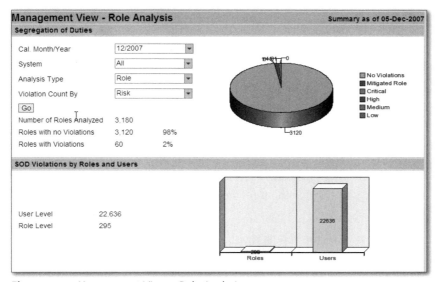

Figure 3.39 Management View – Role Analysis

Management View
– Comparisons

The **Comparisons** management view, which you can access from the **Informer • Management View • Comparisons** menu path, represents the number of SOD violations per user or role per month or quarter in the interval (see Figure 3.40). In the upper part of the report, you can read the trend of how the number of SOD violations has changed over time. In this example, you'll notice that the violations consistently increased after a complete cleanup in May 2007.

In the lower part of the report, you see how many of the identified risks have been corrected or mitigated. By double-clicking the specified percentage, the list of processed risks is displayed.

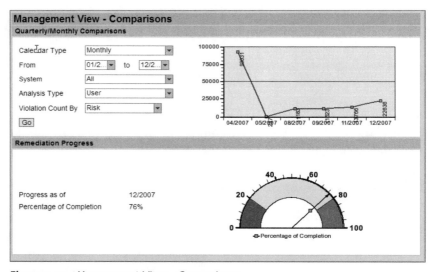

Figure 3.40 Management View – Comparisons

Management View
– Alerts

The **Alerts** management view, accessible from the **Informer • Management View • Alerts** menu path, gives you an overview of how many alerts occurred in a month (see Figure 3.41). From the upper part of the report, you can see the development by the occurrence of alerts per month.

The lower part of the report displays a list of alerts by business process. You can also access a detailed list of the individual alerts by double-clicking the graphic in this report.

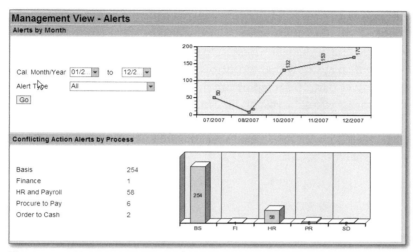

Figure 3.41 Management View – Alerts

The **Rules Library** management view, which you can access from the
Informer • Management View • Rule Library menu path, gives you
an overview of the SOD rules for which a risk has been identified (see
Figure 3.42). The upper part of the report shows the breakdown of rule
violations by risk weighting. The lower part provides information about
how many rules a risk was identified for per business process.

Management View
– Rules Library

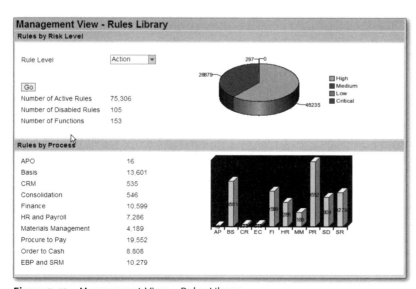

Figure 3.42 Management View – Rules Library

Management View
– Controls Library The **Controls Library** management view, which you can access from the **Informer • Management View • Controls Library** menu path, shows how many controls have been set up (see Figure 3.43). The upper part of the report displays how many controls exist by risk level or risk weighting. The lower part of the report provides an overview of how the number of controls is split across the business processes.

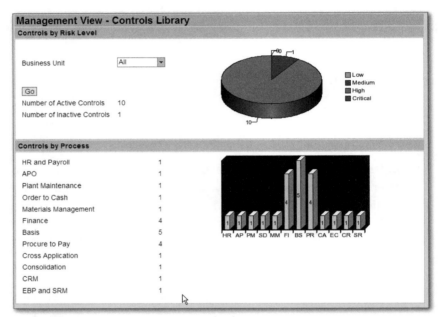

Figure 3.43 Management View – Controls Library

Risk analysis Another group of reports is the one for risk analysis (see Figure 3.44). You access this report group from the **Informer • Risk Analysis** menu path. The objective of these reports is to check whether any user, role, HR object, or organization has access rights that causes the rules for SOD to be violated.

You can change the detailing format for each of these reports, depending on whether you need the result as a summary management display or as a detailed display. You can save the input parameters as reporting variants for each of these reports. If you want the risk analysis to be performed for a large number of users, you can also schedule and perform the reports as background jobs.

Management View • Risk Violations • Users Analysis • Role Analysis • Comparisons • Alerts • Rules Library • Controls Library ▾ Risk Analysis • User Level • Role Level • HR Objects • Org. Level • MIC ▸ Audit Reports ▸ Security Reports ▸ Background Job	**Risk Analysis - User Level**			
	System:	All		
	User:		to:	
	User Group:		to:	
	Custom Group:		to:	
	Risks by Process: *	All		
	Risk ID:		to:	
	Risk Level:	All		
	Rule Set:	GLOBAL		
	Report Type:	Permission Level		
	Report Format:	Summary	+ More Options	
	Execute Simulation Background Reset Search Variant Save Variant			

Figure 3.44 Risk Analysis Selection

Different reports are provided within the **Audit Reports** report group, depending on which factor is the focus of the audit or review.

Audit Reports

Under **Audit Report – Rules**, you can call reports that display the established rules sorted according to business process (see Figure 3.45). The menu path for this is **Informer • Audit Reports**.

Figure 3.45 Audit Reports – Action Rules

The audits/reviews can also be supported by reports that identify critical roles, profiles, and associated risks (see Figure 3.46).

Figure 3.46 Audit Reports – Critical Roles and Profiles

143

Standard reports that highlight risk-mitigation controls are also available from the **Informer • Audit Reports** menu path (see Figure 3.47). You can list the controls by business unit or user.

Figure 3.47 Audit Reports – Mitigation Controls

Security Reports

The last group of standard reports, which you can access from the **Informer • Security Reports** menu path, summarizes security reports (see Figure 3.48). You can use them to query information about certain users by selecting by user ID or organizational unit.

Figure 3.48 Security Reports – Users

Other reports provide details about roles or profiles (see Figures 3.49 and 3.50).

Figure 3.49 Security Reports – Roles

Figure 3.50 Security Reports – Profiles

Reports that are initiated to get all the details of SOD violations in large organizations usually have a longer runtime until the results become available on the screen. All of these reports can therefore also be triggered as jobs in the background or scheduled for a certain period of time.

Rule Architect

You use the rule architect to define rules according to which SAP GRC Access Control identifies risks for SOD violations.

When you call the rule architect for the first time, the **Management View Rules Library** appears (see Figure 3.51). The Rules Library is the overview of predefined rules that are available for implementing SAP GRC Access Control. In the upper half of the report, you can see how high the associated risk is. In the lower half, you see how the rules are broken down by business process.

However, before you create new rules, you should note that the SAP ERP applications to be included are connected to SAP GRC Access Control with the connectors provided (we describe how to create connectors at the end of this section).

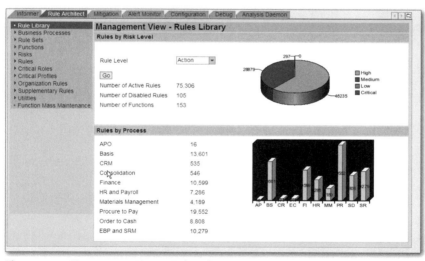

Figure 3.51 Management View – Rules Library

The rules are established based on the if-then principle. *If* an employee has comprehensive authorization to create a vendor master record, for example, and initiate payment of the vendor invoice, *then* this is a high risk for the enterprise.

Therefore, a risk is when one user is assigned two or more functions that should be separated. A function is a combination of activities that a user

Risk and function

performs. In SAP language, this is a collection of transaction codes. A user must be able to perform activities within the function to carry out his tasks in the enterprise.

Generating rules   SAP GRC Access Control generates the rules if the risks are defined. Let's assume that the risk consists of two functions. One function is made up of 5 activities (transaction codes), and the other function comprises 3 activities (transaction codes). The rule architect generates 15 rules (3 x 5) for this example. SAP GRC Access Control also provides a rule set for non-SAP ERP systems. One rule set specifically can be accessed for Oracle, PeopleSoft, and JD Edwards.

Creating a function   When you create a function, you specify the **Function ID**, **Description**, and assigned **Business Process** (see Figure 3.52). The menu path for this is **Rule Architect • Functions • Create**. You also specify whether you want the scope of analysis to be limited to a connected ERP system or whether the analysis is to be performed across all systems. The corresponding actions or transactions that you want to be assigned to the function are then included. As an option, you can also assign critical permissions to a function.

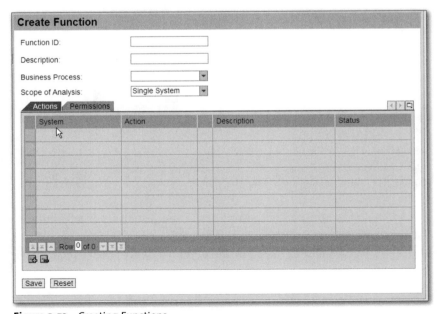

Figure 3.52   Creating Functions

When you create a new risk, you specify the **Risk ID**, **Description**, and **Risk Type** (see Figure 3.53). You call this transaction from the **Rule Architect • Risks • Create** menu path. The risk type is a SOD, a critical action, or critical permission. You then define the assigned business process and risk level (high, medium, low).

Creating a risk

You subsequently assign the conflicting functions that should therefore never be assigned to only one person. You then also specify a detailed risk description. You also maintain the risk owner and information about risk controls. Lastly, you assign the risk to a rule set.

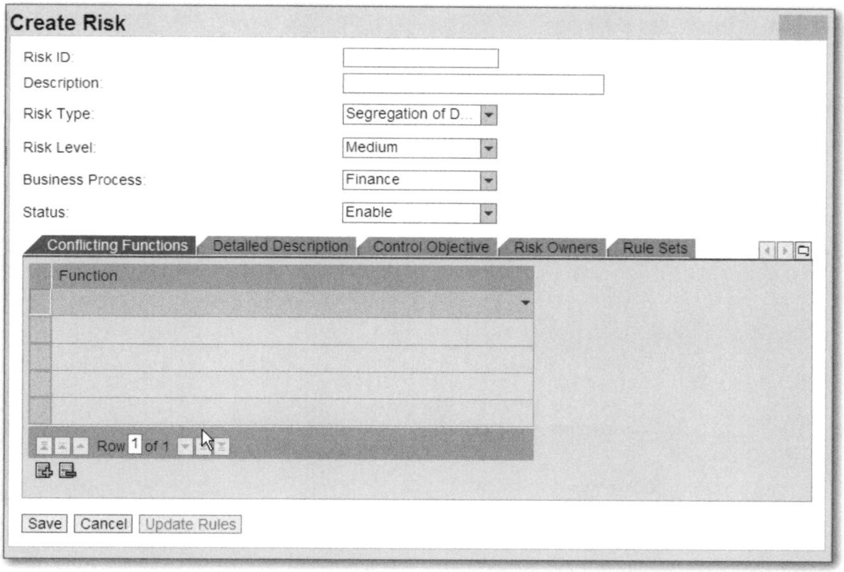

Create Risk

Risk ID:	
Description:	
Risk Type:	Segregation of D...
Risk Level:	Medium
Business Process:	Finance
Status:	Enable

Conflicting Functions · Detailed Description · Control Objective · Risk Owners · Rule Sets

Function

Row 1 of 1

Save Cancel Update Rules

Figure 3.53 Creating a Risk

To manage the risks and functions created, specify a relevant **Business Process** in each case. This mandatory field ensures that all risks and functions can be assigned to a business process. The example *Risk: Create Vendor Master Record* and *Initiate payment of Vendor invoice* are therefore assigned to the procure to pay business process.

Business processes

When you install SAP GRC Access Control for the first time, a list of business processes is provided automatically. You can use these business processes when managing risks and functions. However, you can also define additional business processes using the **Rule Architect • Business Processes • Create** menu path (see Figure 3.54).

Create Business Process

Business Process ID:

Description:

Save   Clear

Figure 3.54   Rule Architect – Creating a Business Process

Descriptive names
for business
process IDs

The **Business Process ID** should be descriptive, for example, FI00 for the Finance business process.

You can use the Search Business Process transaction (**Rule Architect • Business Processes • Search** menu path) to see the overview of the specified business processes (see Figure 3.55). You can also change the description of the business process here. In this case, you need to create a new business process with the required ID. You can delete the business process with the old ID that is no longer used.

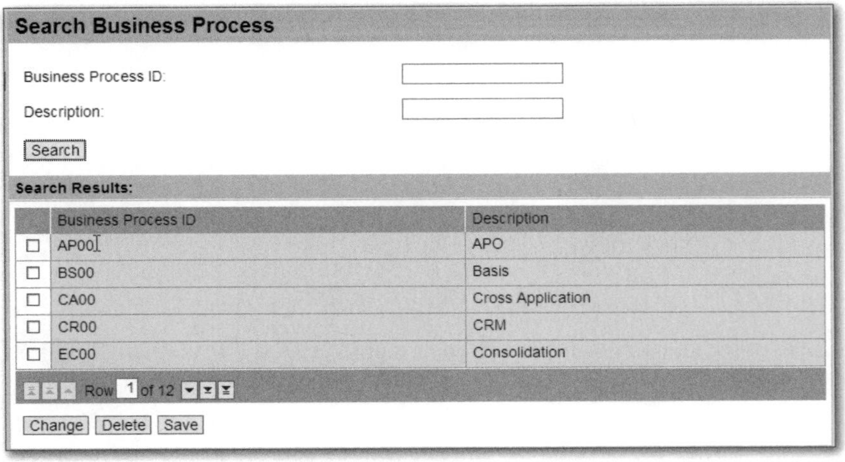

Search Business Process

Business Process ID:

Description:

Search

Search Results:

	Business Process ID	Description
☐	AP00	APO
☐	BS00	Basis
☐	CA00	Cross Application
☐	CR00	CRM
☐	EC00	Consolidation

Row 1 of 12

Change   Delete   Save

Figure 3.55   Rule Architect – Search Business Process

Rule sets   Another classification criterion for creating risks is rule sets. We recommend that you use a rule set globally.

When you create rule sets, you specify the **Rule Set ID** and **Description** (see Figure 3.56). You can access the transaction using the **Rule Architect • Rule Sets • Create** menu path. The ID here should also be descriptive, for example, *GLOBAL*, to create a rule set to which all globally valid risks are to be assigned.

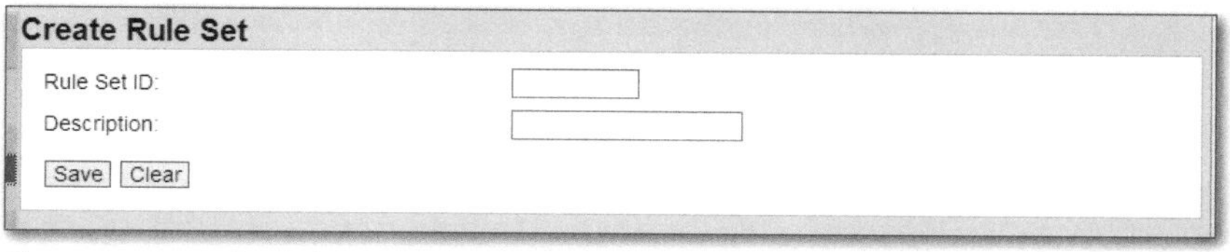

Figure 3.56 Rule Architect – Create Rule Set

To get an overview of existing rule sets, choose the Search Rule Set transaction using the **Rule Architect • Rule Sets • Search** menu path (see Figure 3.57). Here, you can change the **Description** of the rule sets.

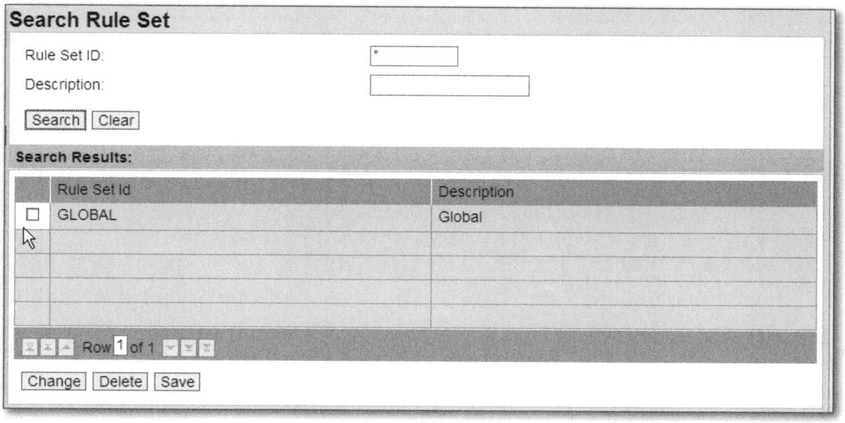

Figure 3.57 Rule Architect – Search Rule Set

You can also create critical roles or critical profiles using the **Rule Architect • Critical Roles** or **Critical Profiles Create** menu paths. If an employee has permission to change or delete data records on the database, this essentially represents a risk for the enterprise. This type of

Critical roles and profiles

149

critical permission assignment to roles or profiles should also always be a component of a risk report.

You can also assign organization rules to risks using the **Rule Architect • Organization Rules** menu path. This is of interest if an enterprise is subdivided into different legal organizational units or plants.

The *Create Vendor Master Record* and *Initiate Payment for Vendor Invoice* actions, for example, may therefore be a risk within a country if these actions are assigned to only one person. However, if you restrict responsibility at organizational level, this doesn't represent a risk for the enterprise any more. An employee can then create master records for vendors in Germany, for example, but initiating the payment of vendor invoices remains limited to U.S. vendors.

Mitigation

You can use *mitigation* to respond to risk violations. First, you find out whether this is a known risk violation or whether a new risk violation has occurred.

Then you determine how long the risk violation is to be tolerated and monitored during this time. You can also specify who is to perform the role of mitigation monitor. Mitigation controls are set up for this, which are approved by a manager.

The **Controls Library** provides an overview of the controls that have been established (see Figure 3.58). You access this transaction using the **Mitigation • Controls Library** menu path. The upper part of the report shows how many controls were set up and what the proportion of the assigned risk evaluation is (high, medium, low). The lower part of the report contains an overview of how the established controls are spread across the business processes. You can go to the list of controls set up by double-clicking the corresponding graphic (e.g., the pie chart) (see Figure 3.59).

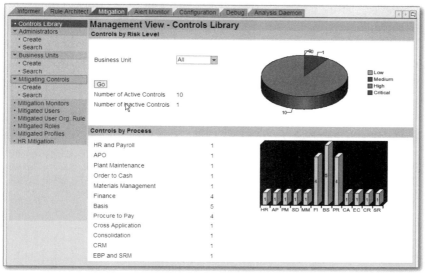

Figure 3.58 Mitigation – Controls Library Management View

Controls for High

Control	Business Unit	Approver Id	Approver Name
BASIS_001: This control is designed to mitigate basis related risk for reporting.	FI00: CORP FINANCE	WSOLIMAN	Wendy Soliman
BASIS_002: Role development is only done in dev environments and transported to production - role change control process monitored	FI00: CORP FINANCE	WSOLIMAN	Wendy Soliman
BASIS_003: Transport change control process monitored by internal controls group - ZAUD - Audit report is run daily to track all	FI00: CORP FINANCE	TMORRA	Tim Morra
FF0001: Firefighter rule access; user access is monitored via VIRSA Firefighter	FI00: CORP FINANCE	BRAMMARDS	Ben Rammards
FI_0005: This mitigating control can be used across the enterprise related to Risks P001, P002 & P003. If there is a need to	FI00: CORP FINANCE	BRAMMARDS	Ben Rammards
FI_0006: All bank changes (Risk F005) need to be properly reviewed and approved. Run the FI04 report on a monthly basis and	FI00: CORP FINANCE	MBOND	Maria Bond
FI_0007: All checks must be validated for approval of check amounts by separate group that controls the physical check printing	FI00: CORP FINANCE	WGASPER	Wes Gasper
FR01_001.1: Report Z_VENDOR_CHG is monitored weekly for appropriate changes to Bank Details and Payment Terms.	FR00: France Market	JMURPHY	John Murphy
MC0001: Mitigation control designed to monitor vendor master changes and disbursement to prevent fraud.	FI00: CORP FINANCE	MBOND	Maria Bond
RISK_MGMT: GRC Risk Management	FI00: CORP FINANCE	CKLINE	Calvine Kline

1 of 1 pages ► ► No. of rows per page: 10 (Total no. of rows : 10)

Figure 3.59 Mitigation – List of Controls

Administrator rights for managing controls

However, before you can work with mitigations, you must define who in the enterprise will receive the right to set up controls. You name the administrators for this using the **Mitigation • Administrators • Create** menu path and store them in the system (see Figure 3.60). An administrator creates mitigation controls and assigns the mitigation monitor and the manager, who must approve the mitigation.

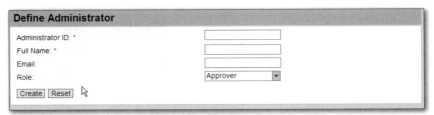

Figure 3.60 Mitigation – Defining an Administrator

Structuring controls by business unit

To assign the list to controls in future, you create business units using the **Mitigation • Business Units • Create** menu path (see Figure 3.61). You then assign the controls to the business units. The advantage of doing this is that a business unit manager can display all controls within his area of responsibility.

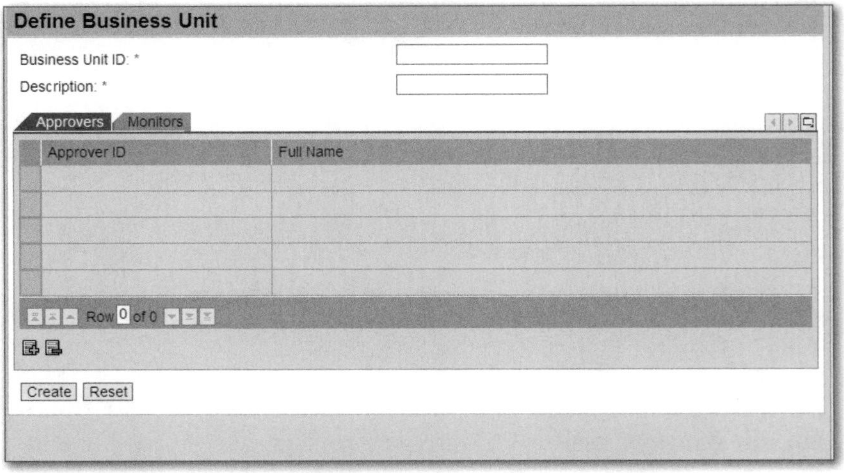

Figure 3.61 Mitigation – Defining a Business Unit

You use the **Mitigation • Mitigating Controls • Create** path to access the transaction to create mitigation controls. To create a mitigation control, you first specify the **Mitigating Control ID** and **Description** (see Figure 3.62). You also need to specify the **Business Unit** and the **Management Approver**, who will approve the mitigation controls. This assignment unambiguously regulates which mitigation controls are carried out in a particular business unit and which manager is responsible for complying with them. The manager can also be notified about a workflow by email. If required, this can be configured as part of the integration with the Compliant User Provisioning application scenario.

You then list the risks that are to be mitigated within the framework of the controls. Next, you assign a control monitor and, finally, in the **Reports** tab, you specify which action is to be performed by which monitor and how often in a particular system.

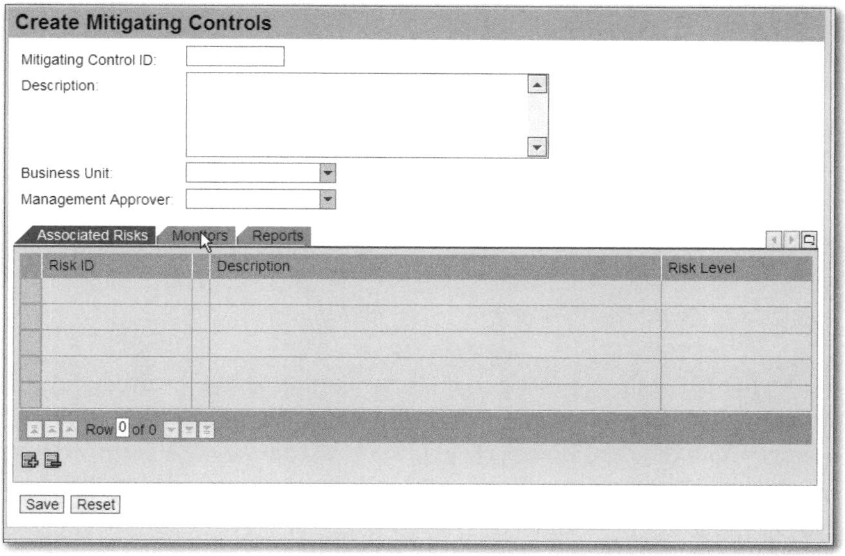

Figure 3.62 Creating Mitigating Controls

SAP GRC Access Control now supports you with different reports. You can therefore select monitors from a particular business unit or by valid-

Reports for evaluating controls and mitigation monitor

153

ity interval using the **Mitigation • Mitigation Monitors** menu path (see Figures 3.63 and 3.64).

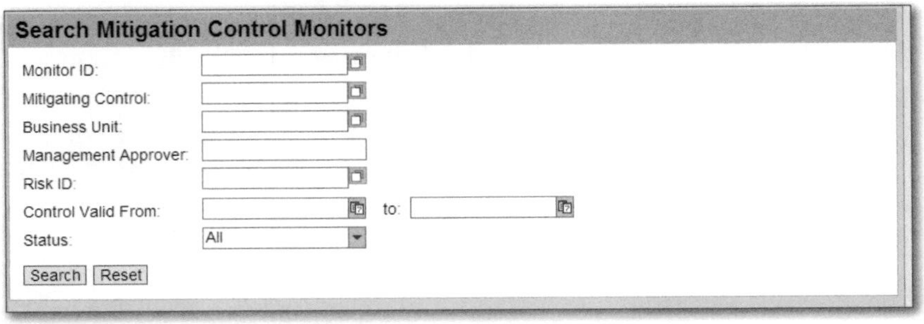

Figure 3.63 Search Mitigation Control Monitors

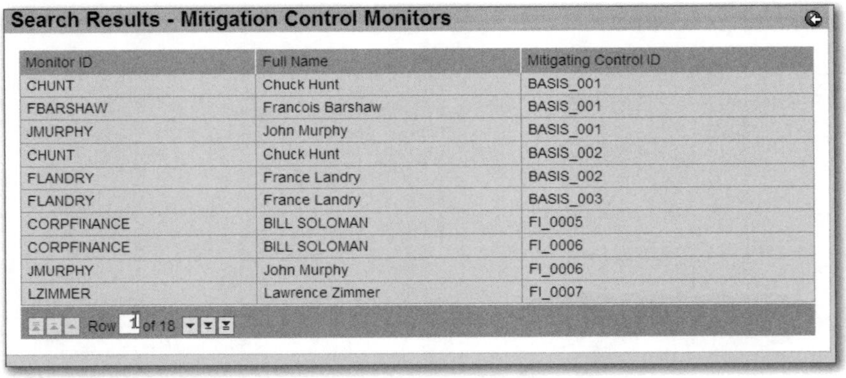

Search Results - Mitigation Control Monitors

Monitor ID	Full Name	Mitigating Control ID
CHUNT	Chuck Hunt	BASIS_001
FBARSHAW	Francois Barshaw	BASIS_001
JMURPHY	John Murphy	BASIS_001
CHUNT	Chuck Hunt	BASIS_002
FLANDRY	France Landry	BASIS_002
FLANDRY	France Landry	BASIS_003
CORPFINANCE	BILL SOLOMAN	FI_0005
CORPFINANCE	BILL SOLOMAN	FI_0006
JMURPHY	John Murphy	FI_0006
LZIMMER	Lawrence Zimmer	FI_0007

Row 1 of 18

Figure 3.64 Search Results – Mitigation Control Monitors

Using the **Mitigation • Mitigated Users** menu path, you can also evaluate those users for whom a risk was identified and the risk was mitigated (see Figure 3.65). The report provides information about control ID that was created for the risk and also who is responsible for monitoring control compliance in the enterprise.

In summary, controls are created for the mitigation area for identified risks. The implementation of controls is monitored and documented and can be submitted to the auditor for possible reviews.

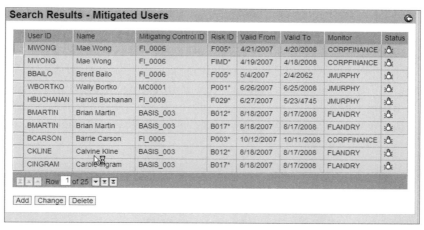

Figure 3.65 List of Mitigated Users

Alert Monitoring

When critical or conflict-ridden actions are performed without a response within a reasonable time frame, you can send an alert to management (see Figure 3.66) in SAP GRC Access Control.

Figure 3.66 Alert Monitoring

In the following situations, you can send alerts for alert monitoring to management (see Figure 3.67):
Alert situations

▶ Call the relevant report under **Alert Monitoring • Conflicting Actions** when conflict-ridden actions violate SOD rules (e.g., an employee calls the transactions to create a vendor master record and initiate payment of vendor invoices).

▶ Call the relevant report under **Alert Monitoring · Critical Actions** when calling critical actions causes an alert. Critical actions involve transactions that represent a high risk (e.g., changing or deleting the contents of IT databases).

▶ Call the relevant report under **Alert Monitoring · Mitigation Monitoring** when mitigation monitoring indicates whether the controls that were set up for mitigating risks were actually implemented.

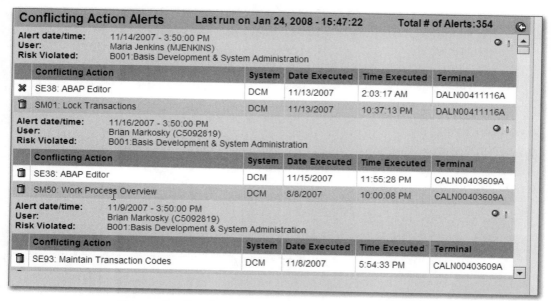

Figure 3.67 Sample Report – Conflicting Action Alerts

Reason required
when alert reset

You can reset an alert by selecting the candle icon on the right. This is useful if management has already been informed of the critical status. However, the system requires you to specify a reason for resetting the alert.

Configuration

The system administrator configures the SAP GRC Access Control Compliance Calibrator – Risk Analysis and Remediation. Only users with corresponding administrator rights can access the configuration menu (see Figure 3.68).

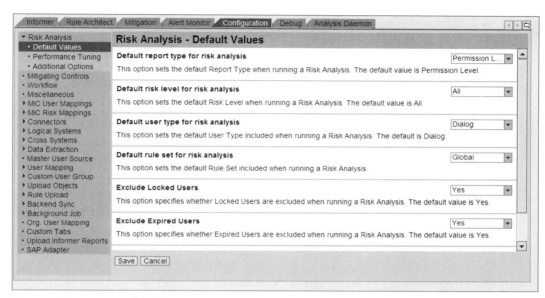

Figure 3.68 Overview of Configuration

Default Settings for Risk Analysis – Default Values

You can implement the default settings for risk analysis under the **Configuration • Risk Analysis • Default Values** menu option (see Figure 3.69):

Risk analysis settings

▶ **Default report type for risk analysis**
You can define the default report type; the recommended default setting is **Permission Level** because this is the most comprehensive form of analysis. You can also narrow down the analysis to subareas such as critical roles or profiles, for example.

▶ **Default risk level for risk analysis**
All is the default setting for the default risk level. You can also limit the analysis to other risk levels for extensive amounts of data. For example, setting the level to **high** means that only risks with a high risk level will be analyzed in the reports.

▶ **Default user type for risk analysis**
Dialog is specified as the default setting for the default user type. This means that all users that have a user ID for dialog operations are included in the analysis. You can also analyze all users, which means that the user IDs that are only provided for operating systems will also be included in the analysis.

▶ **Default rule set for risk analysis**
You can specify the default rule set for risk analysis. You use rule sets as a classification criterion when you create functions and risks. In our example, we use the **Global** setting.

▶ **Exclude Locked Users**
The default setting excludes locked users from the analysis.

▶ **Exclude Expired Users**
The default setting doesn't include users whose permission has expired in the analysis.

▶ **Exclude mitigated risks from analysis**
Risks that have already been mitigated are either excluded from, or explicitly included in, the analysis. The decision depends on the volume of data and method of required reporting.

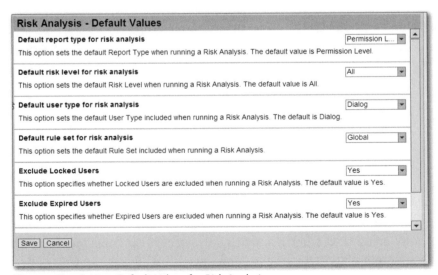

Figure 3.69 Setting Default Values for Risk Analysis

Default Setting for Risk Analysis – Performance Tuning

Under the **Risk Analysis** • **Performance Tuning** menu option, you can implement settings that will improve system performance. These include the following options (see Figure 3.70):

▶ **Define volume for synchronizing users in background**
You determine the volume by the number of permitted users. The default setting is 1,000 users. This means that 1,000 users can be processed by Remote Function Call (RFC). This setting ensures that the maximum time of 10 minutes, which is required for the necessary dialog work process for performing the RFC, isn't exceeded in the connected ERP system. In short, this setting avoids a timeout situation.

▶ **Number of Web Service worker threads**
The number of Web Service worker threads specifies how many requests can be processed in parallel. We recommend that you set five worker threads as the default value.

▶ **Number of analyses running in background in parallel**
If different analyses are to run simultaneously in the background, you determine the number of analyses to be run in parallel by the number of background worker threads allowed here. We recommend that you set three worker threads as the default value.

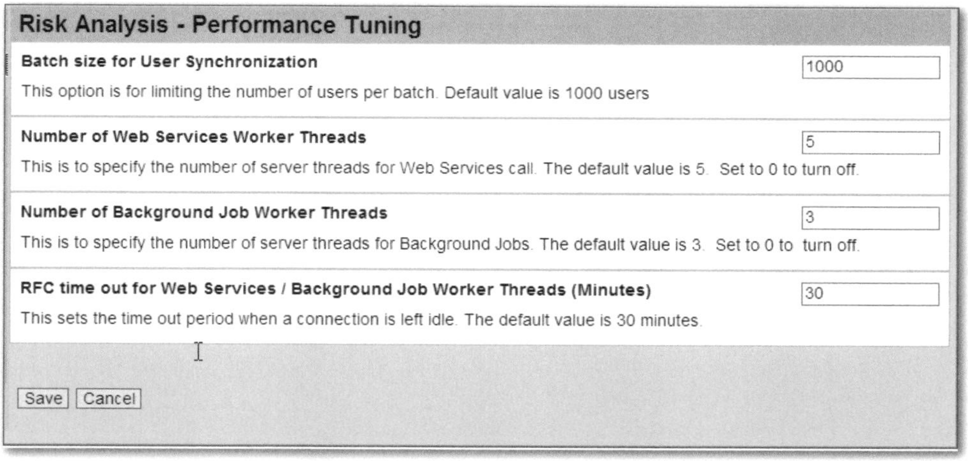

Figure 3.70 Performance Tuning for Risk Analysis

▶ **Idle connection timeout**
The recommended default value for an idle connection timeout with RFCs for Web Service/background job worker threads is 30 minutes.

You can also implement the following default settings, to name a few, under the **Risk Analysis • Additional Options** menu option (see Figure 3.71):

▶ **Ignore Critical Roles & Profiles**
You can ignore critical roles and profiles in the analysis; the recommend default setting is **No**, which means that critical roles and profiles are also included in all risk analyses.

▶ **Show Composite Role in User Analysis**
In addition to single role analyses, you can also display composite roles in the user analysis. Because the content of the information consequently added is low, the default setting is **No**.

▶ **Use SOD Supplementary Table for Analysis**
This option determines whether the *SOD Supplementary Table* is to be used for the analysis. The default setting is **No**. The default Rules Library is therefore used as an analysis criterion.

▶ **Include Role/Profile Mitigating Controls in User Analysis**
With this setting, the user IDs for the mitigating controls are also included in the risk analysis at user level. The default setting here is **No**.

▶ **Enable Offline Risk Analysis**
The default setting for **Enable Offline Risk Analysis** is **Yes**. This ensures that the risk analysis will also be performed when ERP systems aren't connected.

▶ **Include organization rules**
The default setting regarding whether you want organization rules to be included when you update management reports is **No**.

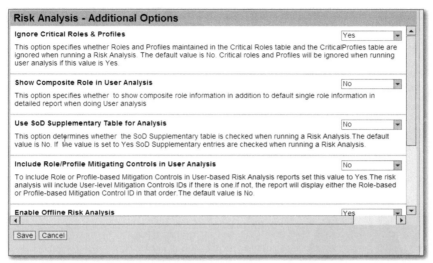

Figure 3.71 Risk Analysis – Additional Options

Under the **Mitigating Controls** menu option, you can set the runtime that will be valid for mitigating controls (see Figure 3.72). The default entry is **365** days. Because you can also assign a runtime to each individual mitigating control, this single value of the relevant control is used if an entry isn't made here.

Mitigating control settings

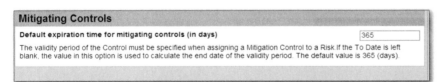

Figure 3.72 Mitigating Controls

Under the **Configuration · Workflow** menu item, you configure the parameters for initiating automatic notifications (see Figure 3.73). Note here that only workflows that were triggered within the *Compliant User Provisioning* (Virsa Access Enforcer) application area are supported here.

Workflow settings

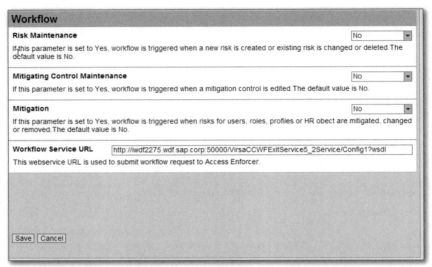

Figure 3.73 Workflow

You can specifically define the situations where notification should be initiated:

▶ When a new risk is created

▶ When a mitigating control is processed

▶ When risks for users, roles, profiles, or HR objects are to be mitigated, changed, or removed

The default value of the setting is **No** for all three parameters. The Web Service URL used to transfer notifications to the SAP GRC Access Control *Compliant User Provisioning* application area is also specified under this menu option.

Background job, change log settings

The **Configure • Miscellaneous** menu option contains some parameters for background processing, printing, and logging (see Figure 3.74). These specifically include the following:

▶ **Frequency of Background Job Daemon in Seconds**
A parameter for setting how often a background job daemon can be invoked (default setting is **60** seconds).

► **Maximum display lines for print preview**
A parameter for specifying the maximum number of lines for print preview.

► **Background Job Spool File Location**
A parameter for specifying the location where background spool files are saved.

► **Alert Log Filename & Location**
A parameter for specifying the location where the alert log is stored.

► **Enable Risk Change Log/Enable Function Change Log**
A parameter for specifying whether changes to risks and functions are to be logged (default setting is **Yes**).

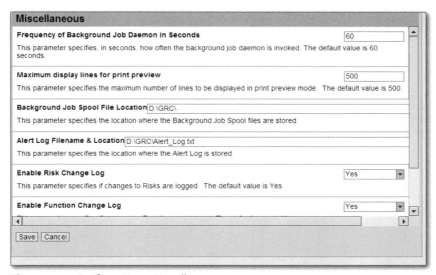

Figure 3.74 Configuration – Miscellaneous

You can subsequently display the change history by selecting the **Change History** button from the **Rule Library** • **Risks** • **Search** • **Select** menu options (see Figures 3.75 and 3.76).

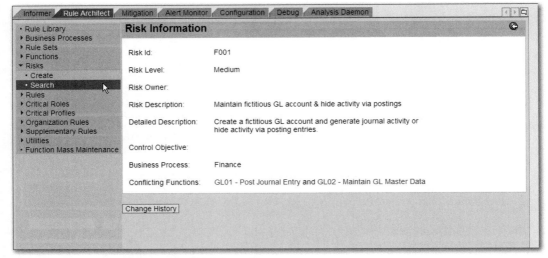

Figure 3.75 Risk Information

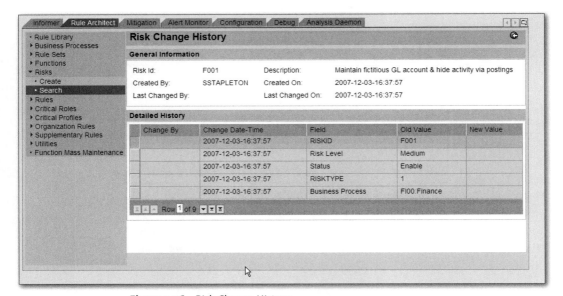

Figure 3.76 Risk Change History

You connect ERP systems to the *Risk Analysis and Remediation* application area of SAP GRC Access Control using the **Configuration • Connectors • Create** menu options (see Figure 3.77).

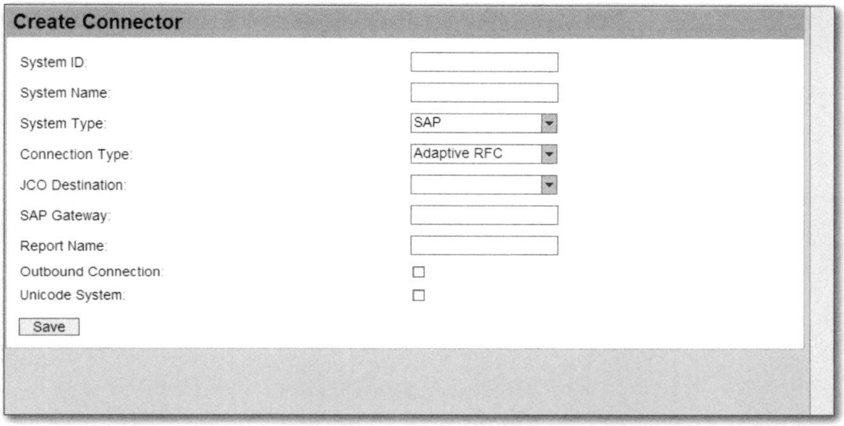

Create Connector

System ID:	
System Name:	
System Type:	SAP
Connection Type:	Adaptive RFC
JCO Destination:	
SAP Gateway:	
Report Name:	
Outbound Connection:	☐
Unicode System:	☐

Save

Figure 3.77 Creating System Connections

In addition to the **System ID** and **System Name**, you also need to specify the **System Type**. As well as SAP systems, you can also connect ERP systems from other providers (Oracle, Siebel, PeopleSoft, Hyperion, JD Edwards) or legacy systems to SAP GRC Access Control.

Creating connections to ERP systems

You can use data extractors to load users, roles, and profiles that are used in other systems into SAP GRC Access Control and adapt them to the necessary format for this purpose (see Figure 3.78). When creating the data extractors using the **Configuration • Data Extraction • Create** menu path, you must specify the source system. You must also specify whether the object to be loaded is a user, role, or profile. When you use the **Flatfile** data extraction mode, the individual fields of the source system (ERP) are assigned to the individual fields in the target system (SAP GRC Access Control).

Data extractor

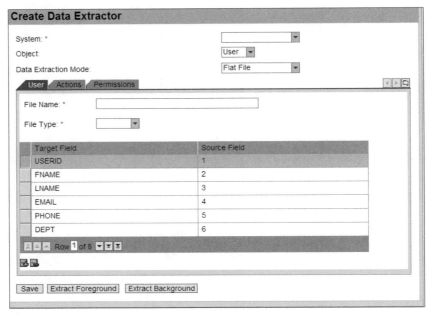

Figure 3.78 Creating a Data Extractor

3.6.2 Overview of Configuration of the Enterprise Role Management Application Area (Virsa Role Expert)

The following section gives an overview of the main configuration steps required to implement Enterprise Role Management.

Initial Setup of Enterprise Role Management

Initial setup Before you can create roles using Enterprise Role Manager, you first essentially need to set up the environment. Administrator rights are necessary for this purpose. The administration user name and corresponding password are generated automatically when you install Enterprise Role Management.

Before you can begin the configuration, you need to load additional system data (see Figure 3.79). You access the transaction from the **Configuration • Initial System Data** menu path.

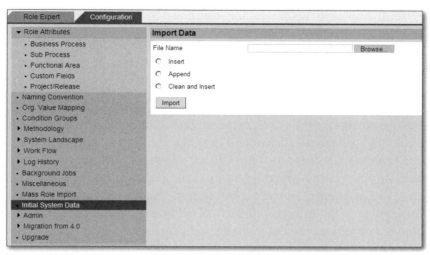

Figure 3.79 Initial System Data

You must load the following files:

```
RE_init_clean_and_insert_data.xml
RE_init_append_data_xml
RE_init_methodology_data.xml
```

After you've completed the loading process, you implement the settings for integrating Enterprise Role Management with Risk Analysis and Remediation or with Compliant User Provisioning by using the **Configuration • Miscellaneous** menu options.

A detailed description of the entries to be made is contained in the *GRC Applications Integration Documentation* Quick Reference Guide (see Section 3.6.6, "Technical How-to Guides").

You can only begin the configuration after you've completed these tasks. The configuration of Enterprise Role Management comprises the following areas:

▶ Defining the system landscape

▶ Setting up role attributes

▶ Setting up condition groups

▶ Determining the Methodology for role definition

- Setting up approval criteria for workflows
- Setting up naming conventions
- Setting up organizational value mapping

Defining the System Landscape

Defining the system group
You usually create roles in Enterprise Role Management in a three-tier system landscape. You define and generate the roles in one system and use transport requests to transport the roles to a second system. You test the roles in this second system. If the results of the test are positive, you transfer the roles to a live system. The individual ERP systems are connected to Enterprise Role Management by connectors, and this connection is then used to exchange data between the ERP systems and Enterprise Role Management.

Creating a connection to ERP systems
The following entries are required to create a connector (see Figure 3.80):

- System type, which is the ERP system that is to be integrated with Enterprise Role Management
- Name of connector, which is the name that will appear as the system name for users of Enterprise Role Management
- Description of connector
- Application, which is the name of the application or application server
- Host application, which is the name of the host where the application is running
- System number, which is the Log ID number of the SAP system
- SAP client
- User ID for the SAP system
- Password for the SAP user
- System language
- Messages server name

- ▶ Messages server group
- ▶ Messages server host
- ▶ SAP version (Enterprise Role Management only supports the connection of SAP ERP releases as of SAP R/3 4.6C and higher)

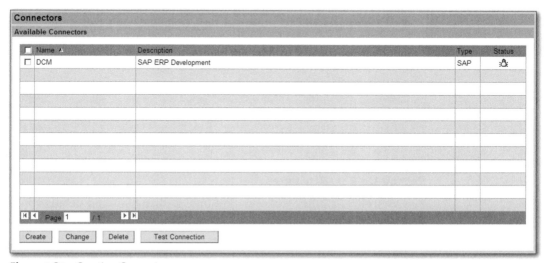

Figure 3.80 Creating Connectors

After you save the data for the connector, you use the **Test Connection** button to check whether the connection works and is valid.

Creating connectors

Important functions performed at the connector or system level include analyzing risks for roles and generating roles in connected ERP systems.

You can use the **System Landscape** configuration (see Figure 3.81) to interconnect several ERP systems/connectors logically. Connected ERP systems are normally three-tier, meaning that they consist of a development system, test system, and live system. You generate roles in the development system and transfer them to the live system using transport requests. In the live system, you analyze the roles with the integration of Risk Analysis and Remediation (Compliance Calibrator) of SAP GRC Access Control.

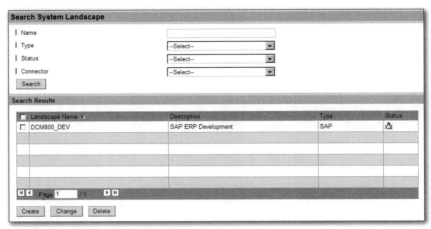

Figure 3.81 Creating a System Landscape

Setting Up Role Attributes

You use role attributes to store additional information and details when defining roles. Five role attributes are available:

- ▶ Business processes
- ▶ Subprocess
- ▶ Functional area
- ▶ Custom fields
- ▶ Project/release

You define role attributes using the **Configuration • Role Attributes** menu path.

Business process role attribute

A business process is a logical sequence or collection of activities. Examples of business processes include finance, sales and distribution, financials, human resources, order to cash, and procure to pay. When you define a business process, you specify an ID, a description, and an abbreviation. This abbreviation should be descriptive because it will be used in the roles library (see Figure 3.82). Note that you can only delete a business process if it's not assigned to a role or subprocess.

You assign subprocesses using the *Process Mapping* function.

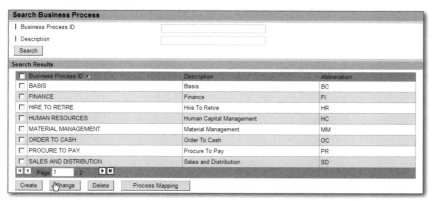

Figure 3.82 Business Process Role Attribute

You can, for example, split the finance business process into the sub- processes *General Ledger*) and *Financial Reporting*). These subprocesses, which logically split a business process into substeps, must be created beforehand. When you create a subprocess, you specify the **Sub Process ID**, **Description**, and **Abbreviation** (see Figure 3.83).

Subprocess role attribute

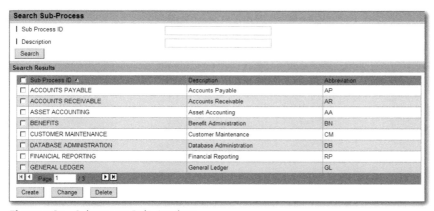

Figure 3.83 Subprocess Role Attribute

The functional area is an additional attribute for cataloging roles. It describes an organizational unit within an enterprise (see Figure 3.84). A business process, in contrast, is performed across functional areas, mean- ing that when a business process is being performed, different depart- ments (functional areas) of the enterprise are involved. The functional

Functional area role attribute

area role attribute is particularly helpful if you want to display all existing roles for a department/functional area in Reporting.

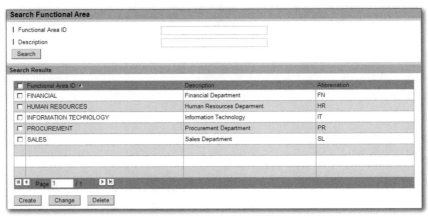

Figure 3.84   Functional Area Role Attribute

Custom fields role attribute   You can also describe a role using custom fields (see Figure 3.85), for example, to catalog roles by region or country.

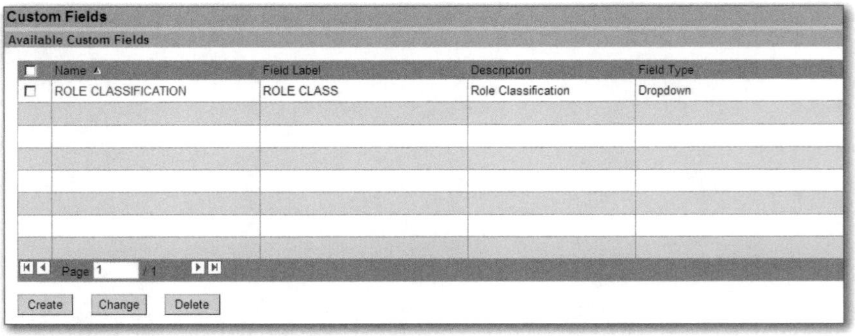

Figure 3.85   Custom Fields Role Attribute

Project/release role attribute   *Project/Release* is available as the last attribute. A project/release consists of the **Project/Release ID** and **Description** (see Figure 8.86). A project/ release role, for example, can be assigned to the software implementation project, with which it was initially created. Keeping a record of the software release that the role was initially set up for is also useful for subsequent management purposes.

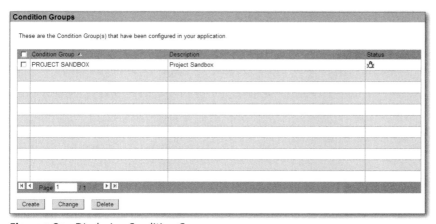

Figure 3.86 Project/Release Role Attribute

Setting Up Condition Groups

A condition group is a collection of conditions. You use it to define valid combinations of conditions for a role. For example, you can use a condition group to prevent a functional area/organizational unit from being assigned to a role that isn't involved in the processing of a business unit. You can display the list of condition groups by selecting the **Configuration • Condition Groups** menu options (see Figure 3.87).

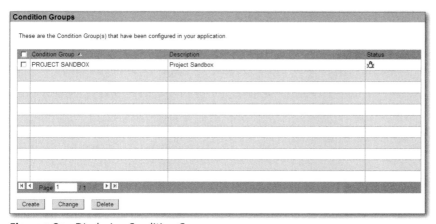

Figure 3.87 Displaying Condition Groups

You create additional condition groups by selecting the **Create** function key. You need to specify a **Condition Groups ID,** and **Description,** and **Status** for this purpose. The status indicates whether the condition group is set to active or inactive for use (see Figure 3.88). You then assign the individual **Role Attributes.** You use the **Status** entry to define whether the role attribute must always be specified (*AND* link) or whether the role attribute can be specified for this condition group (*OR* link).

Figure 3.88 Creating a Condition Group

Methodology for Defining Roles

The methodology for defining roles consists of three components:

- ▶ Actions that are required to define a role
- ▶ Steps that must be performed to define a role
- ▶ Processes that record the sequence of steps to be performed

Actions for defining roles

The following predefined actions are available in SAP GRC Access Control (see Figure 3.89):

- ▶ **Approval of role**
  Sends information about checking and approving the role to the owner.

- ▶ **Generation of a role**
  Causes the role to be automatically created in the SAP ERP backend system.

▶ **Initiating risk analysis**
Checks whether there will be risks associated with the role that is to be created. Also checks the role against the predefined SOD rules.

▶ **Saving role authorization data**
Saves the assignment after you assign authorizations to a role.

▶ **Saving Role Definition**
Saves the role and its attributes.

▶ **Saving role derivation**
Saves the role derivation.

▶ **Saving Test Results**
Saves the results of a test process.

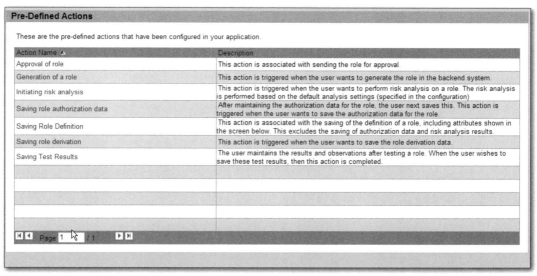

Pre-Defined Actions

These are the pre-defined actions that have been configured in your application.

Action Name △	Description
Approval of role	This action is associated with sending the role for approval.
Generation of a role	This action is triggered when the user wants to generate the role in the backend system.
Initiating risk analysis	This action is triggered when the user wants to perform risk analysis on a role. The risk analysis is performed based on the default analysis settings (specified in the configuration)
Saving role authorization data	After maintaining the authorization data for the role, the user next saves this. This action is triggered when the user wants to save the authorization data for the role.
Saving Role Definition	This action is associated with the saving of the definition of a role, including attributes shown in the screen below. This excludes the saving of authorization data and risk analysis results.
Saving role derivation	This action is triggered when the user wants to save the role derivation data.
Saving Test Results	The user maintains the results and observations after testing a role. When the user wishes to save these test results, then this action is completed.

Page 1 / 1

Figure 3.89 Pre-Defined Actions

These activities are available to describe the individual steps for defining roles. When you create the steps, you assign an ID, the **Description**, and an **Action Name** (see Figure 3.90).

Steps for defining roles

175

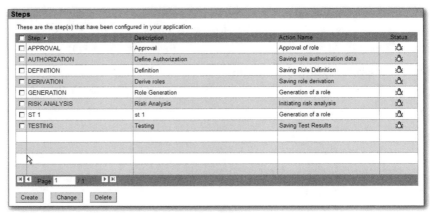

Figure 3.90 Configuring Steps for Defining Roles

You then group the individual steps in a process. The process defines the chronological sequence of processes. It specifically defines the steps and sequence in which the roles are defined and approved. SAP GRC Access Control also provides a standard process for this purpose (see Figure 3.91).

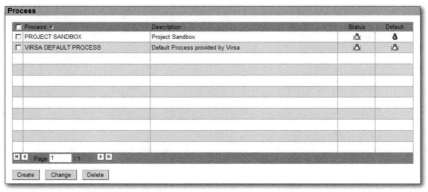

Figure 3.91 Standard Process

Role definition standard SAP process

The standard process consists of seven steps (see Figure 3.92):

▶ **Definition**

▶ **Authorization**

▶ **Risk Analysis**

▶ **Derivation**

▶ **Approval**

▶ **Generation**

▶ **Testing**

If necessary, you can change this standard process. By flexibly developing the method for defining roles, you can adapt the creation process in detail to the requirements of the enterprise.

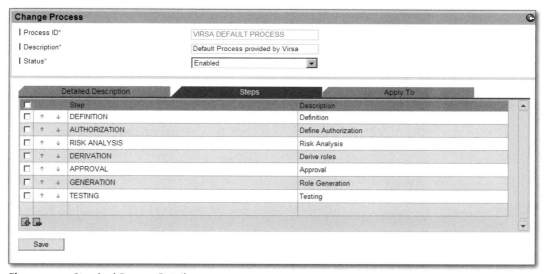

Figure 3.92 Standard Process Details

Setting Up Approval Criteria for Workflows

You must install and configure Compliant User Provisioning to use the workflow for approving roles.

When you create the approval criteria, an approver and alternate approver are assigned to the role attributes. After you call the *Set Up Approval Criteria for Workflow* function, you assign the **Group Name** and **Criteria** (assigned business processes and subprocesses) first (see Figure 3.93).

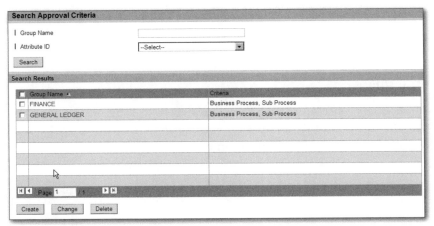

Figure 3.93 Search Approval Criteria

In the course of the process, you then assign the people, who are allowed to approve roles for the relevant area (**Approver**), by group name (see Figure 3.94). You can also specify an **Alternate Approver** here.

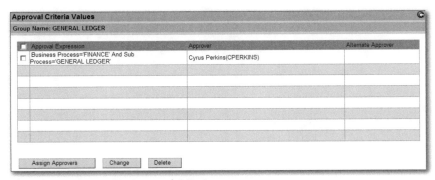

Figure 3.94 Setting Up Approval Criteria

Setting Up Naming Conventions

You can use naming conventions when defining roles. The naming conventions can vary depending on the assigned ERP system and role type (see Figure 3.95).

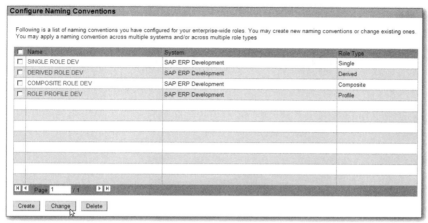

Figure 3.95 Configuring Naming Conventions

Figure 3.96 shows an example of how the role names can be specified. In this case, for example, the specification is that a **User-Defined Text** can be in **Position 1–2**, **Position 3–4** is occupied by the **Business Process** ID, **Position 5–5** in turn is available as a **User-Defined Text**, and **Position 6–7** is reserved for the **Sub Process**. You can subsequently assign four positions as you wish.

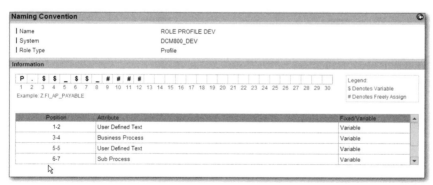

Figure 3.96 Naming Conventions – Details

Setting Up Organizational Value Mapping

You use this option to implement the inheritance of values within an organizational hierarchy, which means that the value mapping that was set up at the company code level will also be inherited on the dependent lower-level organizational units. Figure 3.97 shows an overview of the organizational value mapping that has been set up.

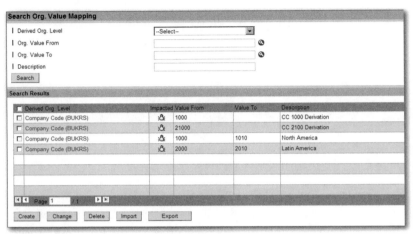

Figure 3.97 List of Organizational Value Mapping

You can display assigned organizational units by selecting a derived organizational unit. In this example, **Purchasing Organization 5000** is assigned from **Company Code 2000** to **Company Code 2010** (see Figure 3.98). This means that roles assigned to company code 2000, for example, are also automatically derived or inherited on purchasing organization 5000.

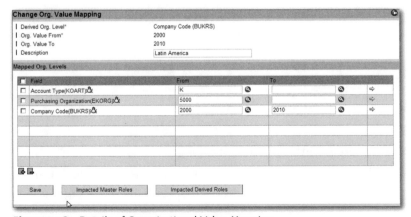

Figure 3.98 Details of Organizational Value Mapping

The organizational hierarchy is imported from connected SAP ERP back-end systems. SAP GRC Access Control provides an Excel spreadsheet for this purpose.

3.6.3 Configuring the Compliant User Provisioning Application Area

The main steps involved in configuring the *Compliant User Provisioning* application area are the following:

- Logging on as administrator
- Configuring connectors
- Configuring authentication
- Defining user data sources
- Mitigating
- Setting up email servers
- Creating workflow initiators
- Creating workflow stages
- Creating workflow paths

Logging On as Administrator

After the installation, you can access the application area for securely assigning permissions by entering the address "http://<servername>:<port>/AE/index.jsp." The user with administrator rights available in the standard system is "Admin" and the password is "initpass."

Configuring Connectors

You must first ensure that all ERP systems in question are connected to SAP GRC Access Control for secure permission assignment. After connection, you can import SAP roles, search for users and roles, and identify user ID numbers (see Figure 3.99).

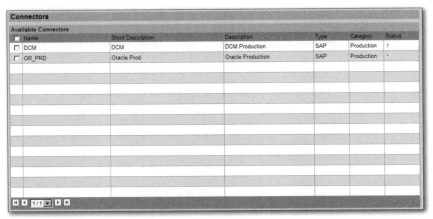

Figure 3.99 Available Connectors

Connectors are available for the connection, which can be classified into three types:

▶ **LDAP connectors (Lightweight Directory Access Protocol)**
These protocols involve the use of the following protocols: Microsoft Active Directory, Sun Microsystems SunOne, Novell E-Directory, and IBM Tivoli.

▶ **Oracle connectors**
Compliant User Provisioning supports the connection of Oracle systems on a limited basis. Interface data fields are therefore hard-coded and can't be adjusted as part of a configuration.

▶ **SAP connectors**
These connectors are created for each of the connected ERP systems. Figure 3.100 shows in detail the specifications that are required when you create an SAP connector. Note in particular that SAP GRC Access Control only supports SAP ERP systems with Release SAP R/3 4.6C and higher. You also specify here whether an SAP HCM application is connected. If this is the case, activities are initiated in SAP GRC Access Control due to changes in the HR master record, and the manager responsible is inferred directly from the HR master data.

Figure 3.100 SAP Connector Details

Also note that all backend systems to be connected are listed in the SAP System Landscape Directory. You activate the corresponding **SLD Connector** checkbox for this purpose.

If you want to connect a large number of SAP systems, we recommend that you use Central User Administration for user administration. You can use Central User Administration to maintain users for all connected SAP systems (children) of an SAP system (parent). To ensure that Compliant User Provisioning can be used in an integrated way with *Central User Administration* (CUA), you need to set up a connector for the SAP system (parent), from which CUA performs the user administration. All other systems (children) must also be connected over it through connectors. It's important here that the names of the connectors of the con-

Central permission assignment

183

nected child systems match their logical system names in CUA. To ensure that SAP GRC Access Control can identify the central system of the CUA group, you must make the corresponding entry under **Configuration • Workflow** (see Figure 3.101).

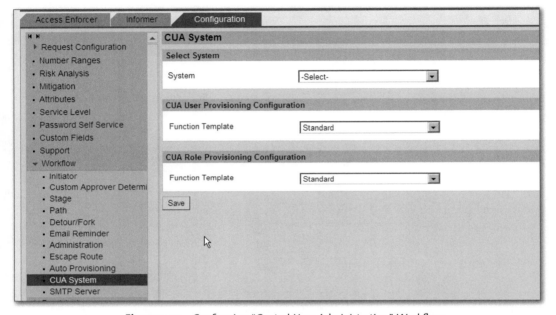

Figure 3.101 Configuring "Central User Administration" Workflow

The CUA system is specified here. If no customer-specific programs are used for configuring users and roles, both entries on this input screen can be made as a default function template.

With SAP GRC Access Control Release 5.2, either all connected ERP systems are each linked with the same CUA, or none of the connected ERP systems are linked. With SAP GRC Access Control Release 5.3, you can also connect several CUA or ERP systems without using a CUA.

Configuring Authentication

The authentication system entry, selected from the **Configuration** • **Authentication** menu path, is required if the requestor also wants to log on to the system before he prepares the change request (see Figure 3.102). There are basically four options here:

▶ SAP system

▶ SAP User Management Engine (UME)

▶ LDAP system

▶ HR/HCM system

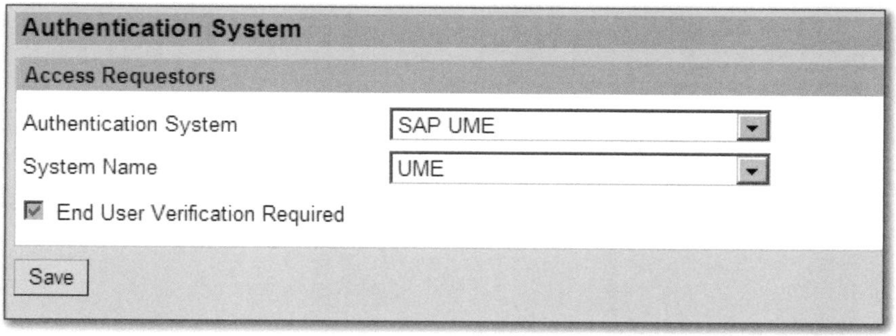

Figure 3.102 Authentication System

Defining User Data Sources

You select the **Configuration** • **User Data Source** menu path here to specify the source from which user data should be extracted (see Figure 3.103).

You can use this specification to search for users, assigned managers, and the people responsible for approval. Again, there are four options for the data source:

▶ SAP system

▶ SAP User Management Engine (UME)

▶ LDAP system

▶ HR/HCM system

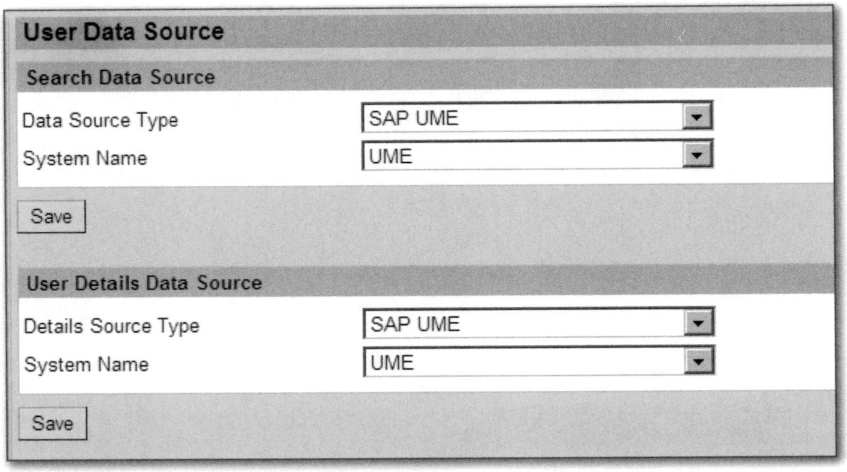

Figure 3.103 Defining the User Data Source

The data source type uniquely identifies what the data type is. You therefore don't need to implement a detailed assignment of individual data record fields elsewhere.

Mitigating

The default setting under the **Configuration • Mitigation** menu option isn't to allow the person responsible for approval to initiate approval despite possible risks (see Figure 3.104).

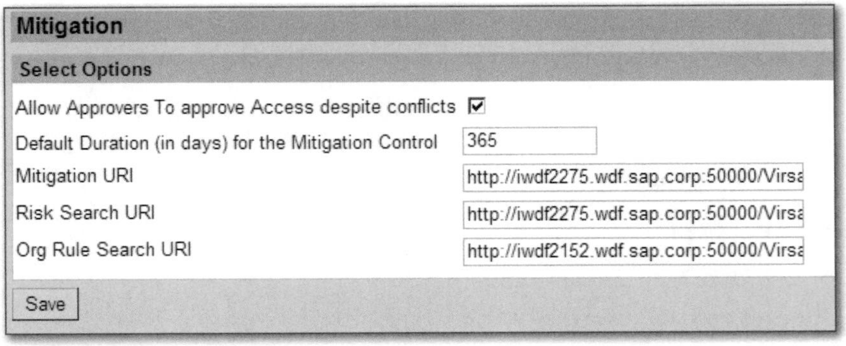

Figure 3.104 Mitigation

Consequently, the approver can't approve the authorization assignment if SOD violations were associated with this in the enterprise. In this case, the request would be rejected.

Setting Up Email Servers

One essential setting you make under the **Configuration • Workflow • SMTP Server** path is to set up the email server (see Figure 3.105).

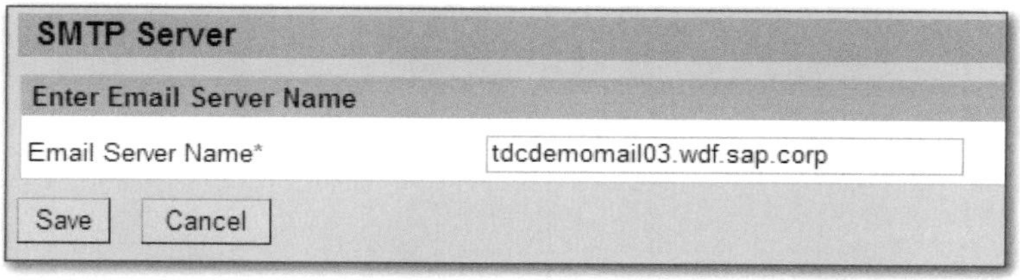

SMTP Server

Enter Email Server Name	
Email Server Name*	tdcdemomail03.wdf.sap.corp

Save   Cancel

Figure 3.105   Email Server Name

Without this setting, all email messages to approvers and the status message to the requestor would not work after processing has been completed.

Creating Workflow Initiators

By configuring a workflow initiator (**Configuration • Workflow • Initiator** menu path), you can specify when a workflow will actually be initiated (see Figure 3.106).

You can describe the initiating situation in detail using attributes. Attributes can be a particular requirement type (e.g., lock account) or also business processes, functional areas, or regional assignments. When specifying attributes, it's important to define whether it's an *OR* status or *AND* status. The workflow will be triggered for an *OR* status if one or the other attribute applies. However, with an *AND* status, the workflow will begin when both attributes apply.

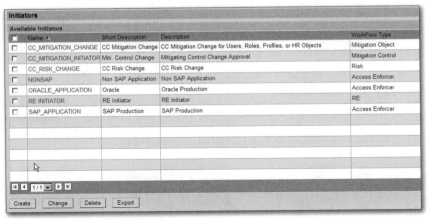

Figure 3.106 Workflow Initiator

Creating Workflow Stages

You create the approval levels to be processed by selecting the **Configuration • Workflow • Stage** menu path. The objective is to define the approver(s) and the notification details. You perform four configuration steps here. First, you create the stage details (see Figure 3.107).

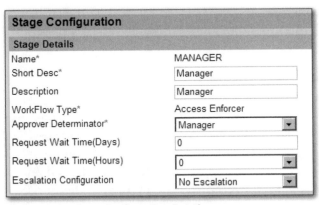

Figure 3.107 Stage Configuration Details

Stage configuration workflow   This includes determining the short description (**Short Desc**). This information, which is limited to 20 characters, appears in the application when the workflow starts. The **WorkFlow Type** is only available if the Compliant User Provisioning application area was set up in an integrated way with the Risk Analysis and Remediation and Enterprise Role Management application areas. You have several selection options in terms of determining approvers. For example, in addition to **Manager**, you can also specify **Security Owner** or **Application Owner**. The reaction if the approver doesn't respond to the request within the specified request wait time is defined in the **Escalation Configuration** field. Four selection options are provided here:

▶ **No Escalation**
This default setting awaits a reaction by the approver, even if the request wait time has been exceeded.

▶ **Forward to Next Stage**
This setting skips this stage due to the approver ignoring the request.

▶ **Forward to alternate approver**
This setting forwards the request to the specified alternate approver.

▶ **Forward to administrator**
This setting forwards the request to the administrator.

Next, you set up the details for configuring notifications (see Figure 3.108) by using the **Configuration** • **Workflow Email Reminder** menu path.

Here, you specify whether the **User**, **Requestor**, **Manager**, or **Other Approvers** should be notified following approval, rejection, escalation, or forwarding to the next approval stage. Because each specification generates additional email, we recommend that you reduce the number of notifications to a minimum. You also predefine the text of the emails here. We differentiate between three possible situations:

▶ The approver approves the request.

▶ The approver rejects the request.

▶ The approver doesn't respond in the specified request wait time and therefore initiates the other escalation.

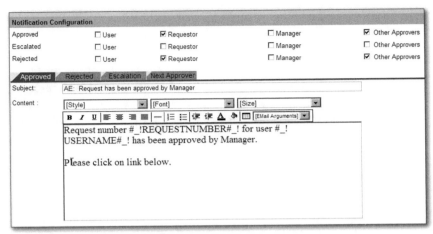

Figure 3.108 Notification Configuration

As the third step for configuring the workflow stage, you need additional details (see Figure 3.109).

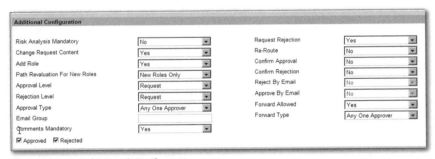

Figure 3.109 Additional Configuration

The following parameters are important to note:

▶ **Risk Analysis Mandatory**
The default setting is **No**. Changing this setting to **Yes** forces a risk analysis to be performed for each stage.

▶ **Change Request Content**
The **Yes** setting means that the approver is notified by email of the change request details.

▶ **Add Role**

The field is ready for input if **Change Request Content** was set to **Yes**. The **Yes** setting means that the approver can include other roles in the approval process.

▶ **Path Revaluation For New Roles**

The field is ready for input if **Add Role** was set to **Yes**. The content indicates how to proceed further if an additional role was specified. For example, you can implement a setting here whereby all workflow stages in the approval process have to be processed again from stage one on.

▶ **Approval Level and Rejection Level**

The default setting is **Request**; the approver can approve or reject at request level.

▶ **Approval Type: Example**

Several approvers are defined. Here, you can specify that it's sufficient if only one of the defined approvers approves the request.

▶ **Email Group**

You can specify a mailing list of who should be notified about requests.

▶ **Comments Mandatory**

If you select **Yes**, you need to give a reason for the approval or rejection.

The fourth and last setting when configuring workflow stages relates to additional security configurations (see Figure 3.110).

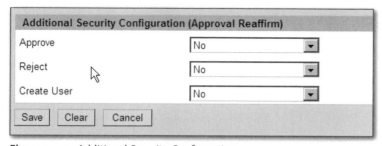

Figure 3.110 Additional Security Configuration

Here, you have the option that approvers must identify themselves by specifying their user IDs if they approve or reject the request.

Creating Workflow Paths

The stages listed earlier are grouped in sequence under the **Configuration • Work Flow Paths** menu options (see Figure 3.111). Important settings here are as follows:

▶ **Name**
Specifies the name of the workflow path; note that no blank spaces are allowed.

▶ **No. Of Stages**
Specifies the stages that you want to go through the approval process.

▶ **Initiator**
Specifies the initial situation that was defined in advance and determines which request attributes initiate the workflow.

▶ **Active indicator**
Specifies whether the relevant path was set to active or inactive.

▶ **Detour**
Specifies that the manager doesn't want to deal with the details of the approval. He waits until the security team or SOX team performs a check in the enterprise.

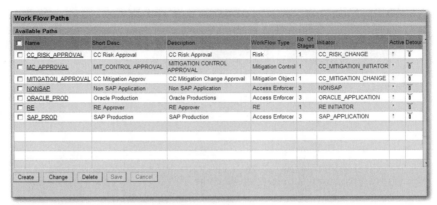

Figure 3.111 Setting Up Workflow Paths

You can also display the defined paths as graphics (see Figure 3.112).

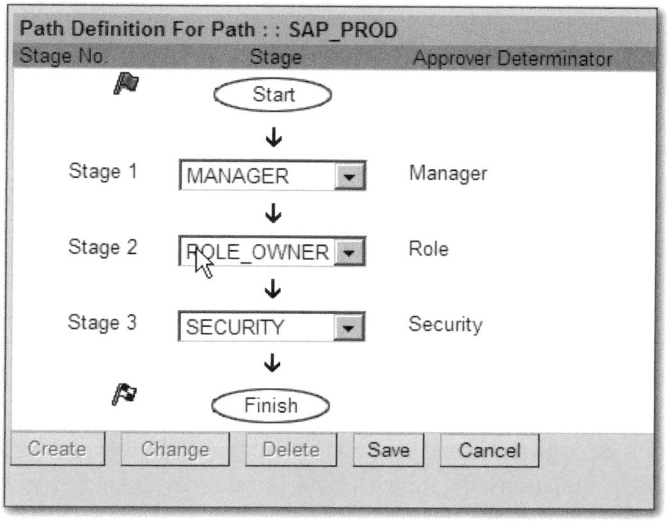

Figure 3.112 Defining Workflow Paths – Details

3.6.4 Configuring the Superuser Privilege Management Application Area

The application area for *Superuser Privilege Management*) enables users, in exceptional cases, to be temporarily assigned more comprehensive privilege profiles outside their normal areas of activity. All activities are documented in which the user uses the ID with the more comprehensive privilege. These specifically include the following:

- Log activities, sorted by transaction (user statistics, called using Transaction STAT)
- Change documents contained in Table CDHDR
- List of performed transactions
- List of programs that were executed using Transactions SA38 or SE38

The application area for Superuser Privilege Management differentiates the following roles, which are used as part of the implementation:

Technical activities log

Roles

► **Administrator**

The administrator is responsible for creating the emergency or "firefighter" user IDs and assigning them to the individual owners. The administrator is also the only one who can assign passwords for the *firefighter user* IDs. He can also call Reporting. Reporting analyzes the recorded activities that a user has performed using the firefighter privilege. SAP GRC Access Control provides the following default role for the administrator activity: /VIRSA/Z_VFAT_ADMINISTRATOR.

► **Owner**

Owners are responsible for a business unit within the enterprise (e.g., Financials). They can assign firefighter user IDs to firefighter users and controllers in their unit. Owners themselves can only see and assign firefighter user IDs that the administrator has assigned to them. Owners can also assume the role of controller. It's important that owners can't assign firefighter user IDs to themselves. SAP GRC Access Control provides the following default role for the owner activity: /VIRSA/Z_VFAT_ID_OWNER.

► **Firefighter User**

Firefighter users ultimately have access to firefighter IDs. After they log on using the firefighter user ID, firefighter users have more comprehensive privileges than they would be entitled to based on their user profiles. The work that the firefighter user performs after logging on with the firefighter user ID is logged in detail. SAP GRC Access Control provides the following default role for the firefighter user activity: /VIRSA/Z_VFAT_FIREFIGHTER.

► **Controller**

The detailed technical log that has been created as a result of firefighter user activities in the system is sent to controllers by email for review. The following default role is used for the controller role: /VIRSA/Z_VFAT_OWNER.

The following steps are required to set up the Superuser Privilege Management application area:

► Create firefighter user IDs.

► Assign Superuser Privilege Management roles to the user IDs.

► Complete the configuration (administrator).

▶ Define owners, controllers, and users for firefighter user IDs.

▶ Define passwords for firefighter user IDs.

▶ Perform tests to verify whether users can log on with the user ID.

▶ Define documentation requirements.

▶ Run background job for creating logs.

Creating Firefighter User IDs

You should create firefighter user IDs for each business unit (e.g., Basis, Procurement, Financials, etc.) in the SAP ERP system using Transaction SU01 (see Figure 3.113).

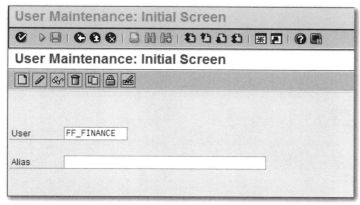

Figure 3.113 User Maintenance

In the next step, you need to assign the corresponding roles and profiles for the firefighting activities to be performed.

In this case, you should never assign a comprehensive privilege such as SAP_ALL to a firefighter user ID. You should always limit the scope of the privilege to the application area (e.g., Financials).

Assigning Superuser Privilege Management Roles to User IDs

In the next step, you assign the specified default roles (*Administrator, Owner, Firefighter, Controller*) to the corresponding user IDs. Note that you can also specify a validity period here.

For security reasons, also note that the administrator is only assigned the **/VIRSA/Z_VFAT_ADMINISTRATOR** default role. You should never assign additional Superuser Privilege Management roles to the administrator because this violates the necessary SOD requirement (assignment of user IDs and execution using user IDs).

You must assign the default role for the firefighter user activity (**/VIRSA/Z_VFAT_FIREFIGHTER**) to each firefighter user ID. Figure 3.114 shows the assignment of the **/VIRSA/Z_VFAT_FIREFIGHTER** default role to the **FF_Finance** firefighter user ID. For the users who must be able to work under a firefighter user ID, you should also assign the **/VIRSA/Z_VFAT_FIREFIGHTER** role to the normal user ID they use every day.

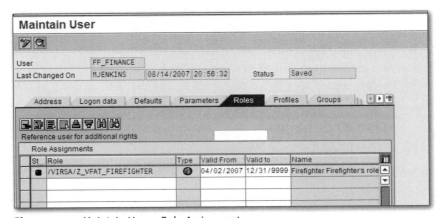

Figure 3.114 Maintain User – Role Assignment

Similarly, you assign the users, who are to perform the role of owners or controllers, the SAP GRC Access Control /VIRSA/Z_VFAT_OWNER default role to their user ID.

Configuration Completed by Administrator

After the **/VIRSA/Z_VFAT_ADMINISTRATOR** default role has been assigned for the administrator ID, the administrator can access the toolbox in Superuser Privilege Management after he logs on to the SAP ERP system. At this point, you perform the next necessary implementation steps by selecting the **Configuration** button (see Figure 3.115).

Figure 3.115   Toolbox

You can set the following parameters here (see Figure 3.116):

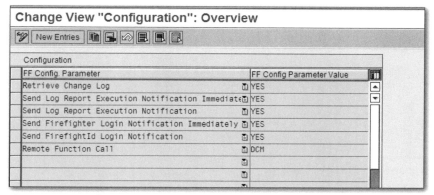

Figure 3.116   Configuration

▶ You can specify whether the change log is to be retrieved if data is changed or created.

▶ You can specify that owners (e.g., the owners of the Financials business application) generally or immediately receive the log of firefighter activities.

▶ You can specify that owners (e.g., the owners of the Financials business application) are to be notified generally or immediately when the firefighter privilege is used.

▶ You can determine the connection for using RFCs. Whenever a firefighter user logs on and executes corresponding applications, these applications are opened using RFC.

Defining Owners, Controllers, and Users for Firefighter User IDs

You then define the following:

▶ Which owner is responsible for which firefighter privileges

▶ Which controller receives the log using which firefighter privilege

- Which user is allowed to work under which firefighter privilege

You define these details in the toolbox by selecting the relevant **Owners**, **Firefighters**, or **Controllers** buttons (refer to Figure 3.115).

Figure 3.117 shows which owners are responsible for which firefight IDs.

Firefight ID	Firefight ID Owner	Used by	Description
FF_CHECKS	FWILSON		EMERGENCY CHECK PROCESSING
FF_FINANCE	CPERKINS		GL MASTER DATA MAINTENANCE
FF_FI_CLOSE	CPERKINS		FINANCIAL PERIOD CLOSING
FF_VENDORS	FWILSON		VENDOR MAINTENANCE

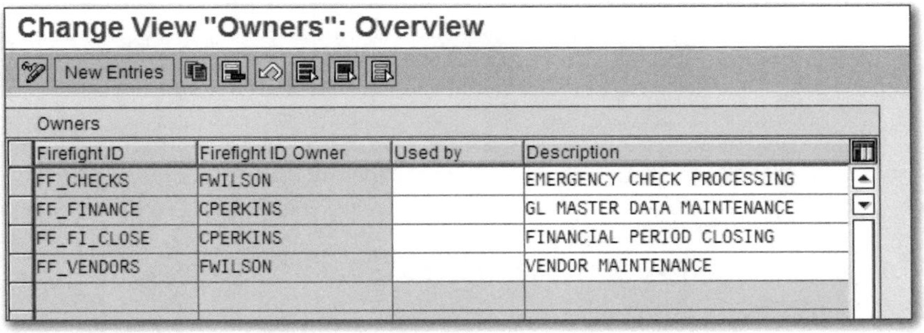

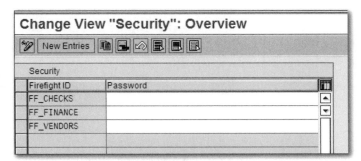

Figure 3.117 Changing Owners

Defining Passwords for Firefighter User IDs

The next step involves assigning passwords for the relevant firefighter IDs. To access the corresponding configuration table, you select the **Security** button in the toolbox (refer to Figures 3.115 and see 3.118). Passwords can only be assigned by an administrator.

Firefight ID	Password
FF_CHECKS	
FF_FINANCE	
FF_VENDORS	

Figure 3.118 Setting Passwords

Testing Whether Users Can Log On Using User ID

By assigning the firefighter user ID to certain users, the use of firefighter users will only be available in the SAP ERP menu of the particular user. Broadly speaking, users shouldn't be able to log on from a general ERP login menu using a firefighter user ID. This is achieved by providing specific programming in user exits during the installation of Superuser Privilege Management. If a user is able to log on with a firefighter user ID via the normal login screen, this means that an error occurred during installation, which must be corrected accordingly.

Defining Documentation Requirements

Each user who wants to log on using the firefighter ID assigned to him must specify a reason for this in the system. The administrator can define what the content of this reason should look like. For example, reasons can be defined in advance, which can then be selected in the relevant situation. Another option is that the user must send a message to the Support Desk in advance, including the ID number of the message in the reason. The user can also specify in advance the transactions that he will perform under the firefighter ID.

Background Job for Creating Logs

You set up the background job for creating logs using Transaction SM36. The recommendation in SAP GRC Access Control is to initiate this background job every hour.

3.6.5 Overview of Software Architecture

SAP GRC Access Control is based on a Java stack, which means that the application is programmed in the Java language. You can connect ERP systems from different manufacturers or also customer developments to this application (see Figure 3.119).

You connect the ERP systems from SAP, JD Edwards, PeopleSoft, or Hyperion using Real-Time Agents (RTA), which ensure the following:

▶ A risk analysis of the specified privileges can be performed in the connected ERP systems.

Real-Time Agents

- ▶ Controls are performed when privileges are being assigned to ensure that no high-risk situations have been overlooked when new users are created or privileges for existing users have been changed.
- ▶ Users are assigned the corresponding privilege.
- ▶ Roles are created in the connected SAP ERP systems.

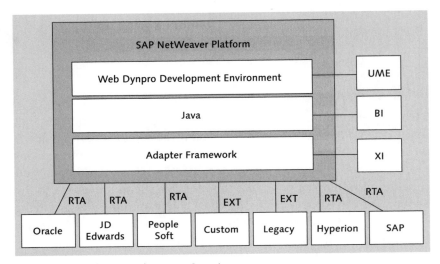

Figure 3.119 Software Architecture Overview

SAP provides RTAs for SAP ERP systems with Release SAP R/3 4.6C and higher. The company Greenlight creates RTAs for connecting ERP systems from Oracle, JD Edwards, PeopleSoft and Hyperion.

You use extractors to connect customer-specific and in-house systems. SAP GRC Access Control provides one-dimensional files, so the data from customer systems must be delivered in this format. SAP GRC Access Control subsequently reads these files in the specified format and processes them further.

SAP NetWeaver as a platform
SAP NetWeaver is used as a platform for SAP GRC Access Control. The following SAP NetWeaver functions support SAP GRC Access Control applications:

- ▶ **SAP User Management Engine (UME)**
  This controls user management on the Java stack locally. Users that

are required to perform certain functions in SAP GRC Access Control are created in UME. For example, all approvers of SAP GRC Access Control Compliant Provisioning must be created in UME. You can manage user master data using the UME interface. For retaining user data, UME is connected to other systems such as LDAP, ABAP back-end (e.g., CUA), or to the local J2EE database (the database where the UME is installed).

▶ **SAP NetWeaver Business Intelligence (SAP NetWeaver BI)**
If required, you can connect the SAP module for business data ware-housing for additional reports about the results of the SAP GRC Access Control application. This is advisable if you want to analyze a high number of SAP ERP systems with a corresponding high number of users.

You can use open interfaces to load master data information to or from SAP GRC Access Control. This master data information includes rules, business functions, risks, and user roles. You can also exchange information about organizational hierarchies using Microsoft Excel, for example.

Open interfaces

You use Web Services for integration with identity management systems (SAP NetWeaver Identity Management or other third-party products).

Web Services

Identity management systems are applications that control access and the assignment of privileges to IT systems. SAP GRC Access Control Release 5.2 supports the following Web Services:

▶ Forwarding requests from the identity management system to SAP GRC Access Control for risk analysis

▶ Listing applications and systems maintained in SAP GRC Access Control

▶ Performing risk analyses for requests that were sent from identity management systems

▶ Accessing detailed documentation that was stored when privileges were assigned (who approved what and when)

3.6.6 Technical How-to Guides

You'll find additional information under the *BPX Community* heading in the SAP Development Network (*https://www.sdn.sap.com/irj/sdn*). An Internet page for Governance, Risk and Compliance has been set up under *Business Process in Practice*. The How-to Guides, which technically address questions about installation and configuration in detail, are stored in a Knowledge Center there.

It is not because things are difficult that we do not dare; it is because we do not dare that they are difficult. (Seneca)

4 SAP GRC Risk Management

Even today, important corporate decisions are frequently made without those responsible having assessed the risks. *SAP GRC Risk Management* provides a uniform platform for automating risk management processes even in inhomogeneous system landscapes.

In this chapter, you'll learn about the relevant phases of the risk management process as well as the roles contained in the standard configuration. In addition to providing information about maintaining the central organizational hierarchy, this chapter also describes in detail how to maintain and manage the required activities and risk catalogs. You can therefore develop a comprehensive risk profile for your enterprise, measure the risk propensity, and draft response strategies for event losses. Furthermore, you can implement a complete cross-enterprise risk management process that extends beyond organizational and departmental boundaries.

You'll also learn how to document activities and risks and how to carry out a risk analysis both with and without a risk management response option. Finally, you'll learn that relevant users in all levels of the enterprise can use the available reports, dashboards, and so on, to obtain transparent information about the current risk profile.

The chapter concludes with five areas of system configuration for SAP GRC Risk Management. For many Customizing activities in these areas, all you have to do is activate standard SAP functions or various services once.

4.1   Goals of SAP GRC Risk Management

Even today, very important corporate decisions are frequently made despite the lack of transparency in terms of existing risks. Quite often, risk managers have to work with fragmented processes and systems. As a result, some essential tracking activities may not be possible. Furthermore, frequently no formal or coordinated risk identification procedure exists within the different business areas or for those responsible for the relevant business processes. Therefore, management and corporate governance don't have a complete overview of the risk profile and can't assess whether negative surprises (in the form of risks that have materialized) will prevent an enterprise from achieving its objectives.

Risk management as part of the enterprise strategy
If enterprises are to overcome future challenges, they must understand that risk management is a fixed part of all business activities. This includes the correct assessment of risk dependencies as well as a risk management policy that is embedded into the enterprise strategy. Therefore, risk analysis should be a key criterion for your strategic decisions at all times.

Proactive enterprise-wide processes
SAP GRC Risk Management enables you (a user in the user departments) to implement risk process control in an end-to-end scenario on an integrated platform and therefore manage risks where they arise. As a result, you can control cross-process risks along the value chain. Furthermore, your enterprise can introduce proactive and enterprise-wide risk management processes.

Uniform platform
SAP GRC Risk Management now provides you (the business process owner) with a uniform platform that supports a high degree of automation for risk management processes in an inhomogeneous system landscape. Furthermore, you can use uniform risk profiles to monitor the entire risk portfolio at operational and strategic enterprise levels. For example, you can trigger a warning message if risks that have far-reaching consequences and a high probability of occurrence exceed previously defined threshold values.

The automatic identification and analysis of as many risks as possible will show the greatest cost-saving potential in both the medium and long term. However, such automation will only be available to you in a later version of SAP GRC Risk Management.

The use of role-based Best Practice specifications enables you to implement proven methods for enterprise-wide risk identification and analysis. You can then apply existing response and solution strategies. Furthermore, this outline concept delivers specifications in relation to monitoring risks on an ongoing basis. In this way, you'll be better able to predict changing conditions and respond accordingly.

Enterprise-wide risk identification

SAP GRC Risk Management also provides dashboards, reports, and warning messages for monitoring activities and prioritizing subsequent responses. This ensures that relevant persons at all enterprise levels (through to management and the executive board) obtain transparent information about the current risk profile.

Transparent information

4.2   Business Processes in Risk Management

You can use SAP GRC Risk Management to develop a comprehensive risk profile for your enterprise, measure the risk propensity, and draft response strategies for event losses.

In the standard version, the risk management process begins with *risk planning* (as shown in Figure 4.1). In this phase, you'll first measure the risk propensity, determine enterprise-specific threshold values, and establish the risk management organization.

Risk planning

In the risk identification phase, proactive transparency is achieved by defining an early warning system from *key risk indicators*. This enables you to more quickly identify opportunities and risks for all risk types at all enterprise levels. In terms of their impact and probability of occurrence, risks can be *analyzed* according to financial and qualitative viewpoints.

Risk identification and analysis

In the case of risk activities, the responses to a risk are identified and the costs associated with preventing the risk are determined. For example, one of these responses could be to actively mitigate the risk to lower the probability of occurrence and/or possible losses.

Risk activity

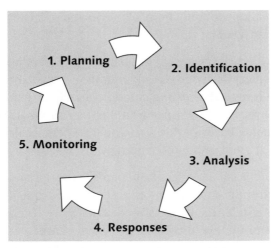

Figure 4.1 Risk Management Process in GRC

Risk monitoring

Risk monitoring involves updating risk data on a regular basis as well as implementing centralized risk reporting. Active and role-based dashboards and notifications can be used to monitor progress during a risk management process. Therefore, this continuous transparency across all enterprise areas ensures a better basis for decision making.

4.2.1 Risk Planning – Enterprise-Wide Risk Management Approach

Risk planning

SAP GRC Risk Management supports the risk planning process. However, this process is usually completed before supporting software is used. Risk planning contains an agreement made at the highest management level of an enterprise to identify the most important risk categories and company objectives to be monitored in the future. Furthermore, you should harmonize the risks to be monitored with the company objectives. In this context, opposing business area objectives would be counter-productive. Therefore, you should always consider those business activities to be monitored in the future from the perspective of risk management. When defining the risk catalogs, you should consider which risk types you want to include in management reports.

In the risk planning phase, you also define the risk processes, the specific risk thresholds, the general risk tolerance, and the organizational units participating in the risk management process.

Risk tolerance

The results from the risk planning process (e.g., risk thresholds, risk categories, and participating organizational units) are now saved centrally in SAP GRC Risk Management. These central structures form the basis for automating the relevant processes as well as ensuring enterprise-wide uniform execution of the risk management processes. In the future, SAP GRC partners such as auditing companies will also provide industry-specific Best Practice content to SAP.

Enterprise-wide execution of risk management processes

4.2.2 Risk Identification and Analysis

In the risk identification and analysis phase, you define an enterprise-wide activities and risk catalog with the aim of achieving proactive transparency. This enables you to more quickly identify opportunities and risks for all risk types at all enterprise levels. In terms of their impact and probability of occurrence, risks can be analyzed according to financial and qualitative viewpoints.

Risk identification and analysis

The application can always support and automate the risk identification process if the existing company systems contain the required risk data. SAP GRC Risk Management enables you to set up automatic risk notifications for both SAP and non-SAP processes. It also provides predefined escalation procedures for different risk types.

Automatic risk notifications

If automation isn't possible, you can initiate and implement collaborative and user-friendly self-assessments as well as collaborative surveys. As a result of the intuitive user interface, occasional users of SAP GRC Risk Management are guided through these activities and can therefore perform these activities themselves.

Collaborative surveys

Furthermore, automated workflow functions ensure that the relevant employees in the risk management department obtain regular consolidated and completed assessments. These assessments contain information about the risk, potential effects, the probability, the time frame, and the company objectives that could be affected. Therefore, an overview

Automated workflow functions

of the current risk analysis is available at all times, thus permitting corporate governance to focus on important, serious risks.

No surprises

In other words, you can avoid unpleasant surprises by using SAP GRC Risk Management to proactively identify, document, and assess all key risks (both internally and externally) for the entire company.

4.2.3 Risk Activities

Risk activities

In the case of risk activities, the responses to a risk are identified and the costs of preventing or reducing the risk are determined. For example, one of these responses could be to actively mitigate the risk to lower the probability of occurrence or possible losses.

Implementing a response

SAP GRC Risk Management equips those responsible (e.g., risk managers) with an instrument that effectively solves and initiates response strategies in their area of responsibility. The application enables you to track the status of each risk activity as well as control the costs associated with implementing the response. Therefore, risk managers can use SAP GRC Risk Management as a reliable monitoring tool to ensure that any risks in their area of responsibility are handled appropriately.

Response owner

You can also use SAP GRC Risk Management to assign several risk activities to a single risk. To save time and to improve the general effectiveness of risk activities, you can distribute risk activities across the company by assigning them to response owners.

4.2.4 Risk Monitoring

Risk monitoring

Risk monitoring involves updating risk data on a regular basis as well as implementing centralized risk reporting. You can use active and role-based dashboards as well as notifications to monitor progress during a risk management process. Therefore, this continuous transparency across all enterprise areas ensures a better basis for decision making.

Proactive monitoring

SAP GRC Risk Management enables you to be informed at all times about the possibility of proactive monitoring for existing business processes. The application automatically and continuously monitors previously identified risks and risk activities. At the same time, it highlights significant changes to the risk situation. This current overview is necessary to achieve the right balance between estimating risks and opportunities for your enterprise.

You can also track and analyze the cause of loss events that have already occurred. The corresponding findings could contribute, among other things, to a continuously improved risk methodology and mature risk management within your enterprise.

Loss events

The analysis functions of SAP GRC Risk Management, along with strategic planning, contribute to assessing the effectiveness of responses and enable you to improve risk planning. The application provides dashboards, risk scorecards, and the individual definition of *watch lists* for monitoring specific key performance indicators (KPIs), risks, responses, and so on. Even at the early stage of creating the risk catalogs, you should consider which risk types you want to include in your management reports.

Dashboards

To obtain an extensive, context-sensitive insight into the risk situation, especially in terms of specific strategies and initiatives, you could also obtain risk data from another application (e.g., a strategy management application). For example, you could use risk data to calculate KPIs to achieve early, initial indications with a view to strategic objectives.

Insight into the risk situation

4.3   User Roles

The standard version of SAP GRC Risk Management comprises several roles (see Figure 4.2). Depending on the user assignment with regard to both the structural organization for risk management and the required function, you can use roles to assign different access rights at global enterprise level and at business area and organizational unit level.

Roles

The role of the *risk manager* is to identify the risks associated with the organizational unit assigned to him and to record these in SAP GRC Risk Management. Risk managers can also create projects that are specific to organizational units. Furthermore, they can support corporate governance by creating activities and risks in the risk management application that will provide a better basis for decision making.

Risk manager

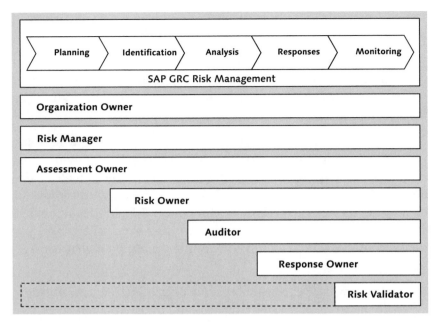

Figure 4.2 Risk Management – User Roles

Assessment owner If an *assessment owner* assesses a risk, he comprehensively identifies, analyzes, and plans the response strategy for all risks assigned to an activity. Assessment owners can only access those activities and risks that have been assigned to them.

Risk owner The *risk owner* analyzes risks and triggers appropriate risk activities and their follow-up activities. If risk processing requires specific knowledge, the assessment owners generally determine the risk owners. You can assign a risk owner to several organizational units, whereas the user can only access those risks assigned to him.

Auditor The *auditor* analyzes all activities and risks, including current risks and risks that have already occurred.

Response owner The *response owner* triggers the responses for mitigating risk and implements the follow-up activities for these responses. You can assign a response owner to several organizational units. The activity owner can only access those activities assigned to him.

The *risk validator* checks and approves risk assessments at activity level or returns specific risks to the assessment owner for post-processing purposes. Each time a risk is recorded, it must be validated in the risk management application.

Risk validator

> **Note**
>
> An activity is a project, process, or object that could be a potential risk for an organizational unit or business area. Objects are therefore generic activities that are neither processes nor projects. For example, an existing production line could be an object activity.

4.4 SAP GRC Risk Management – Application

You can use SAP GRC Risk Management to implement a complete cross-enterprise risk management process that extends beyond organizational and departmental boundaries. The only way to access the application functions of SAP GRC Risk Management is via a URL link and web browser.

Roles are used to assign users the necessary authorizations for accessing web applications. You can use SAP GRC Risk Management to centrally define and maintain an enterprise-wide organizational hierarchy, an activities catalog, and a risk catalog.

Enterprise-wide activities and risk catalog

You can use this enterprise-wide organizational structure or these cross-organizational catalogs to structure processes and activities for risk management, thus making downstream reporting more efficient.

SAP GRC Risk Management has various reporting functions that you can use at any time to display the current risk status. The application currently delivers a range of fully configured reports.

Current risk status

SAP GRC Risk Management is delivered with standard SAP workflow functions that initially facilitate the use of collaborative risk management methods and scenarios.

Using collaborative risk management methods

4.4.1 Risk Management Menu

You can access the five applications within SAP GRC Risk Management under the following tabs: **My Home, Risk Assessment, Risk Structure, Report Center**, and **Dashboards** (see Figure 4.3).

Figure 4.3 Main Menu of GRC Risk Management

My Home

When you select the **My Home** tab, you see a work inbox that contains a list of all risk management tasks assigned to you, along with their respective processing statuses. The same tab page has a second *Document Risk* function that you can use to record any new potential risks and initiate the associated approval workflow.

Risk Assessment

You can maintain activities and risks on the **Risk Assessment** tab page. Here, you can also document risks, analyze risks, and determine possible response activities. Furthermore, you can document any losses that have occurred.

Risk Structure

On the **Risk Structure** tab page, you (the responsible risk manager) can maintain and manage the catalogs for structuring the risks and activities/business processes as well as define the required organizational units (see Figure 4.4).

Figure 4.4 Maintenance Options on the Risk Structure Tab Page

Report Center

On the **Report Center** tab page, you can choose from a total of twelve predefined reports and then choose **Print Reports** to print reports based on risks and activities (see Figure 4.5).

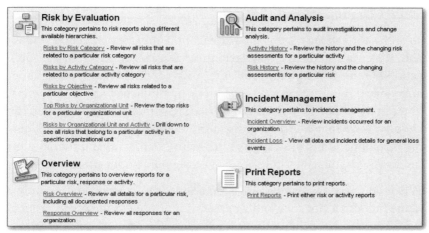

Figure 4.5 Report Center – Predefined Reports

You (the responsible risk manager or managing director) can use the **Dashboards** tab and the display overviews provided by the previously defined and activated dashboard variants to quickly oversee and assess the current risk situation (see Figure 4.6).

Dashboards

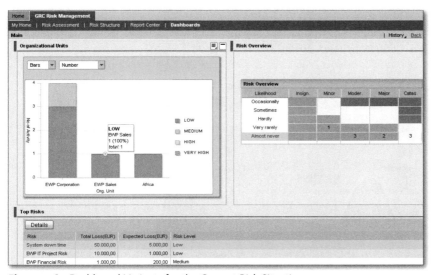

Figure 4.6 Dashboard Variants for the Current Risk Situation

4.4.2 Organizational Unit

Maintaining the central organizational hierarchy

To access the catalog management area for the organizational unit, choose **GRC Risk Management • Risk Structure • Organizations** from the application menu and maintain your enterprise's central organizational hierarchy here. You initially access the hierarchy in display mode. However, you can then choose *Open* to switch to change mode. After that, you can choose *Create* to create a new organizational unit. You can't create new organizational units or change or maintain existing organizational units unless the risk manager role has been assigned to your user.

Organization owner

When you create a new organizational unit, you must assign not only a name but also a currency and a person responsible to the organizational unit. You also have the option of assigning one or more risk managers, setting organizational objectives, and maintaining organizational-specific threshold values.

General tab

Figure 4.7 shows that the managing director **Andreas Schwarz** has been assigned as the organization owner for the **Energy without Plug Corporation**. On the **General** tab page, you can also choose a **Currency**, enter **Name**, and enter a long text **Description** for the organizational unit.

> **Note**
>
> The currency refers to the starting amount for each impact level in terms of the risk threshold values.

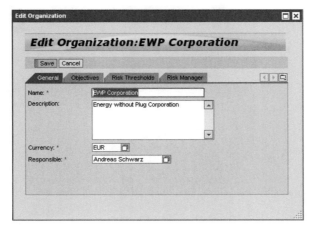

Figure 4.7 Maintenance Dialog Box on the General Tab Page

Figure 4.8 shows that you can define the relevant company objectives on the tab page for maintaining **Objectives**. The primary company objective of the EWP Corporation is to develop and manufacture fuel cells.

Objectives tab

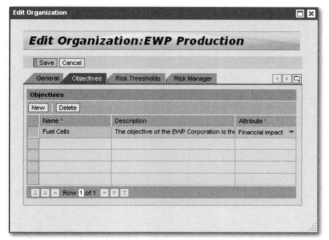

Figure 4.8 Maintenance Dialog Box for Company Objectives

On the **Risk Thresholds** tab page in Figure 4.9, you can define a starting amount (e.g., EUR 100) for each impact level (here **Insignificant** equals lowest impact level).

Risk Thresholds tab

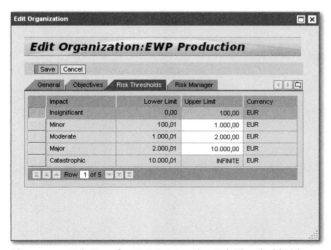

Figure 4.9 Tab Page for Maintaining the Risk Threshold Values

Risk Manager tab   On the tab page for maintaining the **Risk Manager**, you can define the relevant person or the user ID of this person as the responsible risk manager. Figure 4.10 shows that **Thomas Schmidt** has been assigned as the responsible **Risk Manager** for the top EWP organizational unit.

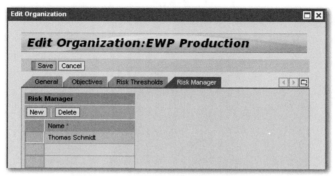

Figure 4.10   Tab Page for Maintaining the Risk Manager

After you've maintained all of the detail data for the organizational unit on the relevant tab pages, you must choose **Save** to save this data.

In addition to creating new organizational units and assigning the persons responsible, you can also use the application menu **GRC Risk Management • Risk Structure • Organizations** and the **Actions** button to "cut" existing organizational units from the organizational structure and "paste" them into another hierarchy position (see Figure 4.11).

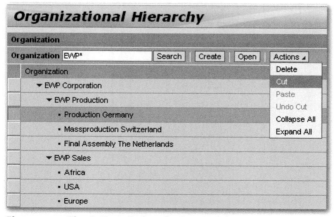

Figure 4.11   The Actions Button for Structure Maintenance

For the EWP Corporation, additional organizational units for the relevant sales regions, other operational countries, and administrative functions have been created and maintained in a hierarchy under the menu path **GRC Risk Management • Risk Structure • Organizations** (see Figure 4.12).

EWP organizational hierarchy

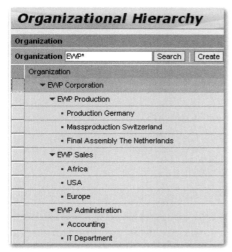

Figure 4.12   Organizational Hierarchy for the EWP Corporation

4.4.3   Activities and Risk Catalogs

To maintain the required activities and risk catalogs, you must determine which risks are to be monitored and which activities are subject to risk. Therefore, you should always consider the business activities to be monitored in the future from the perspective of risk management. When creating the risk catalogs, you should also consider which risk types you want to include in management reports. Furthermore, it makes sense to harmonize the risks to be monitored with the company objectives. In this context, opposing business area objectives would be counterproductive.

Activities and risk catalogs

To access the catalog management area for activities and risks, choose **GRC Risk Management • Risk Structure** from the application menu, and maintain your enterprise's central activities and risk catalogs here.

The term "activity" is used to structure risk management from the perspective of the user departments or operational business. For this rea-

Activity

son, activities are typically processes, projects, or objects. Objects are therefore generic attributes that are neither processes nor projects. For example, an existing production line could be an object activity. You must always assign each activity created in SAP GRC Risk Management to an activity type.

Activities catalog   Furthermore, you use the activities catalog to determine the scope of response for risk management. You can define and maintain the activities catalog under the menu path **GRC Risk Management • Risk Structure • Activity Hierarchy**.

The activities catalog comprises activity categories and activity groups whereby the activity groups are used to group activity categories at a higher level (see Figure 4.13). In the case of the activities catalog, you can define an unlimited number of activity categories. However, you must have created at least one activity group.

Therefore, you can use SAP GRC Risk Management to centrally define and maintain enterprise-wide activities and risk catalog. The activities and risk catalogs represent not only the previously defined organizational units, but also the master data of SAP GRC Risk Management.

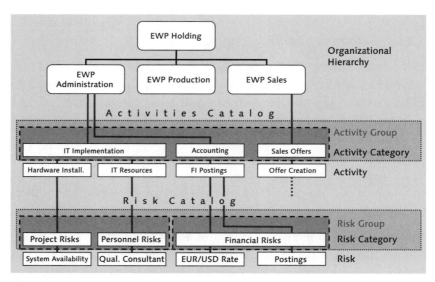

Figure 4.13 Enterprise-Wide Activities and Risk Catalog

You can use this enterprise-wide organizational structure or the cross-organizational catalogs to structure processes and activities for risk management, thus making downstream reporting more efficient.

Figure 4.14 shows that you can only create a new risk category or risk group below a risk group that already exists. In addition to displaying, creating, editing, and deleting risk categories and risk groups, you can also assign risk categories in an existing risk hierarchy from one risk group to another risk group, for example. Only one activity group but several activities categories (quotation creation, financial accounting, IT implementation, and resource management) have been defined for the EWP Corporation. Furthermore, the risk catalog defined for the EWP Corporation has a classical structure that is divided into four risk groups (external risks, financial risks, operational risks, and strategic risks) and other specific risk categories.

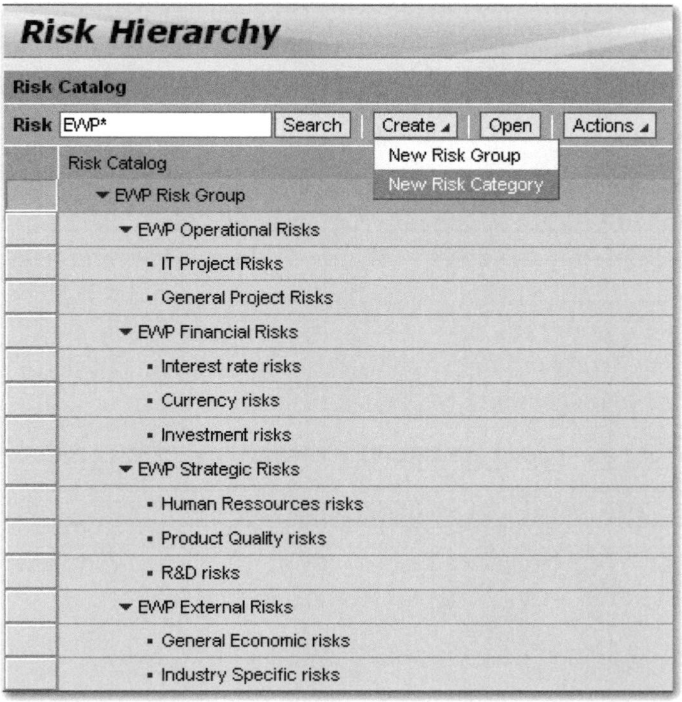

Efficient reporting

Maintaining activities and risk catalogs

Figure 4.14 EWP Risk Hierarchy

> **Note**
>
> When you choose the menu path **GRC Risk Management • Risk Structure • Activity Hierarchy or Risk Hierarchy**, you always access the hierarchy in display mode first. You can then choose **Create** to create a new activity/risk group, a new activity type, or a new risk category. You can't create new organizational units or change or maintain existing organizational units unless the risk manager role has been assigned to your user.
>
> You can use the enterprise-wide catalogs to structure the processes, activities, and risks for risk management of the EWP Corporation, thus making downstream reporting more efficient.
>
> SAP GRC Risk Management also has an Excel template for the initial data upload. You can download this template from the SAP Developer Network (SDN).

Risk manager

In summary, you (the responsible risk manager) can use the *Risk Structure* application area to maintain and manage the catalogs for structuring risks, activities, and business processes. Here, you can also centrally define and manage the required organizational units.

4.4.4 Activities and Risk Documentation

Activities and risk documentation

You can maintain activities and risks under the application menu **GRC Risk Management • Risk Assessment • Activities and Risks**. In the *Risk Assessment* application area, you not only document activities and risks, but you also analyze risks and plan possible response activities. Furthermore, you can document any risks or losses that have occurred. In addition to the aforementioned menu path, you can also create new risks under **GRC Risk Management • My Home • Document Risk**.

Documenting a new activity

When you choose the menu path **GRC Risk Management • Risk Assessment • Activities and Risks**, you always initially access the screen in display mode before switching to edit mode by choosing edit mode. You can then choose **Create** to create a new activity or risk whereby you must have first selected the relevant organizational unit (see Figure 4.15).

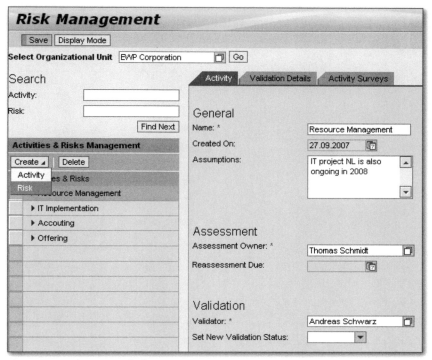

Figure 4.15 Change Mode for Documenting New Risks or Activities

Figure 4.15 shows you that when you document a new activity, you must maintain at least the following data: the activity category, the activity name or description, the relevant assessment owner, the assessment frequency, and the relevant risk validator. All other dialog options associated with maintaining activities (e.g., the assumptions and constraints) are optional.

> **Note**
>
> In SAP GRC Risk Management, all mandatory fields are indicated by a red asterisk at the end of the field name (see Figure 4.16). However, you can't use Customizing to influence the mandatory field selection and existing field names.

Mandatory fields and field names

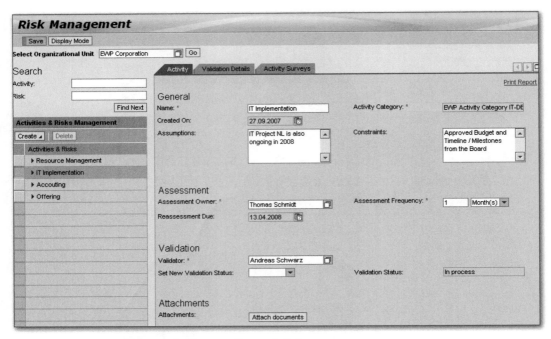

Figure 4.16 Documenting an Activity

Documenting a new risk

When you use the menu path **GRC Risk Management • Risk Assessment • Activities and Risks** to document a new risk, you must maintain at least the following data: the risk category, the risk name or description, and the relevant risk owner. All other maintenance fields associated with documenting a risk such as the causes, consequences, indicators, comment, and the company objective most impacted by the risk are optional. Figure 4.17 shows that you can also attach external documents when documenting a risk. Similarly, when documenting an activity, you can also use a link to attach external documents.

Attaching documents

When attaching a document, select the **Visible** field as illustrated in Figure 4.17. This ensures that the name of the attached document is then displayed in the risk or activity master data summary (see Figure 4.18).

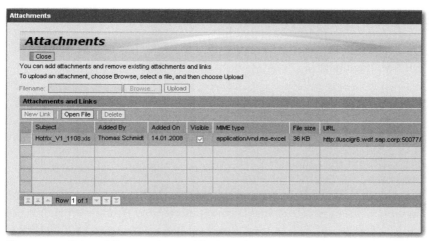

Figure 4.17 External Document as an Attachment

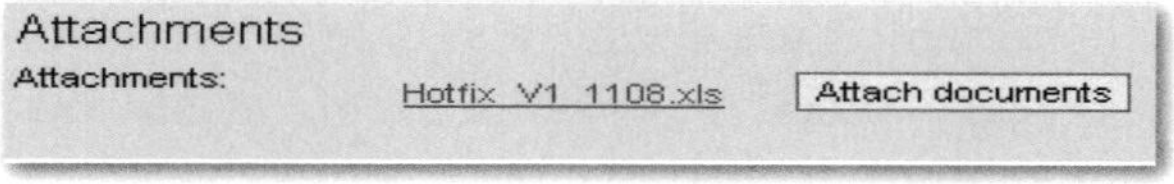

Figure 4.18 Document Name

If you use the menu path **GRC Risk Management • My Home • Document Risk** to document a new risk, you must also maintain the relevant organizational unit and activity for the aforementioned mandatory fields. This documentation option allows occasional users of the risk management application to use the intuitive user interface to document a risk.

Risk documentation by an occasional user

The example illustrated over the next few pages also demonstrates the interaction between those involved in the process with, for example, the central risk management department and the first person to document the risk, who is also generally the person responsible for the process or an employee in the user department. The standard SAP workflow functions delivered in SAP GRC Risk Management enable you to initially use such collaborative risk management methods and scenarios. If you've used the menu path **GRC Risk Management • My Home • Document Risk** to document a new risk, you (the first person to document the risk) receive a message after you choose **Save and Send for Approval**. This message (see Figure 4.19) indicates that the workflow function successfully delivered the risk to the relevant risk owner (**Risk proposed successfully**). This means that when a person or user ID is assigned as the

Collaborative risk management scenarios

risk owner, the relevant workflow task is automatically delivered to this person. You can therefore assign the risk owner completely independent of the actual functional role assignment for the relevant user of SAP GRC Risk Management.

Figure 4.19 Risk Proposed Successfully

Risk owner   In your work inbox (**GRC Risk Management • My Home • Work Inbox**), you (the assigned risk owner) now receive a corresponding workflow task (*Risk requires validation*) with the request to validate the previously documented risk. Thomas Schmidt, the risk manager responsible for the EWP Corporation and the assigned risk owner here (see Figure 4.20), also receives this workflow task and can now accept (**Approve and Submit**) or reject (**Reject and Submit**) the risk.

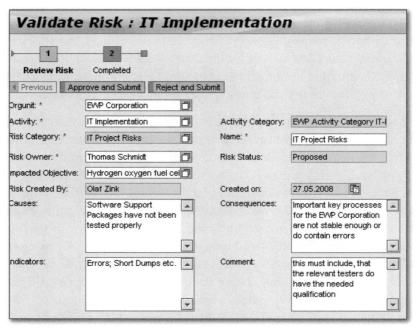

Figure 4.20 Accepting or Rejecting a Risk

Thomas Schmidt realizes that the risk documented by the occasional user of the risk management application is a relevant risk. He therefore accepts the risk. The corresponding workflow task (*Complete documentation for risk XYZ*) is now automatically returned to the person who created the risk along with a request to complete the risk documentation (see Figure 4.21).

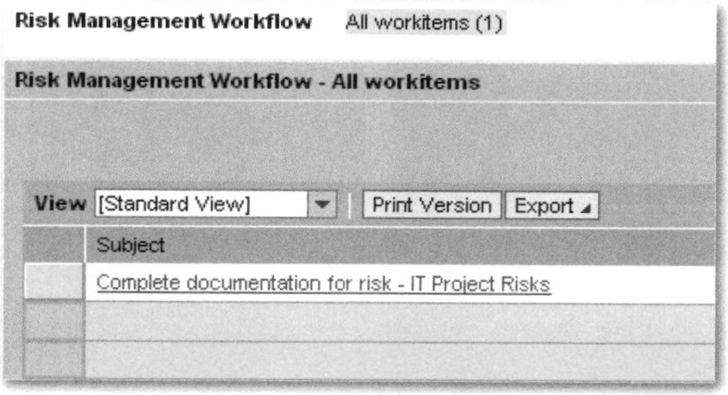

Risk Management Workflow   All workitems (1)

Risk Management Workflow - All workitems

View [Standard View] ▼ | Print Version | Export ◢

	Subject
	Complete documentation for risk - IT Project Risks

Figure 4.21   Workflow Request to Complete the Risk Documentation

You (the person originally responsible for documenting the risk) now receive the corresponding workflow task (**Complete documentation for risk XYZ**) and therefore must analyze the risk and complete the risk documentation. In our example, you initially analyze the risk without a response option (*Analysis Without Response*). Figure 4.22 shows that you must also maintain the probability of occurrence, the total loss amount, and the expected time frame (short, medium, or long term) for incurring the loss.

Risk analysis without a response

You then use the probability of occurrence (5%), the total loss amount (EUR 5,000) for a total failure, and the expected time frame (**Short**) for incurring the loss, to perform a quantitative analysis. In this case, the **Impact**, **Risk Level**, and **Priority** fields are derived automatically. This information is based on the Customizing entries and the organization affected by the defined loss threshold values. The impact is based on an estimation of the consequences associated with a risk, the risk level corresponds to the severity of a particular risk, and the risk priority indicates the urgency of the risk, that is, when the risk must be processed. The risk priority defined here depends on the valuated time frame and risk level.

Quantitative risk analysis

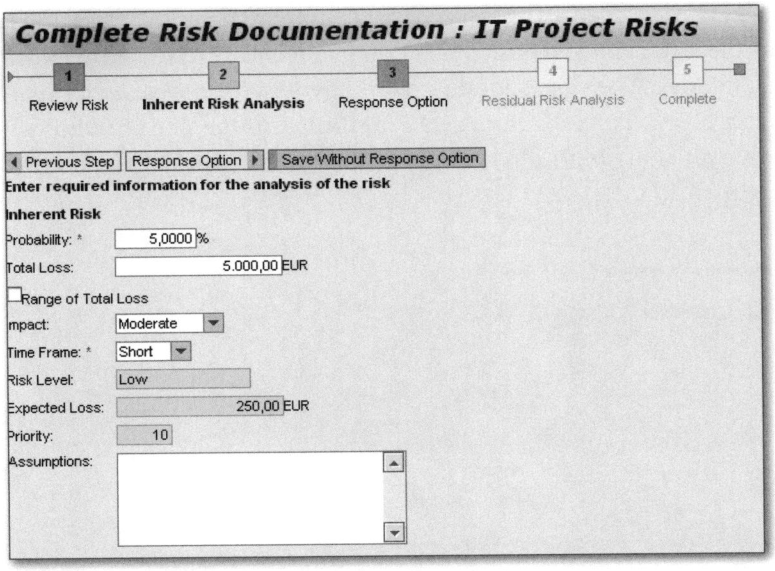

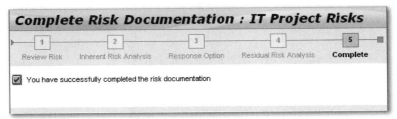

Figure 4.22   Risk Analysis Without a Response Option

Triggering warning
messages
Based on the sample function described previously, you can trigger warning messages if risks that have far-reaching consequences and a high probability of occurrence exceed previously defined threshold values.

Intuitively
managed user
interface
After you choose *Save*, the risk is analyzed without a response option (**Analysis Without Response**), and you are notified that you have successfully completed the risk documentation via an intuitively managed user interface (see Figure 4.23).

Figure 4.23   Completed Risk Documentation

Excursus: Risk Status

When documenting the risk in SAP GRC Risk Management, you can assign a new status after the status **Draft** (originally assigned by the system). Figure 4.24 shows that, at first, you can only assign the status **to validation** after the status **Draft**.

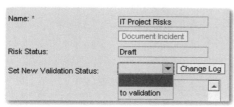

Figure 4.24 Draft Risk Status

Figure 4.25 shows the risk status options available to you as you progress through the risk documentation or risk analysis, depending on the processing situation and collaboration scenario.

The small rectangle in the upper-right half of Figure 4.26 indicates that the risk has occurred. Because the risk status is **Occurred**, you can now choose **Document Incident** to document the corresponding risk incident in a maintenance dialog box and subsequently forward it "to validation."

Documenting an incident

Figure 4.25 Assignment Options for the Risk Status

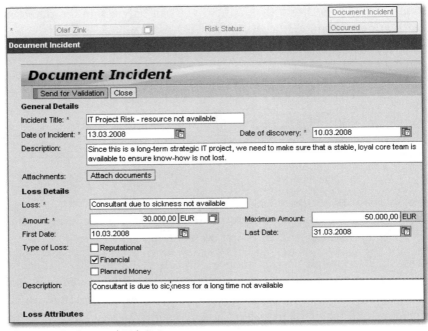

Figure 4.26 Occurred Risk Status

Conclusion

Central early warning system

SAP GRC Risk Management enables your enterprise to identify and quantify operational and strategic risks. In the risk identification or risk documentation phase outlined previously, an enterprise-wide organizational hierarchy and a central activities and risk catalog were used to define a central early warning system for the EWP Corporation. In addition to the main objective of achieving proactive transparency, you can also use this holistic, enterprise-wide approach to more quickly identify opportunities and risks for all risk categories at all enterprise levels.

4.4.5 Risk Analysis With and Without a Response

Risk analysis with a response

In the earlier description of a risk analysis, a risk analysis without a response option (*Analysis Without Response*) was performed within the risk documentation process. Over the next few pages, however, you'll reject a risk following the previous risk analysis without a response option and then use a risk management response (*Analysis With Response*) to eliminate or mitigate this risk.

You always have the option of counteracting a potential risk with a risk management response (*Analysis With Response*) if the risk isn't being validated at that point in time nor completed or if it hasn't actually occurred.

Figure 4.27 shows that, if you document a risk, the area in which you maintain the response isn't displayed until you choose **Analysis With Response** (see the lower half of the screen in Figure 4.27). When you choose **New**, the system displays a maintenance dialog box in which you can enter a risk management response (see Figure 4.28).

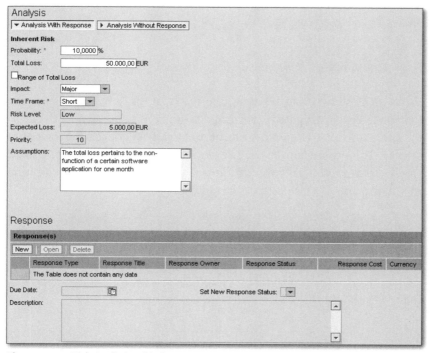

Figure 4.27 Risk Analysis with Response

In addition to the **Response Title** and **Response Type** (**Accept**, **Observe**, **Research**, **Transfer**, **Delegate**, and **Mitigate**), you must maintain the **Response Owner** when creating a response. You also have the option of

Creating a new response

defining the **Response Cost**, the **Due Date**, and a detailed **Description** for the response. Furthermore, you can assign a new response status after you successfully create the response.

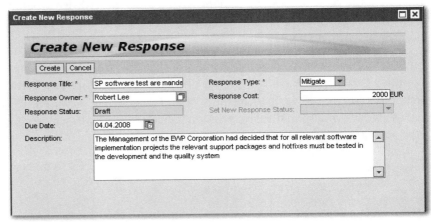

Figure 4.28 Creating a New Response

Response owner — Figure 4.29 shows that following the risk analysis, a response with the **Response Type "Mitigate"** was created for the preceding sample risk. Furthermore, the EWP IT employee **Robert Lee** was assigned as the **Response Owner**. The system automatically assigned the **Response Status "Draft."** However, after you save the data once, you can manually redetermine this status. You can also assign several responses to one risk.

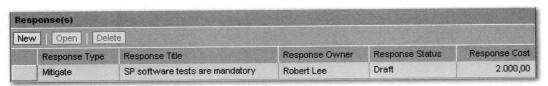

Figure 4.29 Response Owner

Residual risk — After you create a response, you determine the residual risk by entering the probability of occurrence and the total loss amount. After initiating the response for our sample risk, the probability of occurrence was halved, and the total loss amount remained the same (see the example shown in Figure 4.30). As a result, the estimated impact was lowered from **Catastrophic** to **Major**.

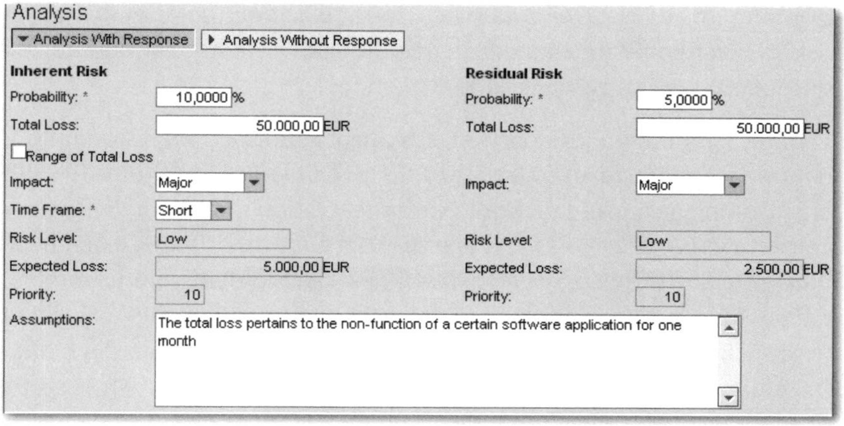

Figure 4.30 Residual Risk after a Risk Analysis with Response

In the preceding example, you rejected a risk analysis without a response option and then used a risk management response to eliminate or mitigate the risk. In SAP GRC Risk Management, you always have the option of counteracting a potential risk with a risk management response (*Analysis With Response*) if the risk isn't being validated at that point in time nor completed or if it hasn't actually occurred.

Risk management response

In SAP GRC Risk Management, you can also use uniform risk profiles to monitor the entire risk portfolio at operational and strategic enterprise levels. The automatic identification and analysis of as many risks as possible will show the greatest cost-saving potential in both the medium and long term. However, such automation will only be available in a later version of SAP GRC Risk Management.

4.4.6 Risk Monitoring

Risk monitoring involves updating risk data on a regular basis as well as implementing centralized risk reporting. You can use active and role-based dashboards and notifications to monitor progress during a risk management process. SAP GRC Risk Management enables you to be informed at all times about the possibility of proactive monitoring for existing business processes.

Risk monitoring

The analysis functions of SAP GRC Risk Management contribute to assessing the effectiveness of responses and enable you to improve risk

Analysis functions

planning. In addition to dashboards, the application provides the use of risk scorecards and the individual definition of watch lists for monitoring specific KPIs, risks, responses, and so on.

Report Center

Thomas Schmidt, the risk manager responsible for the EWP Corporation, now wants to obtain an overview of the risk situation for the entire EWP organization group and therefore executes a tabular report in the **Report Center**. Figure 4.31 shows you that the risks for the entire EWP organization group are displayed as activities. The report contains, among others, the possible quantitative loss and the estimated consequences associated with such a loss. Figure 4.31 contains three risks that would have catastrophic consequences if they were to occur.

▼ EWP Corporation	183.000,00	Moderate
▼ IT Implementation	180.000,00	Major
• Support Package testing	0,00	
• SP sotware tests	50.000,00	Catastrophic
• IT Project risks	0,00	
• IT Project Risk	5.000,00	Moderate
• SP testing	50.000,00	Catastrophic
• EWP IT Project Risk 2	5.000,00	Moderate
• EWP IT Project Risk	10.000,00	Major
• Software testing	10.000,00	Major
• Qualified Consultants	0,00	
• System down time	50.000,00	Catastrophic
▶ Resource Management	0,00	
▶ Offering	1.000,00	Minor
▼ Accounting	2.000,00	Moderate
• General ledger posting	0,00	
• EUR - USD exchange rate	0,00	
• EWP Financial Risk 3	2.000,00	Moderate

Figure 4.31 Risks per Organization and Activities

Response overview

To monitor the effectiveness of risk responses in general but also the three risks with possible catastrophic consequences, the risk manager Thomas Schmidt now executes another report from the *Report Center*. To obtain an overview of the risk responses for the EWP Corporation, Thomas Schmidt uses the *Response Overview* report.

The report results immediately show Thomas Schmidt that risk responses already exist for at least two risks with possible catastrophic consequences. These responses have the status **In Process** and **Committed** (see Figure 4.32). The results of the preceding report indicate that Thomas Schmidt must only follow up the third risk with possible catastrophic consequences and, if necessary, request that a response is initiated or trigger the response himself.

Risk responses

As already shown for the preceding risk responses, you can also use other risk management reports to track and analyze the cause of loss events that have occurred. The corresponding findings could contribute, for example, to a continuously improved risk methodology and mature risk management within your enterprise.

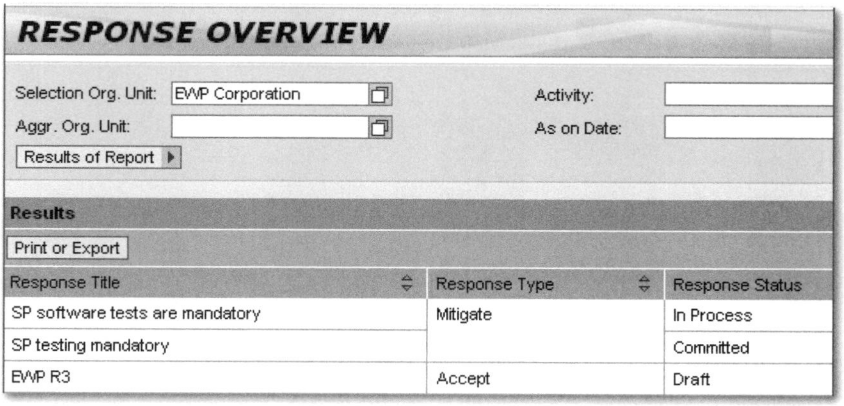

Tracking the cause

RESPONSE OVERVIEW

Selection Org. Unit: EWP Corporation   Activity:
Aggr. Org. Unit: As on Date:
Results of Report ▶

Results

Print or Export

Response Title	Response Type	Response Status
SP software tests are mandatory	Mitigate	In Process
SP testing mandatory		Committed
EWP R3	Accept	Draft

Figure 4.32 Response Overview

To more quickly oversee and assess the current risk situation, Thomas Schmidt now switches to the *Dashboards* area. The previously defined and activated *Risk Overview* dashboard variant shows you a total of nine risks for the EWP Corporation. Three of these risks (the aforementioned risks) are estimated in such a way that they would have catastrophic consequences if they were to occur. However, the dashboard display in Figure 4.33 also shows that the probability of occurrence for these three risks is extremely low (**Almost never**).

Risk overview

233

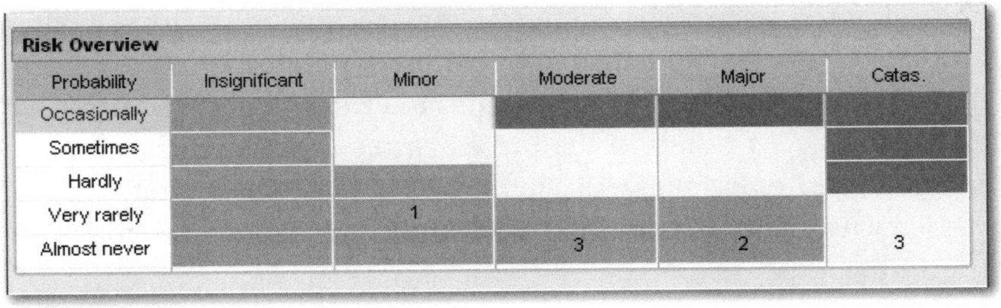

Figure 4.33 Dashboard – Risk Overview

Top risks

In the *Dashboards* area, Thomas Schmidt also has, among other things, the previously defined and activated *Top Risks* dashboard variant, which he now executes to obtain a list of the most important risks (see Figure 4.34). He can choose **Details** to display detailed information about any risk.

Details

Risk	Total Loss(EUR)	Expected Loss(EUR)	Risk Level
SP sotware tests	50,000.00	5,000.00	Low
SP testing	50,000.00	5,000.00	Low
System down time	50,000.00	5,000.00	Low
EWP IT Project Risk	10,000.00	1,000.00	Low
EWP Financial Risk	1,000.00	200.00	Medium
EWP Financial Risk 3	2,000.00	200.00	Low
Software testing	10,000.00	500.00	Low
EWP IT Project Risk 2	5,000.00	250.00	Low
IT Project Risks	5,000.00	250.00	Low

Figure 4.34 Top Risks for EWP Corporation

4.5 SAP GRC Risk Management – System Configuration

The system configuration for GRC Risk Management comprises the following five areas: *General Settings, Risk Analysis, Risk Responses, Loss Event Database, and Workflow Activation.*

General settings

You must make the **General Settings** under the path **GRC Risk Management • General Settings** before the actual Customizing settings for risk management. You should therefore execute the relevant Customizing activities in Figure 4.35 in sequence, that is, from top to bottom.

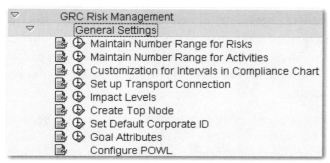

Figure 4.35 General Settings Customizing Activities

Over the next few pages, we'll describe the following Customizing activities in more detail: *Set up Transport Connection, Create Top Node, Configure POWL, Loss Event Database, and Workflow Activation*.

However, you must first maintain the *number range intervals* for risks and activities. When you create or save a risk or activity, an internal system number is automatically assigned to this risk or activity. We recommend that you define at least one additional number range interval because, in risk management, number range 01 is used for all risk and activity types.

Number range intervals

In the Customizing activity *Adjust intervals to compliance chart*, you can use intervals to determine the number of overdue days for which activities require validation or reassessment. The intervals specified in Figure 4.36 enable you to display the corresponding activities with overdue assessments and overdue validations in the dashboard view of SAP GRC Risk Management.

Compliance chart

Dashboard - Compliance customization for intervals		
Chart Type	Low	High
Overdue Assessments	10	40
Overdue Validations	15	50

Figure 4.36 Adjusting Intervals in Compliance Chart

4.5.1 Setting Up a Transport Connection

Setting up a transport connection

Because the Customizing functions used to establish the risk management hierarchy are the same functions used to set up objects in the organizational plan for organizational management[1], you can use this Customizing activity to maintain the transport settings for the objects for establishing the hierarchy as well as the objects for organizational management under **GRC Risk Management • General Settings • Set up Transport Connection**.

The automatic transport connection is activated in the standard version of SAP GRC Risk Management. Figure 4.37 shows you that the **Value abbr.** column does not contain an entry in the field next to the **CORR** abbreviation (same line).

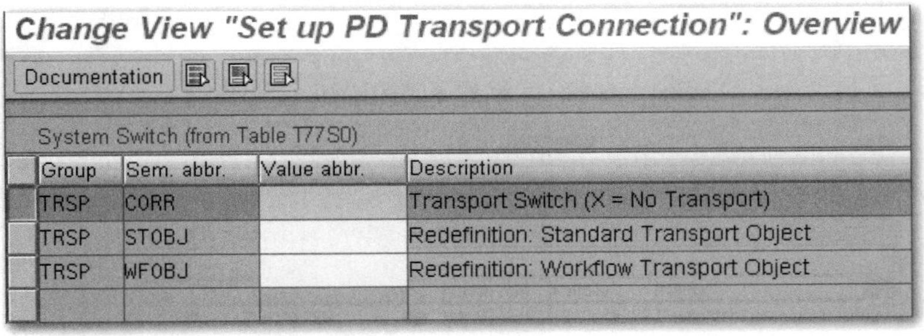
Change View "Set up PD Transport Connection": Overview
Documentation
System Switch (from Table T77S0)
Group
Sem. abbr.
Value abbr.
Description
TRSP
CORR
Transport Switch (X = No Transport)
TRSP
STOBJ
Redefinition: Standard Transport Object
TRSP
WFOBJ
Redefinition: Workflow Transport Object

Figure 4.37 Activated Transport Connection

> **Note**
>
> Because the objects for establishing the hierarchy and the objects for setting up the organization have the same master data, we recommend that you deactivate the automatic transport connection. This is imperative if you want establish the structure or hierarchy in the web application. To do this, you must enter the value "X" in the **Value abbr.** field next to the **CORR** abbreviation (see Figure 4.38).

Deactivating the transport connection

We also recommend that you deactivate the transport connection because experience has shown that the hierarchy structure and the assignment data that depends on the hierarchy structure (e.g., the persons respon-

1 Note that the abbreviation for SAP Organizational Management is PD.

sible) can change several times during prototyping in a development system, for example. In this scenario, it has been proven that the automatic transport connection should be deactivated and the required master data should be uploaded into or maintained in the relevant client, especially in the corresponding quality and production systems.

Change View "Set up PD Transport Connection": Overview			
Documentation 📋 📋 📋			
System Switch (from Table T77S0)			
Group	Sem. abbr.	Value abbr.	Description
TRSP	CORR	X	Transport Switch (X = No Transport)
TRSP	STOBJ		Redefinition: Standard Transport Object
TRSP	WFOBJ		Redefinition: Workflow Transport Object

Figure 4.38 Deactivated Transport Connection

If you use both risk management and organizational management in your SAP system, you should also refer to the transport documentation for the Customizing activity **Personnel Management • Transport • Set up Transport Connection**.

You must now define and maintain the impact levels under **GRC Risk Management • General Settings • Impact Levels**. An impact level estimates the consequences associated with a risk on a scale of *Insignificant* to *Catastrophic*. The standard version of SAP GRC Risk Management contains five impact levels that you can change and supplement with other impact levels of your choice.

Impact levels

4.5.2 Creating the Top Node

In SAP GRC Risk Management, you may only define one top organizational unit. In the following section, we'll describe how you can define this top node of the structural organization for risk management.

Creating the top node

In Customizing, define this node under **GRC Risk Management • General Settings • Create Top Node**. You'll then see the maintenance screen displayed in Figure 4.39.

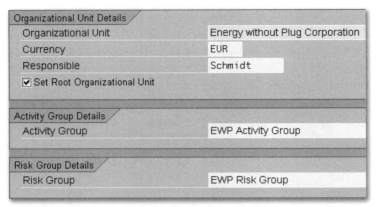

Figure 4.39 Dialog Box for Maintaining the Top Risk Management Objects

Top organizational unit

In this dialog box (see Figure 4.39), you can maintain a description for the top organizational unit. The description **Energy without Plug Corporation** was chosen for the top **Organizational Unit**.

When you use the input help (press F4) to assign a currency (**EUR** in this case), this currency is used for the starting amount for each impact level. The currency that you select here is also displayed when you maintain the threshold values in SAP GRC Risk Management.

In addition to defining the top organizational unit, you should also determine each of the higher-level nodes for the activities and risk catalogs.

Root organizational unit

When you select the **Set Root Organizational Unit** checkbox, the organizational unit, activity group, and risk group defined here are displayed as the top nodes in the relevant catalog management area within the application. In SAP GRC Risk Management, however, you can define only one root organizational unit.

Organization owner

You can use the input help (press F4) to search and define the person or the user ID of the person responsible for the top organizational unit. Figure 4.39 shows that Mr. Thomas Schmidt has been assigned as the person responsible for the top EWP organizational unit. The responsible risk manager, on the other hand, is maintained using SAP GRC Risk Management. Here, you can also assign several responsible risk managers to an organizational unit.

After you've successfully created the higher-level object nodes, you should use SAP GRC Risk Management to maintain threshold values for the top organizational unit as well as assign a responsible risk manager to this organizational unit.

> **Note**
>
> For the Customizing activity *Create Top Node*, note that you can only maintain one organizational unit as the higher-level node. For this top organizational unit, you must determine an existing user as the person responsible for this organizational unit. However, you can use SAP GRC Risk Management to assign several risk managers to an organizational unit.

You can now define your company's corporate ID under the Customizing activity *Set Default Corporate ID*. The top node created earlier (**Energy without Plug Corporation**) must be available in this activity as an entry for the corporate ID. Furthermore, the selected organization must have lower-level activity and risk groups.

Setting the default corporate ID

In the next Customizing activity, *Target attributes*, you can maintain the list of possible consequences (e.g., financial consequences, impact on the market share) for the target attributes.

Target attributes

4.5.3 Configuring POWL

The menu option **GRC Risk Management · General Settings · Configure POWL** isn't a Customizing activity. Therefore, you should regard it as a landmark for configuring the Personal Object Worklist (POWL). This activity is necessary to enable SAP GRC Risk Management to display the workflow inbox. To do this, you must copy Transaction FPB_MAINTAIN_HIER to the transaction field and then execute it.

Configuring POWL

You must check whether the **Personaliz. App** column contains the **ORM_INBOX** entry. Furthermore, Figure 4.40 shows that the **Personalization Characteristics** column must also contain the **DEFAULT_QUERY** and **LAYOUT** characteristics for the **ORM_INBOX** entry.

ORM_INBOX entry

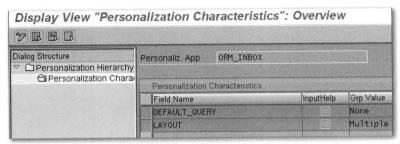

Figure 4.40 Mandatory Personalization Characteristics

Worklist type repository

If the preceding entries exist, choose the following menu path **Cross-Application Components • General Application Functions • Settings • Generic Functions of mySAP Suite • Personal Worklist • Configure Worklist Type Repository** in Customizing.

Worklist type at role level

Figure 4.41 shows that the **ORM_INBOX** entry was made in the **Type** field and the **/ORM/CL_ORM_POWL_INBOX** entry was made in the **Feeder class** field. Now create the entries in accordance with Figure 4.41, and execute the Customizing activity under the menu path **Cross-Application Components • General Application Functions • Settings • Generic Functions of mySAP Suite • Personal Worklist • Define Visibility of the Worklist Type at Role Level**. Now make the same **ORM_INBOX** entry in a line in the **Application** and **Type** field (or column).

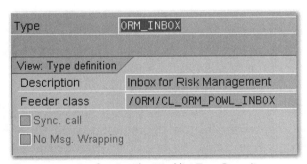

Figure 4.41 Configuring the Worklist Type Repository

Defining the default queries

Now execute the activity **Cross-Application Components • Application Functions • Settings • Generic Functions of mySAP Suite • Personal Worklist • Define Default Queries** and maintain the data for the **Query ID**, **Description**, and **Type** fields in accordance with Figure 4.42.

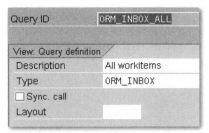

Figure 4.42 Defining Customizing Entries for Default Queries

Save the preceding entries, and then choose the following menu path **Cross-Application Components • General Application functions • Settings • Generic Functions of mySAP Suite • Personal Worklist • Define Categories**. Now enter the **ORM_INBOX** characteristic in the **Category** field and the text **Risk Management Workflow** in the **Description** field. Don't forget to also save these entries.

Defining categories

You must now execute the activity **Cross-Application Components • General Application Functions • Settings • Generic Functions of mySAP Suite • Personal Worklist • Define Query Visibility at Role Level**. Now enter the data in the **Application**, **Query ID**, and **Category** fields in accordance with Figure 4.43, and set the **Activate** indicator.

Defining query visibility at role level

Application	ORM_INBOX
Role	
Query ID	ORM_INBOX_ALL

View: Query - Role assignment	
Category	ORM_INBOX
Description	All workitems
Category sequence no	
query sequence no	
Tab sequence no	
☑ Activate	

Figure 4.43 Define Query Visibility at Role Level

To use the risk analysis functions in SAP GRC Risk Management, you must first execute the Customizing activities shown in Figure 4.44 in the sequence specified. To do this, choose the path **GRC Risk Management • Risk Analysis** in Customizing.

Risk analysis

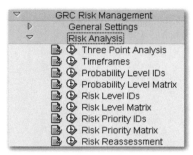

Figure 4.44 Customizing Activities for Risk Analysis

Three point analysis

In Customizing, you can determine the percentages for the three loss categories in *three-point analysis* under the path **GRC Risk Management • Risk Analysis • Three Point Analysis**. In the Customizing table shown in Figure 4.45, the three columns contain the percentages for the three loss categories used in three point analysis to calculate the total loss (minimum, average, and maximum loss).

Three Point Analysis				
Date	Min Loss	Avg Loss	Max Loss	Boolean
22.08.2007	20,0000	40,0000	30,0000	◉

Figure 4.45 Percentage Values for the Three Loss Categories

Example

In accordance with the percentage assignment in Figure 4.45, a minimum loss of EUR 10,000, an average loss of EUR 15,000, and a maximum loss of EUR 20,000 result in a total loss of EUR 14,000 as follows:

10,000 x 0.2 + 15,000 x 0.4 + 20,000 x 0.3 = EUR 14,000

Time frames

After the Customizing activities for three-point analysis, you can choose **GRC Risk Management • Risk Analysis • Time Frames** (see Figure 4.46) to determine the relevant time frames and assign each a numeric value. In SAP GRC Risk Management, you can then use these input values for the time frames to select and assign a risk response time.

Probability level IDs

You can then define and configure the probability level IDs under **GRC Risk Management • Risk Analysis • Probability Level IDs**. Figure 4.47 shows you the probability levels delivered in the standard version of

SAP GRC Risk Management. Here, each probability level corresponds to a specific probability value.

Maintenance dialog for time frames	
Time Frame	Description
1	Long
2	Medium
3	Short

Figure 4.46 Time Frames for Selecting and Assigning a Risk Response Time

Probability Levels	
Prob Level	Description
0	Rarely
1	Almost never
2	Very rarely
3	Hardly
4	Sometimes
5	Occasionally
6	Yearly
7	Monthly
8	Daily
9	Permanent

Figure 4.47 Probability Levels

You must use the probability level IDs that you've just maintained to now define and determine the *probability level matrix* under the Customizing path **GRC Risk Management • Risk Analysis • Probability Level Matrix**. Figure 4.48 shows you that the probability level matrix is created by assigning a time frame and a probability percentage for each probability level. You can use the generic placeholder (*) for the time frames.

Probability level matrix

Probability Definitions		
Time Frame	Prob. Value From	Prob Level
*	0,00000	1
*	15,00000	2
*	30,00000	3
*	45,00000	4
*	70,00000	5
*	80,00000	6

Figure 4.48 Probability Level Matrix

Risk level ID In the Customizing activity shown in Figure 4.49, you should now maintain a list of values for risk levels under **GRC Risk Management • Risk Analysis • Risk Level ID**. The risk level that corresponds to a specified value (**Very High, High, Medium, Low**, etc.) indicates the consequences or the severity of a particular risk. The risk levels depend on the valuated probability of occurrence and the total loss associated with the corresponding risk.

Maintenance dialog for risk level IDs		
Risk Level	Description	Position
H	High	2
L	Low	4
M	Medium	3
VH	Very High	1
VL	Negligible	5

Figure 4.49 Risk Levels for Indicating the Severity

Risk level matrix For the Customizing activity with the menu path **GRC Risk Management • Risk Analysis • Risk Level Matrix**, you should use the equation *probability level × impact level = risk level* to define and maintain a matrix. Figure 4.50 shows you a section of a risk level matrix defined in the system.

Maintenance dialog for risk level matrix		
Prob Level	Imp. lev.	Risk Level
1	1	Low
1	2	Low
1	3	Low
1	4	Low
1	5	Low
2	1	Low
2	2	Medium
2	3	Medium
2	4	Medium
2	5	Medium
3	1	Low
3	2	Medium
3	3	Medium
3	4	Medium
3	5	Medium
4	1	Low
4	2	Medium
4	3	High

Figure 4.50 Risk Level Matrix

You can determine risk priorities under **GRC Risk Management • Risk Analysis • Risk Priority ID**. Here, you can maintain the numeric values for the risk priority with the associated text descriptions. In SAP GRC Risk Management, the risk priority indicates the priority assigned to the risk in terms of its urgency. The risk priority is defined by a numeric value and a corresponding text description to indicate the urgency. Figure 4.51 shows that the lower numeric value represents the greatest urgency.

Risk priority ID

In the risk priority matrix, you can consolidate the values for the calculated risk level and time frame under **GRC Risk Management • Risk Analysis • Risk Priority Matrix**. The equation *time frame × risk level = risk priority* is used to determine the priority. The lower the value for the risk priority is, the higher the priority. The highest risk priority (= 1) is assigned if the response has only a short time frame (= 3) and the highest risk level (= VH). In SAP GRC Risk Management, you can calculate the risk priority both before and after each response.

Risk priority matrix

Maintenance dialog for priority IDs	
Risk Prior.	Description
1	Very urgent and very important
2	Very urgent and important
3	Urgent and very important
4	Urgent and imporant
5	Very urgend but less important
6	Not urgent but very imporant
7	Urgent but less important
8	Not urgent but important
9	Neither urgent nor important

Figure 4.51 Risk Priorities

The risk priority defined in Figure 4.52 depends on the valuated time frame (numeric values: 1 = long, 2 = medium, and 3 = short) and the risk level (L = Low, M = Medium, H = High, and VH = Very High).

For the last Customizing activity within the risk analysis area, you can define the number of days after which a notification should be sent via the workflow to the risk owner under **GRC Risk Management • Risk Analysis • Risk Revaluation**. According to this notification, a revalua-

Risk revaluation

tion is due in *x* days. You can only define one entry in this Customizing table.

Maintenance dialog for risk priority matrix

Time Frame	Risk Level	Risk Prior...
1	H	6
1	L	12
1	M	9
1	VH	5
2	H	4
2	L	11
2	M	8
2	VH	2
3	H	3
3	L	10
3	M	7
3	VH	1

Figure 4.52 Risk Priority Matrix

Response types

To use the risk response functions in SAP GRC Risk Management, you must define and maintain the response types and their various combinations. The response type indicates the risk response strategy. Therefore, you must define and maintain the response types and their corresponding descriptions under **GRC Risk Management • Risk Responses**. Response types are defined and maintained with a numeric value and a corresponding description (e.g., **Watch, Delegate, Accept**, etc.).

You can define a response type as a default value by selecting the option selection button shown in Figure 4.53 next to the relevant response type. These settings are available under **GRC Risk Management • Risk Responses • Response Types**.

Maintenance dialog for response types

Resp. Type	Default	Description
0001	○	Accept
0002	○	Watch
0003	○	Research
0004	○	Transfer
0005	○	Delegate
0006	◉	Mitigate

Figure 4.53 Response Types

You must maintain the response type combinations shown in Figure 4.54. Otherwise, the risk management functions won't work properly in terms of the risk responses. By defining response type combinations, you can exclude specific response types under **GRC Risk Management • Risk Responses • Response Type Combinations** when creating a new risk response in the application.

Response type combinations

The best way to define and configure response type combinations is to maintain a matrix that contains all of the response types. For those response type combinations that you exclude (e.g., 0001 with 0004), you must leave the relevant checkbox field in the right column in Figure 4.54 blank.

Maintenance dialog for response ty		
Resp. Type	Resp. Type	+
0001	0001	☑
0001	0002	☑
0001	0003	☑
0001	0004	☐
0001	0005	☐
0001	0006	☐
0002	0002	☑
0002	0003	☑
0002	0004	☑
0002	0005	☐
0002	0006	☐
0003	0003	☑
0003	0004	☑

Figure 4.54 Response Type Combinations

4.5.4 Loss Event Database

For the loss event database, you must define and maintain the segment tables, the validators, and the number ranges for the events. You can make these settings under **GRC Risk Management • Loss Event Database**.

Loss event database

You can define and maintain the necessary segment settings for the events under the Customizing activity **GRC Risk Management • Loss Event Database • Make Segment Settings**. Because segments are assigned to events, the segment is automatically derived when you create an event. The segment table configuration contains three areas (**Segment Dimen-**

Making segment settings

sions, **Segment Tables List**, and **Segment Table Operations**), each with different functions (see Figure 4.55).

Segment dimensions

The first step when creating or setting up segment tables is to maintain the segment dimensions because these segments are actually dimension groups. The settings are available in the **Segment Dimensions** area under **GRC Risk Management · Loss Event Database · Make Segment Settings**.

Segment Dimensions

Click on the button and maintain the dimensions for segment tables

| Dimension Maintenance | Create Default Dimensions |

Segment Tables List

Click on the button and maintain the list of the segment tables

| Segment Tables Maintenance |

Segment Table Operations

Segment Table

| Check | Create | Numberrange | Display | Last Log |

Add Dimension | Add
Delete Dimension | Delete

Figure 4.55 Defining and Maintaining Segment Tables

First, you must choose the **Dimension Maintenance** button in the **Segment Dimensions** area and maintain three dimensions with links to organizational units and to the activities and risk catalog. Figure 4.56 also shows that you must assign a **Dim ID**, a language-dependent description, a class or interface, and other parameters to each dimension.

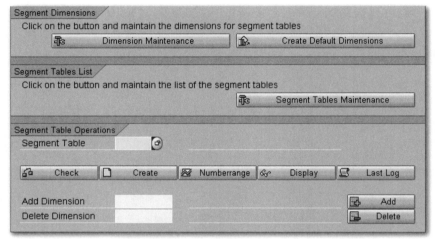

ILD Segment Dimension Definitions

Dim (ID)	Dimension	Class/Interface	Params
CACTIVITY	Activity Catalog	/ORM/CL_ORM_ILD_SGMT_DIM_HRORG	06;50000738;ORM_06ST
CRISK	Risk Catalog	/ORM/CL_ORM_ILD_SGMT_DIM_HRORG	00;50000739;ORM_00ST
ORGUNIT	Org Hierarchy	/ORM/CL_ORM_ILD_SGMT_DIM_HRORG	0;50000737;ORGEH

Figure 4.56 Dimension Maintenance

SAP GRC Risk Management currently provides the two classes shown in Table 4.1. However, you can develop your own classes, if necessary.

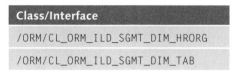

Class/Interface
/ORM/CL_ORM_ILD_SGMT_DIM_HRORG
/ORM/CL_ORM_ILD_SGMT_DIM_TAB

Table 4.1 Class/Interface for Dimension Maintenance

In the second area, you can now define an ID, a language-dependent description, an activation indicator, and the validation indicator for each segment table. The settings are available when you choose **Segment Tables Maintenance** in the **Segment Tables List** area under **GRC Risk Management** • **Loss Event Database** • **Make Segment Settings**. If you've set the **Validate** indicator as shown in Figure 4.57, you must validate each risk event that has occurred and been recorded in the segment table. A validation workflow will be triggered if the risk occurs.

Segment tables list

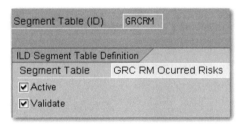

Figure 4.57 Segment Table Validation Indicator

You must have maintained the organizational unit in the GRC RM **segment table,** or it must be there already (see Figure 4.58).

Field	Data eleme...	Data Type	Short Description
MANDT	MANDT	CLNT	Client
SEGMENT	/ORM/ORME	NUMC	ILD Segment Identification
.INCLUDE	ZZILD_1_YS	STRU	ILD Generated
ORGUNIT	OTJID	CHAR	Concatenation of Object Type and Object ID
CRISK	OTJID	CHAR	Concatenation of Object Type and Object ID
CACTIVITY	OTJID	CHAR	Concatenation of Object Type and Object ID

Figure 4.58 Organizational Unit Within the Segment Table

249

Segment table operations

The third area, **Segment Table Operations** under **GRC Risk Management • Loss Event Database • Make Segment Settings**, contains additional maintenance functions for configuring the segment table (see Figure 4.59). To use the segment, you must create the dictionary structures and the database table. We also recommend that you use the check function provided in this area to perform a consistency check on the dictionary structures that have been generated.

Furthermore, you must maintain a number range for the segment table that has been generated. Within this maintenance function for the segment table, you can implement other activities such as adding or deleting a dimension. However, you should use the latter function with caution because all of the segment references to the corresponding events are recalculated when you delete a dimension.

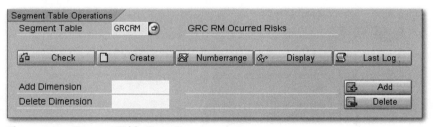

Figure 4.59 Segment Table Operations

Default validator

If a loss event that has already occurred is stored in a segment to be validated, you must have first assigned the relevant event validator before validating the relevant segment. In the Customizing activity **GRC Risk Management • Loss Event Database • Maintain Default Validator**, you can assign the relevant event validator to a segment in which information about the loss that occurred was recorded (see Figure 4.60).

You can derive the event validator from the organizational units dimension. If you used the Customizing activity *Maintain Default Validator* to define the validator, the validator is derived from this table entry if the relevant organizational unit does not contain any other entry or if the organizational unit for the segment table doesn't exist.

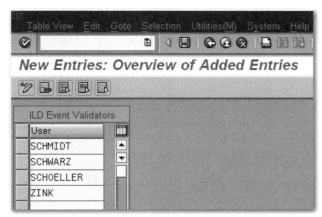

Figure 4.60 Event Validator Assigned Before Validation of the Relevant Segment

When you create or save an event, a number is automatically assigned to the risk incident that occurred. In the Customizing activity **GRC Risk Management • Loss Event Database • Maintain Number Range for Events**, you can define and maintain number range intervals for events that have occurred. Because number range 01 is used by all incident types in risk management, you should always define another number range interval.

Number range for events

4.5.5 Workflow Activation

To ensure that the workflow functions in risk management work properly, you must have implemented the workflow and task-specific Customizing as well as the email settings for the survey function. You can make these settings under **GRC Risk Management • Workflow Activation**.

Workflow activation

For risk management, you must maintain the Customizing activity **GRC Risk Management • Workflow Activation • Implement Automatic Workflow Customizing** under the **Maintain Runtime Environment** top node in accordance with Figure 4.61. You can also configure the other nodes in the Customizing activity. However, this is optional. The system automatically makes all of the required settings if you select the top node **Maintain Runtime Environment** and then press F9 to implement automatic workflow Customizing.

Runtime environment

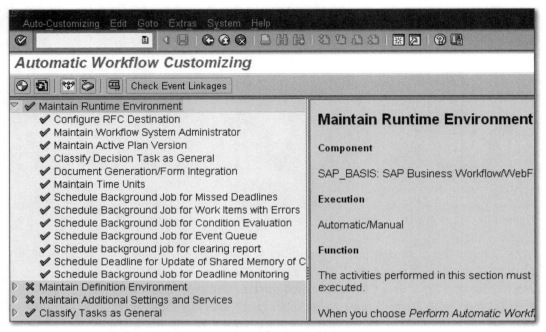

Figure 4.61 Automatic Workflow Customizing

Background job if schedule exceeded

After automatic workflow configuration is complete, you should use the Plan Background Job if Schedule Exceeded node (**GRC Risk Management • Workflow Activation • Implement Automatic Workflow Customizing • Maintain Runtime Environment • Plan Background Job if Schedule Exceeded**) to plan the relevant background job as shown in Figure 4.62 with an interval of **20** minutes until the next deadline check.

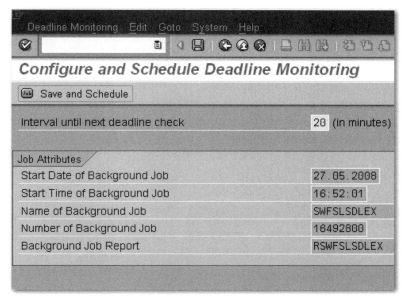

Figure 4.62 Plan Background Job if Schedule Exceeded

After automatic workflow Customizing is complete, you can make all of the settings required to adjust the default tasks provided and the workflow templates under **GRC Risk Management • Workflow Activation • Implement Task-Specific Customizing** (see Figure 4.63).

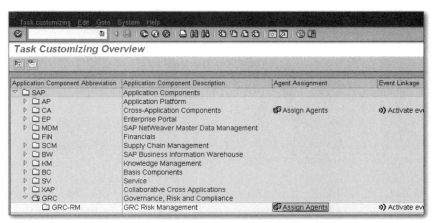

Figure 4.63 Implementing Task-Specific Customizing

Assigning agents

You must specify all possible agents for each task because only these agents can then start the workflow in dialog mode. If you don't want to assign specific users to the standard risk management tasks and workflow templates, we recommend that you define all standard dialog tasks (nonbackground tasks) and the workflow templates as a **General Task** under **Assign Agents** as shown in Figure 4.64. Furthermore, you can also assign an organizational unit, job, or position as a possible agent for a task or workflow, which means that if personnel changes were made in the structural organization, these would not require the workflow components to change.

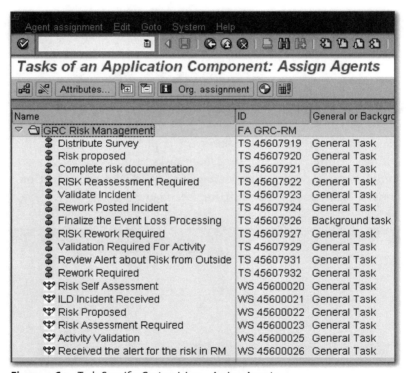

Figure 4.64 Task-Specific Customizing – Assign Agents

Activating event linkage

You can start tasks or workflows as a response to events that were generated by the application functions. Here, you define specific incidents as events that trigger a task or workflow. For this reason, we recommend that you activate the relevant linkages under **GRC Risk Management** • **Workflow Activation** • **Implement Task-Specific Customizing** • **Activate Event Linkage** as shown in Figure 4.65.

> **Note**
>
> You should once again implement or at least check the activities described previously in every new client[1] in which you want to use the workflow functions.

Figure 4.65 Activating Event Linkage

In the Customizing activity **GRC Risk Management** • **Workflow Activation** • **Maintain Email Settings for Survey**, you can configure the email settings in such a way that a recipient receives an invitation to participate in a survey in his inbox. First, you must activate the nodes listed in Table 4.2 in the maintenance screen for the HTTP service tree (Transaction SICF).

Email settings

---

1 In commercial, organizational, and technical terms, a client is a self-contained unit in an SAP system with separate master records and its own set of tables.

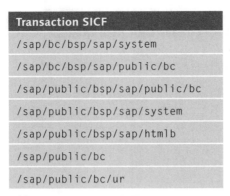

Transaction SICF
/sap/bc/bsp/sap/system
/sap/bc/bsp/sap/public/bc
/sap/public/bsp/sap/public/bc
/sap/public/bsp/sap/system
/sap/public/bsp/sap/htmlb
/sap/public/bc
/sap/public/bc/ur

Table 4.2 Transaction SICF

Transaction SWNADMIN

You can use *Notification Administration* (Transaction SWNADMIN) to open the administration screen for extended notifications for the business workflow in a new web window. You must first choose **Create** to create a new **category** as shown in Figure 4.66.

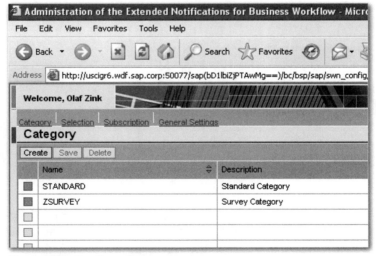

Figure 4.66 Creating a Category

You must then use the category that you have just created (**ZSURVEY**) to now create and record a new **selection** (see Figure 4.67).

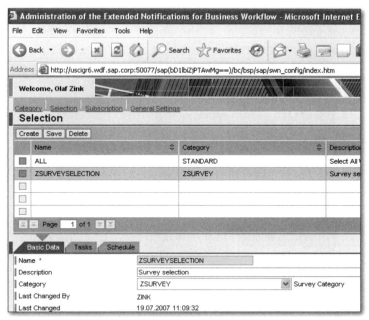

Figure 4.67 Creating a Selection

On the **Tasks** tab page, enter the task number "TS45607919" in accordance with Figure 4.68, and choose **Adopt** to save your entry.

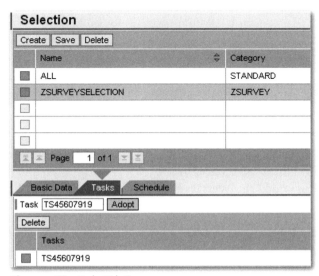

Figure 4.68 Tasks Tab Page

To successfully configure the email settings, you must define a new *subscription* (see the upper menu bar) for the category that you've just created in accordance with Figure 4.69.

Figure 4.69 Creating a Subscription

Transaction SWNCONFIG To conclude the activities for configuring the email settings, you must use the *Configuring Notifications* function (Transaction SWNCONFIG) under **General Settings** to enter "WD_HOST" with the URL *http://{hostname}:{port}/webdynpro/dispatcher*, as shown in the example provided in Figure 4.70. The host name and the port are the SAP NetWeaver Application Server on which the Web Dynpro application for SAP GRC Risk Management is implemented.

The last step is to use Transaction SM36 to schedule the job for sending an email notification.

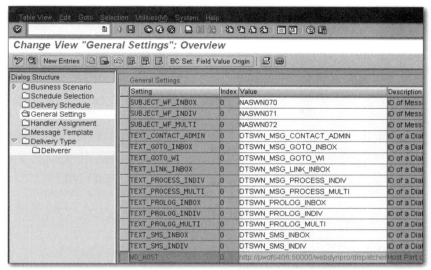

Figure 4.70 Notifications – Configuration (Transaction SWNCONFIG)

Each to his own. However, man should not be burdened with more taxes and charges than he deserves. (Wigand)

5   SAP GRC Global Trade Services – An Overview

The *SAP GRC Global Trade Services* application is the solution for customs and foreign trade management. This central, automated customs and foreign trade platform enables you to respond more quickly to changes with greater confidence and flexibility because these changes are implemented only once in the central platform and then are immediately available throughout the company.

This chapter provides an overview of those areas in which you can use SAP GRC Global Trade Services. It also introduces you to the application scenarios that are available for compliance with legal controls and for customs management while simultaneously optimizing financial risks and opportunities.

5.1   Goals of SAP GRC Global Trade Services

SAP GRC Global Trade Services standardizes all operational processes associated with foreign trade and supports these during cross-border trade. It also complies with local laws and foreign trade regulations and facilitates system-based electronic communication with the relevant authorities. All essential information is available to the right people (forwarding agents, customs brokers, insurance agencies, banks, and authorities) at the right time. As a result, individual processes such as customs clearance for imported goods are performed much faster. It's also possible to integrate non-SAP ERP applications. The initial menu for SAP GRC Global Trade Services provides an overview of the application (see Figure 5.1).

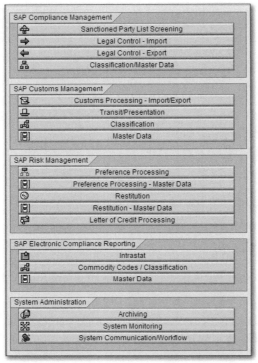

Figure 5.1   Initial Menu for SAP GRC Global Trade Services

The following sections provide an overview of the three focal points of SAP GRC Global Trade Services:

▶ Legal Control

▶ Customs Management

▶ Utilization of Monetary Benefits and Limitation of Monetary Risks

5.2   Legal Control

This application groups together all of the functions that a company requires to comply with the legal regulations for cross-border trade. These include not only the import and export control but also compliance with boycott lists and the provision of embargo checks.

5.2.1 Screening Sanctioned Party Lists

Governments in different countries publish boycott lists that prohibit companies from conducting a business relationship with certain legal or natural entities.

Public sources for these sanctioned party lists include the Bundesanzeiger Verlag (German federal publishing house) or FedEx. The lists provided by these sources incorporate the directory of names associated with EU anti-terrorist regulations within the European Union as well as the United States. Other sources for sanctioned party lists are the Internet pages provided by MK Technologies (*www.mkdenial.com* and *www.saptradedata. com*). You can also receive regular updates. Easy-to-use upload functions enable you to upload this information to the GTS database.

Sources for sanctioned party lists

The following is an overview of the most important boycott lists:

Important boycott lists

- ▶ Commerce Dept. Denial List (TDO)
- ▶ Treasury Dept. Specially Designated Nationals of:
  - ▶ Angola (UNITA)
  - ▶ Cuba (SDNC) & Merchant Vessels (MVC)
  - ▶ Iran (SDNR)
  - ▶ Iraq (SDNI) & Merchant Vessels (MVI)
  - ▶ Libya (SDNL)
  - ▶ North Korea (SDNK) – Assets prior to 6/17/00 remain blocked
  - ▶ Sudan (SDNS)
  - ▶ Western Balkans (BALK)
  - ▶ Yugoslavia & Blocked Vessels (FRYM & BYV)
  - ▶ Zimbabwe (SDNZ)
- ▶ State Dept. Statutorily Debarred Parties (DOS)
- ▶ State Dept. Designated Terrorist Organization (DTO)
- ▶ State Dept. Missile Proliferators (MT)
- ▶ State Dept. Chemical & Biological Weapons Concerns (CBW)
- ▶ Treasury Dept. Specially Designated Terrorists (SDME)

▶ Treasury Dept. Specially Designated Narcotic Traffickers (SDNT)

When you use SAP GRC Global Trade Services, all business relationships are screened and compared against international boycott lists. This ensures that you don't trade with any partners recorded in the boycott list.

Overview of blocked business partners

Figure 5.2 provides an overview of the various possible reports for sanctioned party lists. For example, you can display blocked business partners (see Figure 5.3). The Compliance Manager can access extensive functions and reporting options. For example, you can manually release business partners that have been blocked by the application.

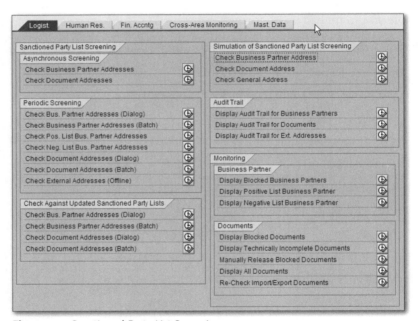

Figure 5.2 Sanctioned Party List Screening

Display Business Partner

Status	LS Group	B.	Business Partner	BusPartner	L.Reg.	AddressNo.	Date of SPL Screening	Sanct. Block	Valid to
∞	GRPLOGSYS	07	70101614	1400	SPLUS	14043	02.02.2006 14:05:09	☑	31.12.9999 00:00:00

Figure 5.3 Blocked Business Partners

You can also use positive lists. Sometimes, a business partner may be classified as "discredited" because he shares the same name as a company recorded in a boycott list. If you're sure that this business partner was accidentally discredited, you can place the business partner on a positive list. This ensures that this business partner isn't discredited the next time you screen the sanctioned party list.

Of course, you can also create internal sanctioned party lists. Here, you can include business partners or persons with whom you have had negative experiences in the past.

Internal sanctioned party lists

All of the sanctioned party list screening results are saved and stored in the system. If you manually release a partner that has been blocked by the function for sanctioned partner lists, you can also include a comment. Therefore, when you perform a subsequent external check, you can immediately verify whether the sanctioned party lists have been considered or which exceptions are permitted. Different audit trails are provided for this purpose. For example, you can view all changes made to the master data or documents (see Figure 5.4).

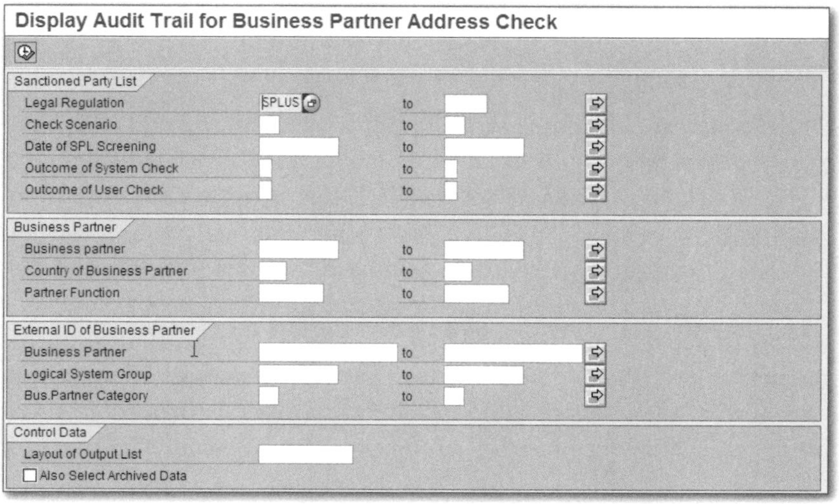

Manually releasing blocked partners

Figure 5.4 Audit Trail for Business Partner Addresses

You can also perform ad hoc simulation runs. In day-to-day business, these enable you to more quickly identify whether the business partner

Simulating the sanctioned party list

is recorded in a public sanctioned party list or an internal sanctioned party list.

5.2.2 Import/Export Control

Examples of controls requiring compliance

Some import or export transactions are subject to an import or export control. To prove compliance with these controls, you must have the necessary licenses. Examples include the following:

- Disposal Act
- Raw Materials Surveillance Act
- Drug Registration and Administration Act
- Narcotics Act
- Dual-Use Regulations[1]
- Chemical Weapons Convention
- War Weapons Control Act

You can use SAP GRC Global Trade Services to determine whether you require a trading license. If you do, it immediately checks whether you have license with sufficient volume licenses and sufficient value. It also ensures that you don't contravene any trade embargos.

Product classification

One prerequisite for compliance with the legal requirements is that all of the products imported or exported by a company are classified accordingly. The *Harmonized Tariff Schedule* (HTS) is the most frequently used classification system. HTS is based on an international naming convention used by approximately 200 customs authorities to determine customs tariffs, produce import and export statistics, and check compliance with legal regulations. Generally, each country adds a country-specific number to the HTS ID. Different countries also use other classification systems. The main classification systems are the ECCN (Export Classification Control Number), which is used in the United States, the commodity code, and the export list number.

---

1 According to Wikipedia, dual-use is a term often used in politics and diplomacy to refer to technology that can be used for both peaceful and military aims.

The process of assigning these classification numbers to the individual goods imported or exported by a company is known as *product classification*.

SAP GRC Global Trade Services supports product classification by providing the following:

► One central goods classification overview. This makes it possible to create this classification once only and then make it available in all integrated systems.

► Optional upload functions for uploading classification schemas which are generally in use to SAP GRC Global Trade Services.

► A proposal list for numbering according to the goods description.

► An overview of those goods that are yet to be classified. This overview is then used as a worklist for processing those goods that are yet to be classified.

► A mass change function if the authorities redesign, refine, or enhance (reclassify) the predefined classification lists.

SAP GRC Global Trade Services uses product classification to automatically determine whether a business transaction is export- or import-relevant. Furthermore, it automatically assigns a license to the business transaction (see Figure 5.5).

Export and import licenses

This includes the following core functions:

► A check to determine whether an import or export license is required when triggering the movement of goods for a specific product.

► Automatic determination and assignment of license if required.

The licenses are usually limited to a certain volume or value of goods. When a license is used, the volume or value of goods for the license is automatically depreciated.

If there are any inconsistencies, for example, a license expires or it's used up, the business transaction ceases immediately, and the agent is notified by email that he can save but not post the document. Follow-up actions such as creating a delivery or issuing an invoice are blocked.

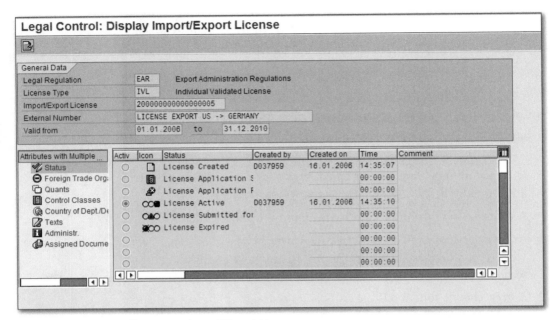

Figure 5.5 Import/Export License

Overview reporting can provide the license status, its validity period, and its residual and quantity values.

Embargo

In contrast to third countries, embargos exist for some countries. Companies that operate different production and trading locations worldwide can have very complex import and export scenarios. SAP GRC Global Trade Services checks each business transaction to determine whether the company is complying with the trade embargo. It can also determine which customer or vendor outside the trade and production chain is affected by an embargo. Furthermore, all trade relationships worldwide are documented here. If required, this history can be produced for external checks. Different reports are available for this purpose (see Figure 5.6), and you can also release blocked documents accordingly.

Simulations

SAP GRC Global Trade Services provides extensive simulation functions for a corresponding preliminary leg. These enable you to check in advance whether successful transaction processing is endangered by an embargo. You must also simulate in advance the effects of export or import business on a company's licensing situation.

Figure 5.6 Legal Control – Export

5.3 Customs Management

Customs management involves processing all customs-relevant processes within procurement or the sale of products.

Its purpose is to ensure that you comply with all customs-relevant regulations for cross-border trade and that the right documents are available on time. This is the only way to avoid consignments being detained at borders due to certain violations or missing/incorrect documents. Each delay extends the transport time for goods and is very cost-intensive.

You can avoid these delays by using IT-based applications such as SAP GRC Global Trade Services. The integration of such applications into the

269

IT systems for procurement or sales ensures that all customs-relevant situations can be recognized on time and processed without errors. This is the basis for electronic communication with the customs authorities.

IT-based customs procedures are generally country-specific. SAP GRC Global Trade Services supports some of these country-specific solutions:

▸ The German customs processing system: Automated Tariff and Local Customs Processing System (ATLAS)

▸ The European electronic shipping procedure: New Computerized Transit System (NCTS)

▸ The Dutch customs processing system: Sagitta

▸ The Swiss customs processing system: ZM90

▸ The U.S. export system: Automated Export System (AES)

▸ The Australian customs processing system: Integrated Cargo System (ICS)

Most of the information transferred to the electronic customs document originates in the integrated IT systems for procurement or sales. The creation of electronic customs documents prevents errors that would have occurred in the past as a result of manually transferring and completing these documents. The electronic customs documents are then transferred to the customs authorities. This electronic customs processing procedure means that the movement of goods is a highly automated process.

Similar to the import and export control, a basic prerequisite for product classification is the classification of products (see Section 5.2.2, "Import/Export Control"). A unique product classification is required to determine the product tariffs because the individual customs authorities refer to common naming conventions (import code numbers, commodity codes, HTS numbers, etc.) when determining product tariffs. Therefore, an exact product classification can contribute greatly to cost savings because it can achieve considerable savings in relation to import tariffs (see Figure 5.7).

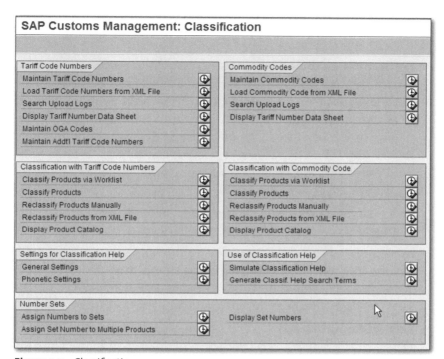

Figure 5.7 Classification

The customs authorities generally also provide the product tariffs in electronic form. SAP GRC Global Trade Services provides interfaces for uploading country-specific customs tariffs to the application. For example, SAP provides interfaces for the standards for the *Electronischer Zolltarif* (Germany) (EZT) and the *Tarif Intégré Communautés Européennes* (France) (TARIC).

Furthermore, SAP GRC Global Trade Services provides functions that calculate the customs duties associated with importing goods from third countries. As a result, future customs duties can be calculated before they are due.

Customs value determination

The current duty rates can be procured for data providers and provided via SAP application interfaces.

The customs value is determined by subtracting other expenses such as transport costs, insurance charges, and import turnover tax from the import value. SAP GRC Global Trade Services can also calculate the most common customs duty rates:

► **Preferential customs duty rate**
"When goods originating in a preferential zone are imported into the EU, they are subject to a preferential customs duty rate that ranges from zero to a customs duty rate lower than the rate for goods from states that are not authorized to receive preferential duty treatment such as the U.S. and Japan whose goods are subject to the normal third country customs duty rate when imported into the EU."[2]

► **General duty rate**
Goods from states not authorized to receive preferential duty treatment.

► **Anti-dumping customs duty rate**
"Imported goods are considered to be dumped if the price of the goods imported into the EU is lower than the price payable for the same goods or similar in the country of origin."[3]

► **Exempt from customs**
"The EU has produced a directory of goods that are imported into the EU for a specific reason and are therefore exempt from customs (for example, low-value sample goods, advertising print, relocation goods or inherited goods)."[4]

Document print When you export and import goods, you must print out various customs documents. SAP GRC Global Trade Services is integrated into the procurement and sales systems for each integrated SAP ERP application. This enables you to copy the data to those documents required for foreign trade. As a result, the process of creating and printing the documents required for foreign trade is largely automated. SAP GRC Global

---

2 Schmöger, J.; Mlkakar, H. C.: Terminology for EU Customs Legislation, p. 16 at: *http://www.eycom.ch/library/chd/items/199905/de.pdf.*
3 Schmöger, J.; Mlkakar, H. C.: Terminology for EU Customs Legislation, p. 14 at: *http://www.eycom.ch/ library/chd/items/199905/de.pdf.*
4 Schmöger, J.; Mlkakar, H. C.: Terminology for EU Customs Legislation, p. 18 at: *http://www.eycom.ch/library/ chd/items/199905/de.pdf.*

Trade Services supports you in creating the necessary documents in the respective local language:

- Shipping documents (T1, T2)
- Movement certificate EUR.1
- Assessment notices
- Certificates of origin (NAFTA, EU)
- Import customs declaration
- U.S. Shippers Export Declaration
- Single administrative document (EX/EU/COM)

The export documents can also be made available to forwarding agents and customs brokers in electronic form.

5.4 Using Monetary Benefits and Limiting Monetary Risks

Due to the complex laws that govern cross-border trade, numerous regulations are beneficial to trading companies, if used correctly.

These include customs tariff preferences, which means that certain goods traded between certain countries are subject to reduced customs duties or are exempt from customs. This simplifies (and therefore promotes) trade between these countries for preferential products.

Customs tariff preferences

Another benefit is restitution. The European Union has fixed its prices for various products. As a result, these prices are considerably lower within the European Union than they are on the world market. To promote the export of such goods within the European Union, restitutions are granted to level the price difference between the price on the world market and the price within the EU.

Restitution

The SAP GRC Global Trade Services application area ensures that both customs preference and refunds on imports and exports are determined correctly.

It also contains functions for using documentary letters of credit to financially hedge goods associated with risky exports.

5.4.1 Trade Preference Management (Preference Determination)

Preference processing

States use preference agreements to promote trade for specific products. To benefit from reduced customs duties and customs exemptions (known as *preferences*), SAP GRC Global Trade Services provides the preference processing application (see Figure 5.8), which essentially comprises three steps.

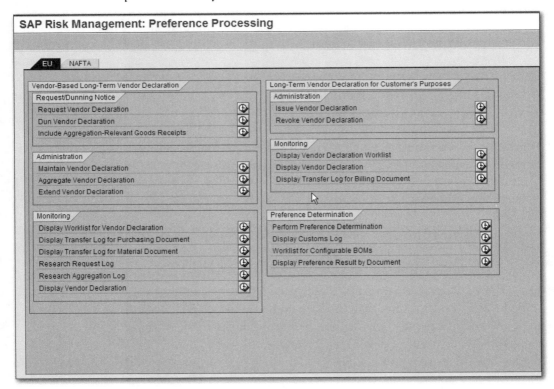

Figure 5.8 Preference Processing

Step 1: Requesting Vendor Declarations

First of all, you must verify the origin of the product, which can be an extremely difficult task if a product comprises different components delivered by different vendors from different countries. However, SAP GRC Global Trade Services can help you verify the origin of a product.

The application provides functions for requesting, managing, and archiving vendor declarations. It does this by providing forms that can also be customized for each company. In addition to shipping forms, vendors can also use the Internet to transfer the relevant information to the company. To facilitate this, a company's website includes an input page in which vendors can enter the necessary information. If the vendors also use SAP software, the process of exchanging data can be fully automated via SAP NetWeaver Exchange Infrastructure (SAP NetWeaver XI). After vendor declarations are entered once, they can be adjusted accordingly using track changes. Furthermore, an easy-to-use archiving function can provide detailed historical information at the click of a mouse.

Step 2: Determining the Preference Authorization for Products

You can then use the proof of vendor results to determine the associated customs benefits and customs exemptions. Therefore, the companies can use international trade preference agreements such as the EU preference agreement or the North American Free Trade Agreement (NAFTA).

This is done by comparing the information contained in the proof of vendor for traded products against the current options for preference processing. SAP GRC Global Trade Services accurately determines the associated customs benefits and customs exemptions. The result is then the valuated origin of the goods.

Companies can always seize the opportunities associated with trade benefits in accordance with the currently applicable basis for a decision by procuring the official third-party rules of origin. SAP GRC Global Trade Services provides interfaces for uploading this information so that the latest information is always used for the preference determination algorithms.

SAP GRC Global Trade Services also uses the information defined within an SAP bill of material (BOM). The SAP BOM is used, for example, if products always have the same subproducts. Examples include configurable products such as vehicles or computers.

Even if the subproducts are produced in different plants and then combined to form one complete product, the logistical challenge is to also map preference determinations in SAP GRC Global Trade Services.

Companies are required to fully document preference determinations. The functions we've discussed enable you to easily comply with this obligation and avoid possible penalties.

Step 3: Issuing Certificates of Origin for the Customer

In this step, a certificate of origin is issued for your customers. Your customers, in turn, use this certificate of origin as a "proof of vendor" for using preference agreements. The documents that must accompany the goods are also printed (e.g., the EUR_1 movement certificate or the NAFTA certificate of origin).

5.4.2 Restitution Management (Refunds on Imports and Exports)

Companies that are based in the European Union and export specific goods such as agricultural produce to another EU country can benefit from restitutions. This is the case if the fixed price for these goods within the European Union is considerably lower than the price for these goods on the world market. In this situation, the exporting company can benefit from restitutions or export subsidies. The procedure for requesting restitutions is complicated by the markets and their ever-changing legal requirements. SAP GRC Global Trade Services supports you through integration and automation, so that no errors occur when requesting and using restitutions (see Figure 5.9).

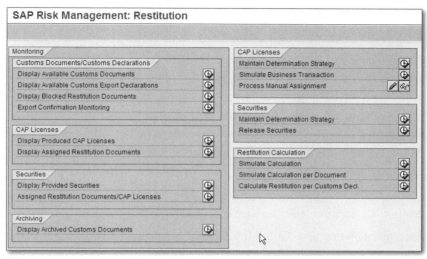

Figure 5.9 Restitution

This involves the following steps.

Step 1: Requesting an Export License

Only companies that have a valid export license can request restitutions. An export license authorizes a company to export a specific quantity of specific goods in a specific period. Companies must define collateral when requesting a license. This collateral can be paid in cash or covered by a guarantee of payment.

You can use SAP GRC Global Trade Services to request and manage export licenses. In particular, you can use its functions for managing collateral, including automatically assigning collateral to the relevant export licenses and determining the percentage of collateral for the restitution.

Step 2: Managing an Export License

If an export license has been approved, SAP GRC Global Trade Services manages the document. Products that are relevant for a refund are automatically identified. This license is then assigned if goods that are relevant for a refund are exported. This enables a company to determine, at any time, which export licenses have been issued, when they are due, and the extent to which they are used.

Step 3: Assigning the Composition of Goods Manufactured

A basic prerequisite for a refund is that the company verifies the composition of goods manufactured. This is necessary if some parts of a product are relevant for a refund, but others aren't. SAP GRC Global Trade Services provides the necessary functions for managing the composition of goods manufactured.

Step 4: Calculating the Restitution

Interfaces enable SAP GRC Global Trade Services to always provide the currently valid restitution rates for the European Union. This ensures that the restitution amounts to be expected are automatically determined correctly. This calculation is used as the basis for submitting a restitution application to the customs authorities. In addition, the amount contained in the restitution application is invoiced in the finance system. Accounts receivable financial accounting monitors whether the restitution has also been incurred.

5.4.3 Trade Finance Services (Documentary Payments Processing)

A fundamental risk in foreign trade is that customers are unable to meet their payment obligations. Therefore, it's common practice to hedge transactions with certain customers or in certain regions. Common financial hedges include letters or credit, collections, and guarantees of payment. If a company uses financial documents to hedge its transactions, this hedging complicates financial accounting and the export documents accompanying the goods. However, SAP GRC Global Trade Services also provides extensive functions for fulfilling these requirements, including assigning financial documents to import and export transactions, issuing all of the required documents, electronic shipping of financial documents to partners, maintaining changes and printing out documents, and finally overview reporting for all current and completed financial documents in import and export business (see Figure 5.10).

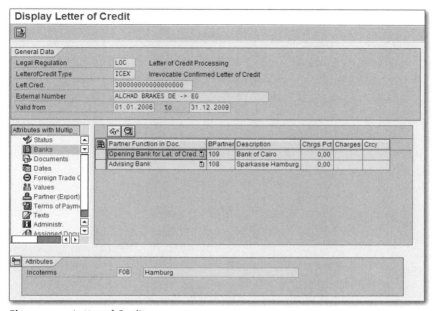

Figure 5.10 Letter of Credit

Nature is immutable. (Eiselein)

6 SAP Environment, Health & Safety – An Overview

Regulations governing environmental protection, health protection, and industrial hygiene and safety are subject to frequent change because governments are quick to incorporate the latest findings and technological innovations into legislation. SAP supports compliance with these regulations with its *SAP Environment, Health & Safety* (SAP EH&S) application. Due to its high degree of integration with enterprise business processes, SAP EH&S is incorporated into SAP ERP and SAP Product Lifecycle Management (SAP PLM).

SAP PLM includes all of the applications involved in the design, construction, production, and maintenance of a product. These functionalities are integrated with SAP ERP. This merging of all of the required functions in a single software application provides optimal support for the product lifecycle and removes the need for redundant data storage.

6.1 Goals of SAP Environment, Health & Safety

The seamless integration of the SAP EH&S application with other SAP applications results in significant benefits. The benefits include a very high degree of transparency and control over whether internal and external guidelines are being adhered to.

The high degree of automation in this application makes a considerable contribution toward keeping costs down. Financial risks are avoided because the threat of financial penalties due to nonadherence to legal regulations doesn't exist. Decision-makers in the enterprise have access to all of the existing information in consolidated form, which enables

Adherence with legal regulations by means of automation

them to analyze and evaluate major decisions in advance. This decision-making confidence ultimately benefits the customer because the enterprise is in a position to provide high product quality and optimized services.

SAP EH&S can be divided into the following main application areas:

▶ Chemical safety

▶ Environmental protection, health protection, and industrial hygiene and safety

▶ Adherence to product-specific environmental regulations

▶ Compliance management and emissions management

6.2 Chemical Safety

SAP EH&S supports all employees with safe chemicals handling and, at the same time, with adhering to all of the relevant legal regulations and specifications.

The first prerequisite for the safe handling of chemicals is that all parties involved are aware of what they are dealing with. This requires that all products and their compositions are documented down to the minutest detail.

This information has to be available and accessible in the correct form and in accordance with the law during putaway, consumption, and transport.

Figure 6.1 gives you an initial idea of the functions available for chemicals management.

Specification database

The core area for product safety and hazardous substance management is therefore a special product safety function that can automatically calculate product composition. Substances are described in a specification database that incorporates logical dependencies and sets of rules. Substances are chemical products. A distinction is drawn among real substances, preparations, and mixtures. A possible result of a search in this database could be information on the composition of a substance that is classified as highly flammable. The SAP EH&S application makes classifying and managing hazardous substances much easier by means of open interfaces. These interfaces make it possible to automatically transfer substance and recipe information, and statutory lists from third parties, for example. The result is a classification or hazard rating, or both, of the relevant chemicals. The application also enables you to determine which finished products contain a particular ingredient and creates reports to give you an overview of the stock of hazardous substances.

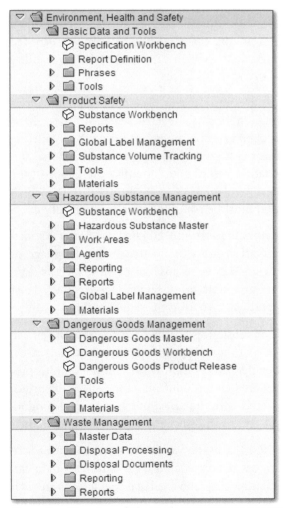

Figure 6.1 Overview of Chemicals Management Functionality

The information that is stored in the specification database is available to all employees whose activity profile means that they come into contact with the hazardous substances. This applies in particular to activities that are associated with the internal transport, further processing, and the delivery and disposal of hazardous substances.

Products are documented in the form of material safety data sheets. The documentation process is carried out automatically on the basis of the information stored in the specification database. The material safety data sheets are also updated automatically. Updates are made when product compositions or legal requirements change. The changes are recorded in the system in change documents, which can be used for traceability purposes in future internal or external checks.

When hazardous substances are transported, besides special dangerous goods papers such as material safety data sheets and tremcards, products also must have the proper labeling. Labeling is carried out by a labeling management function that supports goods transport for both national and international markets. The labels describe and identify the goods in the specified packaging. The legal regulations of each country through which the goods will be transported must be complied with in the labeling.

A significant aspect of documentation and labeling is that transport-related labels and documentation must be created in the language of each of the countries involved. This is because all parties, such as drivers, customs officials, warehouse staff, and accident service staff, must be able to identify the dangerous good from the labels.

In certain countries, different substances may be transported only if the authorities have been notified of the transport in advance. In such cases, the authorities require a detailed description of the product and a precise list of the quantities that are being produced, imported, or exported. Because SAP EH&S is integrated with the sales, purchasing, and production functions of SAP ERP, it gives you direct access to these documents.

As well as the detailed specification of the hazardous substances, the SAP system also stores and manages the associated legal data. This data can be used as a basis for calculating the relevant legal regulations in each case, as well as for working out the appropriate and permitted transpor-

Documentation and labeling — *(margin note)*

Notifiable transports — *(margin note)*

tation option. This information is then automatically included in all of the transportation documentation, such as the delivery note.

This data basis is also used to carry out the appropriate pre-transport controls, which means that goods can leave the company premises only after the dangerous goods check has been successfully completed. This control in turn ensures that the transport is carried out in accordance with all of the legal requirements that apply to dangerous goods. These requirements include a check of whether the dangerous good is being transported using the approved means of transport.

Another aspect of chemicals handling is waste disposal. The legal require-   Waste disposal
ments for waste disposal are particularly stringent when it comes to waste from hazardous substances. The SAP system supports you in complying with all of the legal requirements in this area, too. One such requirement is ensuring that only the quantity of hazardous substances is transported that is approved in advance. In the SAP system, the required documentation is made available in accordance with the laws and languages of each individual country, depending on whether the waste in question is to be disposed of domestically or in another country.

Because waste disposal is usually a highly costly process, it's necessary to assign the costs to the originators of the costs within the enterprise. This is done using the integrated financial and cost accounting applications within SAP ERP. Another benefit of the waste disposal function is its integration with the procurement function in SAP ERP. This allows the user to identify the disposer who can provide the most cost-effective service.

6.3   Environmental Protection, Health Protection, and Industrial Hygiene and Safety

What is the best way of recognizing and minimizing health risks to employees? How can a preventive health protection policy be set up in an enterprise? SAP EH&S can help you answer these questions and comply with the extensive legal regulations on industrial hygiene and safety, health protection, and hazardous substance handling.

The following basic principle applies: create greater safety and avoid health risks to employees by complying strictly with the law. To achieve this, you need detailed information about the applicable laws, the working environment, the health of the employees, and the hazardous substances with which employees come into contact in the course of their work. The essential information is stored in the previously mentioned specification database. Figure 6.2 shows an overview of the scope of functions for industrial hygiene and safety, and occupational health.

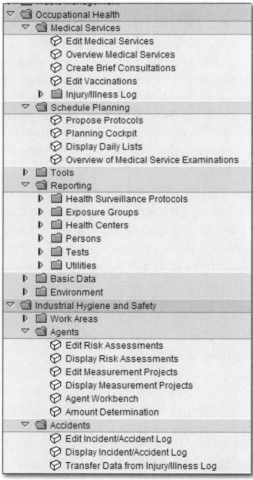

Figure 6.2 Overview of Industrial Hygiene and Safety, and Occupational Health

As well as details on substances, permitted packaging, dangerous goods classification, and waste codes, the SAP EH&S solution also contains details on health protection, and industrial hygiene and safety. These details include, in particular, descriptions of work environment agents that employees are exposed to due to noise, climate, and hazardous substances (see Figure 6.3).

Agents in the work environment

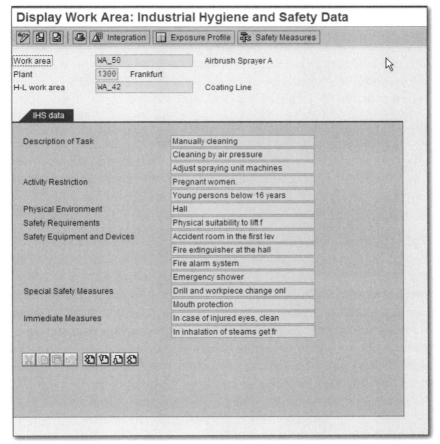

Figure 6.3 Industrial Hygiene and Safety Data

Open interfaces also greatly facilitate the transfer of health and safety data, which can be purchased from data providers. Some providers specialize in updating and selling health- and safety-related data after legal changes are made. These changes have to do with country-specific legal regulations on occupational safety and health protection in the work-place, and with the labor standards set down by the *International Labor Organization* (ILO).

Plant maintenance

Another aspect of industrial hygiene and safety is the maintenance of production facilities. Because the SAP EH&S solution is integrated with SAP ERP Corporate Services and SAP Enterprise Asset Management, you can check whether the required maintenance and repair measures are carried out on schedule and to a sufficient level of quality.

Accident reports and first-aiders

If, in spite of all preventive measures, an occupational accident occurs, the required data is recorded and stored in SAP EH&S. An electronic injury/illness log is then created on the basis of this data, and an accident report is drawn up on the basis of the injury/illness log.

Also, a first-aider must be available for serious incidents. There must be a specific number of first-aiders in every enterprise. SAP EH&S provides an overview of these first-aiders and at what work station they are usu-ally to be found. Also, SAP Training and Event Management can be used to display at a glance the further training that these first-aiders have undergone, and when.

Preventive measures

The appropriate preventive measures also make a significant contribu-tion to industrial hygiene and safety, and health protection. Thanks to the integration of SAP EH&S with SAP ERP Human Capital Manage-ment (SAP ERP HCM), the functions for industrial hygiene and safety and occupational health can be processed automatically. These func-tions include regular health surveillance protocols. The SAP function-alities help you schedule and implement only those protocols that are genuinely required. The results and diagnoses are stored in the applica-tion, and this data can then be called on when work centers need to be re-assigned. In addition to this, other important information about employee health can be recorded; for example, data on the vaccinations that an employee has had. Needless to say, sensitive data such as this is protected by a restrictive access concept to ensure that all data protection regulations are complied with.

6.4   Adherence to Product-Specific Environmental Protection Regulations

Examples of product-specific environmental protection regulations include the RoHS directive (Restriction of the Use of Certain Hazardous Substances in Electrical and Electronic Equipment) and the *Integrated Product Policy* (IPP).

The aim of RoHS is to reduce the risk posed by the huge increase in disposable electronic goods by banning toxic and dangerous components in these products.

RoHS

The aim of IPP is to monitor and evaluate the environmental aspects of a product in all its phases, from planning to production to disposal. The idea is to then use the detailed knowledge of the environmental effects gained in this way to minimize and avoid negative results. Ideally, throughout the entire value chain of a product, all producers are responsible for their part of the product lifecycle to ensure that the product in question doesn't represent an additional burden on the environment. If IPP is applied in a consistent manner to all products, it should be possible to reduce the overall environmental burden created by the national economy in the mid-term.

Integrated Product Policy

The *Compliance for Products* (CfP) solution, which SAP provides in conjunction with TechniData, enables you to manage all product-specific environmental protection regulations. The product contents are specified in detail in this solution. During production processes, checks are built in that determine whether hazardous substances were involved in the production of the intermediates or the finished products. These checks can be integrated into the relevant business processes as early as the initial stages of product research and development. The results of the checks are documented and can be made available automatically to suppliers and customers. In the European Union, the German "Blue Angel," a certification for environmentally-friendly products and services, is one such check.

Compliance for Products

6.5 Compliance Management and Emissions Management

SAP Environmental Compliance provides functions that help enterprises comply with emissions regulations. To do this, it obtains all of the required information from the connected SAP ERP applications and compiles this data for emissions management purposes. SAP Environmental Compliance ensures that enterprise-wide business processes do not violate the applicable environmental protection regulations and that the process of creating the sustainability reports required for the purposes of *corporate social responsibility* (CSR) is automated.

Plant assets

The first step is to describe the plant assets for each location. All assets that release emissions into the environment have to be included. Different regulations apply, depending on the emission type. SAP Environmental Compliance provides functions for describing plants and facilities. It also provides functional support for the administration of official approval of plant assets. The level of overall emissions per plant and the resulting burden on the environment are calculated automatically. SAP Environmental Compliance also provides functions that calculate the effect on future emissions of a planned change to the plant, and stores target key figures for emissions. The actual emissions figures are then compared to these target figures and documented on a regular basis. These reports are available both to investors and to the general public.

Emissions monitoring

The emissions level of each location is monitored and recorded, and the system checks regularly whether all regulations are being complied with. If changes are made to the plant, these changes have to be checked to establish whether they will have any effects on emissions levels. If the emissions are outside the specified limits, an alarm workflow is triggered.

Documentation and reporting

Because the individual pieces of information are all stored in the SAP system, the required reports for the regulation authorities and investors can be automatically generated in the system. The following important report types are supported:

▶ Title V reports for the U.S. environmental protection authority

▶ Environmental data for the European Pollutant Emission Register

▶ Environmental data for the Global Reporting Initiative

▶ Guidelines for sustainability reporting

To ensure that the report reaches the correct addressees, the relevant authorities and the contact data of the person responsible in each case are also stored.

EU member states are required to have a national allocation plan for greenhouse gases. This plan specifies the quantity of greenhouse gases that are emitted in a country within a given time period. These quantities are then distributed across the individual enterprises. An enterprise that emits more than the permitted level must apply for an emissions certificate from another company. Enterprises that emit less than the permitted level, on the other hand, can sell emissions certificates. SAP Environmental Compliance functions support this trade in emissions certificates. When an enterprise is selling a certificate, it has to provide detailed evidence that it has not exceeded the emissions limit. The corresponding reporting function in the SAP system, which can be called automatically, enables enterprises to do this. Another support provided by the SAP system comes in the form of data exchange interfaces, for example, interfaces providing price data for emissions certificates and interfaces that connect the SAP system to emissions marketplaces and emissions trading platforms.

Emissions certificate

SAP Environmental Compliance thus enables enterprises that operate globally in a more environmentally friendly and sustainable manner to represent this, as far as possible, in a transparent way, using the available information. For this purpose, SAP Environmental Compliance processes data from the following connected SAP applications, among others:

Integration with SAP ERP

▶ Material consumption data out of SAP Supply Chain Management (SAP SCM).

▶ Data on emissions-related substances out of SAP Product Lifecycle Management (SAP PLM).

▶ Equipment data and functional hierarchies from the technical plant management function out of SAP Product Lifecycle Management (SAP PLM).

▶ Data on maintenance costs out of SAP ERP Financials.

If God did create the world, his main concern in doing so was certainly not that we should understand it. (Albert Einstein)

7   An Outlook Ahead and a Product Roadmap

The great success of SAP products in the area of governance, risk, and compliance shows that there is huge demand in enterprises for support for this area in the form of integrated IT applications. SAP is continuing to respond to this demand and will further develop its existing applications on an ongoing basis. The goal is to integrate the GRC applications into a CFO (Chief Financial Officer) cockpit. SAP has acquired the Business Objects company and the product portfolios of SAP and Business Objects have been merged, with the result that all of the essential information required by the CFO of an enterprise is available at a glance. Details on the content of the merged portfolios and a schedule are currently being worked out as part of the process of integrating the Business Objects products. This chapter provides an overview of the current status of the plans for 2008 and 2009, and a holistic overview of the future CFO portfolio.

7.1   Overview of 2008 and 2009

Before we look in detail at the individual components, let's first gain an insight into the product launch process for SAP solutions.

7.1.1   SAP Ramp-Up – The Product Launch Process for SAP Solutions

The lifecycle of SAP solutions specifies that after the planning, development, and testing phases, the software is validated. This validation occurs when the development departments transfer the software to the quality team. As part of the validation process, the new software is installed and implemented using the official product documentation. Teams of experienced internal consultants are used in this implementation process. After the software has been successfully validated, the SAP Ramp-Up process — the product launch process for SAP solutions — begins (see Figure 7.1).

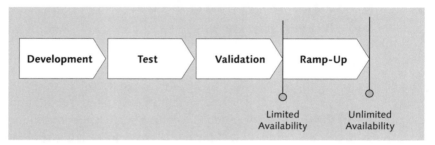

Figure 7.1   SAP Development and Product Launch Process

Having a successfully completed validation phase as a prerequisite for the Ramp-Up in this way ensures that the first customers of the new software receive a high-quality product.

An important element of the Ramp-Up is that the product is available on a limited basis. Customers who want to have the advantage of being the first in their industry to implement the new SAP functionality and go live with it have to register their interest with their responsible SAP sales executive. The aim of the Ramp-Up program is to have a number of customers who use the new functionality and can serve as reference customers. The limited availability period is also used to ensure that there are enough experts (such as consultants) in the subsequent mass-availability stage to deal on an unlimited basis with the inquiries from the market after the Ramp-Up phase ends.

During the Ramp-Up program, a specific implementation scope and a customer-specific support and training model are used to bring the selected customers to the successful operations stage. The Ramp-Up process proceeds as follows.

Customer requirements analysis

The first step is a customer requirements analysis. This analysis compares the customer's requirements with the functional scope of the new SAP

294

solutions. The project is approved only if all of the experts agree that an implementation will meet the customer's needs. Right from the analysis phase on, the customer has the support of SAP experts who know the latest functionalities in detail.

This support model is continued during the remainder of the implementation phase; a SAP Consulting expert supports the customer on-site. This expert, in turn, has direct contact with a specialist from the SAP development group. The development specialist is part of a virtual team of experts that forms part of the Ramp-Up back office. This support structure means that all of the required SAP specialists are available as needed at short notice to answer customer queries. This model also guarantees that even the most complex questions can be answered competently and quickly.

Support model

Needless to say, training materials are available right from the start of the ramp-up phase. Knowledge transfer relating to the latest functionalities is carried out by means of e-learning materials and training courses that are held in SAP training centers.

Knowledge transfer

Additional detailed information on the SAP Ramp-Up process is available at *www.service.sap.com/rampup*.

7.1.2 SAP Solutions for Governance, Risk, and Compliance – Status and Roadmap

The following is a brief overview of the availability of the current releases of SAP GRC products (see Figure 7.2). Note in relation to all information about future releases that the statuses specified here represent a non-binding plan that is subject to change.

Chapter 2, SAP GRC Process Control, is based on the latest release, 2.5. SAP GRC Process Control 2.5 has been available on a limited basis since the first quarter of 2008. Unlimited availability is scheduled for the end of the third quarter of 2008. Based on what is known at the time of print, the subsequent release, SAP GRC Process Control 3.0, will be restricted available in the second quarter of 2009. There are also plans to integrate SAP GRC Process Control with SAP GRC Risk Management 3.0 and

An outlook ahead at SAP GRC Process Control

additional industry-specific functionalities, such as functionalities for the pharmaceutical industry.

Q1 2008	Q2 2008	Q3 2008	Q4 2008	Q1 2009	Q2 2009	Q3 2009	Q4 2009
Ramp-Up Start Process Control 2.5		End of Ramp-Up Process Control 2.5			Start of Ramp-Up Process Control 2.5		End of Ramp-Up Process Control 2.5
Ramp-Up Start Access Control 5.3			End of Ramp-Up Access Control 5.3				Start of Ramp-Up Access Control 6.0
End of Ramp-Up Risk Mgt. 2.0					Start of Ramp-Up Risk Mgt. 3.0		End of Ramp-Up Risk Mgt. 3.0
	End of Ramp-Up Global Trade 7.2			Start of Ramp-Up Global Trade 8.0		End of Ramp-Up Global Trade 8.0	

Figure 7.2 Planned Roadmap 2008-2009

An outlook ahead at SAP GRC Access Control

Chapter 3, SAP GRC Access Control, is based on the latest release, 5.2. The subsequent release, SAP GRC Access Control 5.3, has been available on a limited basis since the first quarter of 2008. Unlimited availability is planned for the start of the fourth quarter of 2008. Besides some fundamental performance optimizations, SAP GRC Access Control 5.3 also contains a range of extended functions, including a more comprehensive standard reporting concept. Based on what is known at the time of print, the subsequent release, SAP GRC Access Control 6.0, will be restricted available in the fourth quarter of 2009.

An outlook ahead at SAP GRC Risk Management

Chapter 4, SAP GRC Risk Management, is based on the latest release, 2.0. This release has been generally available on the market since the first quarter of 2008. Based on what is known at the time of print, the subsequent release, SAP GRC Risk Management 3.0, will be available on a limited basis in the second quarter of 2009. Based on what is currently known, planned extensions in this release will include integration with SAP GRC Process Control 3.0 and extended integration scenarios with SAP ERP.

The current release of SAP GRC Global Trade Services is 7.2, with unlimited availability scheduled for the second quarter of 2008. Based on what is currently known, the subsequent release, SAP GRC Global Trade Services 8.0, will be available on a limited basis in the first quarter of 2009. This release will include extensions that are necessitated by legal changes in customs management.

An outlook ahead at SAP Global Trade Services

7.2 Strategic Look Ahead After Integration with Business Objects in SAP

Enterprises today are faced with the difficult fact that never before has there been so much information that needs to be read, analyzed, and evaluated before decisions are made. What is more, this flow of information isn't restricted to internal company data; it's essential to include all of the relevant information from the entire value chain.

This means that information from external sources about customers and suppliers also has to be included in the decision-making process. The persons responsible within enterprises need data to be formatted in such a way that enables them to evaluate all of the external and internal facts at a glance. Also required are tools that the persons responsible can use easily to detail the evaluations on the basis of the individual decision or to shift the focus of the evaluation to a different topic area or key figure area.

External information

With the acquisition of Business Objects, SAP has taken a significant step toward offering a holistic, tailored software product portfolio to deal with the previously mentioned issues. This portfolio consists of the following solution packages (see Figure 7.3):

Holistic product portfolio

- ▸ Business performance optimization applications
  - ▸ Financial Performance Management
  - ▸ Governance, Risk, and Compliance (GRC)
- ▸ Business Intelligence Platform
  - ▸ Visualization and Reporting
  - ▸ Enterprise Query, Reporting, and Analysis

▸ Data Integration and Data Quality

▸ Master Data Services

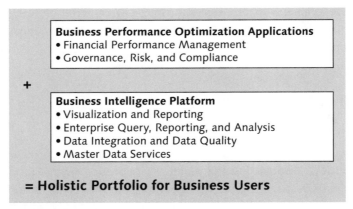

Figure 7.3 The Business User Product Portfolio

These product packages help enterprises to use accurate and relevant enterprise data. The special applications and tools they contain enable users to analyze information, structure data, and manage data. The persons responsible in enterprises thus have access to all of the information they require to analyze and manage the enterprise's output, including financial management. What is more, they also get an insight into the most critical processes within the enterprise. This business-relevant data can be evaluated accurately and in a timely fashion and thus can also be used as a solid information basis for more far-reaching decisions. The responsible persons on all hierarchical levels of the enterprise are therefore in a position to conduct their daily work as productively as possible and to adhere to the enterprise's code of conduct.

7.2.1 Business Performance Optimization Applications

The aim of the business performance optimization applications is to provide information that can be used for business optimization purposes and, in doing so, to make transparent what the individual user contributes to business optimization and what he is responsible for in this area.

The Financial Performance Management functions enable financial managers to understand their enterprises' situation in terms of corporate performance and to identify the right parameters for enhancing total output. The applications cover all of the required aspects, including profitability, planning processes, budgeting, and balance sheet consolidation.

Managing financial services

The Governance, Risk, and Compliance applications provide an enterprise-wide insight into compliance (and noncompliance) with internal and external regulations.

Governance, risk, and compliance

7.2.2 Business Intelligence Platform

A central success factor for enterprises is that all employees are able to access the information they require, when they require it. The source of the information should be irrelevant. Also, the process of accessing information should be simple and usable from the user's viewpoint.

The Business Intelligence Platform provides a technical infrastructure for data access and enables users to create accurate and up-to-date business analyses on the basis of this data. Needless to say, comprehensive security and revision functions ensure that access is granted only when a user genuinely requires it. All of the relevant users are thus provided with information that is tailored and formatted to meet their needs. It's also possible to incorporate users who have a business relationship with the enterprise but aren't employed there.

An important aspect of business intelligence is that the Business Intelligence Platform is integrated with text analysis functions. This enables data from the Internet and email to be used as sources for information analysis. Other external sources can be used, too. This may be useful if, for example, key figures on competitors need to be included in analyses. Companies that provide this kind of information include Thomson Reuters (formerly Thomson Financial), and Dun and Bradstreet.

The Visualization and Reporting package contains features that report authors can use to prepare reports based on all kind of sources. The report content is converted to graphical reports that provide users with a clear, interactive key figures cockpit. This key figures cockpit or dashboard is a visualized, compressed representation of the information. The

Reports and visualization

figures are displayed in the form of a speedometer, a thermometer, or traffic lights, and can be made available to the entire enterprise with a minimal amount of work. Microsoft applications can also be used as data sources for graphical reports.

Business analyses, reports, and queries

The Enterprise Query, Reporting, and Analysis package enables users to navigate through business data. It doesn't matter whether the data in question is structured or unstructured. Nor does it matter from the navigational viewpoint whether the data source to be analyzed is located in SAP applications or third-party applications. From the viewpoints of reporting and navigation, this application overcomes the disadvantages of heterogeneous IT landscapes and the resulting standalone data clusters.

Data integration and data quality

The Data Integration and Data Quality package enables users to obtain data both from SAP systems and third-party systems and thus to create a flexible and reliable data basis. The package also contains functionality for subsequently harmonizing the data and integrating it into reports.

Master data maintenance

When data is stored and processed in multiple heterogeneous systems, inconsistencies are often the result. The Master Data Services package supports the consolidation and harmonization of master data. The focus is on critical master data, such as, among other things, data on business partners, products, employees, and finances. This application thus provides a centralized overview of all strategically important master data.

The Authors

Sabine Schöler has worked at SAP AG since 1993, where she has managed complex SAP implementation and development projects. From 2003, she used this experience in the Service Solution Management department to coordinate and further develop the SAP Service portfolio and the SAP methods for SAP solutions. Since 2003, she has been responsible for the ramp-up programs of various SAP products.

Olaf Zink studied Industrial Engineering at the University of Kaiserslautern, Germany. In the main part of his studies, he specialized in the areas of controlling, internal accounting, human resources management, and work organization. Since 1997, Olaf Zink has held various roles and positions at SAP, mainly in SAP Consulting. Initially, he worked as a Solution Consultant in Financials before moving on to roles as Project Manager and Business Solution Architect with responsibility for international SAP implementation projects. From 2004, he closely studied the Sarbanes-Oxley Act and successfully rolled out Management of Internal Controls, the predecessor software to GRC Process Control, for several SAP customers around the world.

Index

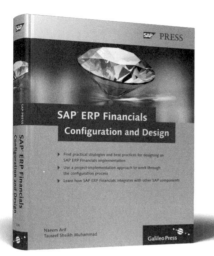

Find practical strategies and best practices for designing an SAP ERP Financials implementation

Use a project-implementation approach to work through the configuration process

Learn how SAP ERP Financials integrates with other SAP modules

Naeem Arif, Sheikh Tauseef

SAP ERP Financials: Configuration and Design

Master the most important issues involved in designing and configuring an SAP Financial implementation using the real-world, holistic business information provided in this compre-hensive reference. You'll learn everything from the general areas of SAP Financials and how they fit in the SAP landscape, to how the General Ledger can work for you.
This invaluable guide is the one resource you need to understand the configuration and design process, the enterprise structure, reporting, data migration, Accounts Payable and Receivables, Financials integration with other modules, and all other critical areas of SAP Financials.

467 pp., 2008, 79,95 Euro / US$ 79.95
ISBN 978-1-59229-136-6

>> www.sap-press.de/1462

Provides a detailed overview of proper Year-End Closing proce-dures for AA, IM, and PS

Includes hands-on guidance for managing the frustrating neces-sity of infrequent, once-per-year closing processes

Teaches effective, replicable, real-world techniques for stream-lining Year-End Closing

Thomas Michael, Kent Bettisworth

Year-End Closing for AA, IM, and PS in SAP

SAP Press Essentials 44

Year-End Closing for AA, IM, and PS in SAP is a hands-on guide to the proper steps for correct Year-End Closing procedures for SAP AA, IM, and PS. The book will walk the reader through the essential steps for performing an effective Year-End Close for each of the Applications covered. It will help practitioners develop correct, reusable processes for accomplishing Year-End Closes in AA, IM, and PS, with the goal of minimizing the need to "reinvent the wheel" at every new closing period.

approx. 200 pp., 68,– Euro / US$ 85
ISBN 978-1-59229-201-1, Dec 2008

>> www.sap-press.de/1765

Get the most out of your SAP ERP Financials implementation using the practical tips and techniques provided

Achieve operational efficiencies by adopting the process-driven approach detailed throughout the book

Find useful value-added activities and important strategy ideas in the case studies and real-world examples

Shivesh Sharma

Optimize Your SAP ERP Financials Implementation

The real work in SAP Financials begins after the implementation is complete. This is when it's time to optimize and use SAP Financials in the most efficient way for your organization. Optimization entails understanding unique client scenarios and then developing solutions to meet those requirements, while staying within the project's budgetary and timeline constraints. This book teaches consultants and project managers to think about and work through best practice tools and methodologies, before choosing the ones to use in their own implementations.

The variety of real-life case studies and examples used to illustrate the business processes and highlight how SAP Financials can support these processes, make this a practical and valuable book for anyone looking to optimize their SAP Financials implementation.

676 pp., 2008, 79,95 Euro / US$ 79.95
ISBN 978-1-59229-160-1

>> www.sap-press.de/1583

Discover how product costing works and
integrates with other modules

Learn about Integrated Planning, Product
Cost Planning, Manufacturing Methods,
Reporting, and more

Reduce long run times during month-end
processing

John Jordan

Product Cost Controlling with SAP

If you are looking for a resource that shows you how to set up Controlling for
Product Costing and how it integrates with other modules, this book is for you.
This comprehensive resource is for anyone in Financials, Production Planning,
Purchasing, and Sales and Distribution with an interest in the integrated areas
of product costing.
Learn how overhead costs flow from financial postings to cost centers and then
on to manufacturing orders. Also learn about the material ledger, transfer pricing,
reporting, and discover how to address common problem areas, including month-end
processing, long run times, and message and variance analysis.

approx. 450 pp., 79,95 Euro / US$ 79.95
ISBN 978-1-59229-167-0, Nov 2008

>> **www.sap-press.de/1610**

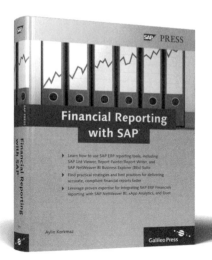

Understand and implement strategies for maximizing Financials reporting capabilities

Learn and apply best practices for simplifying, streamlining, and automating financial and management reporting

Leverage proven expertise concerning the integration of Financials reporting with BI, xApp Analytics, and Duet™

Aylin Korkmaz

Financial Reporting with SAP

This book provides finance and IT teams with best practices for delivering financial reports faster, more accurately, and in compliance with various international accounting standards. Featuring step-by-step coverage of all major FI reporting functions (including Sub-Ledger, Corporate Finance Management, and Governance, Risk & Compliance), this timely book will help you streamline and simplify financial business processes and automate financial and management reporting in SAP ERP Financials. It includes coverage of integrating FI reporting with Business Intelligence, xApp Analytics, and Duet™.

668 pp., 2008, 79,95 Euro / US$ 79.95
ISBN 978-1-59229-179-3

>> www.sap-press.de/1654

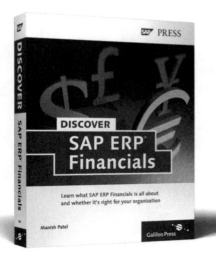

Discover what SAP Financials (FI) is all about and whether it's right for your organization

Lean how this powerful, time-tested tool can improve your financial processes and save you money

Explore the major modules, including receivable and payables, tax accounting, cost accounting, payroll accounting, travel management, and more

Manish Patel

Discover SAP ERP Financials

Business financials are an essential part of every business, large or small. Whether you just need basic accounting or you perform complex financial audits and reporting, your business needs a software tool that meets your needs.   Discover SAP Financials explains how SAP can provide this solution. Using an easy-to-follow style filled with real-world examples, case studies, and practical tips and pointers, the book teaches the fundamental capabilities and uses of the core modules of SAP Financials. As part of the Discover SAP series, the book is written to help new users, decision makers considering SAP, and power users moving to the latest version learn everything they need to determine if SAP Financials is the right solution for your organization.

This is the one comprehensive resource you need to get started with SAP Financials.

544 pp., 2008, 39,95 Euro / US$ 39.95
ISBN 978-1-59229-184-7

>> www.sap-press.de/1672

Obtain a comprehensive framework
for implementing Business Process
Management

Find insights and experience from
leading companies on their BPM
journey

Learn how to benefit from service-
oriented architecture using BPM

Jim Hagemann Snabe, Ann Rosenberg,
Charles Møller, Mark Scavillo

Business Process Management - the SAP Roadmap

This unique book finally sheds light on Business Process Management - a term often
misunderstood and misused. It explains what BPM is, how to implement
it in your company, and it gives real-life examples of BPM implementations. The
authors explain the phase model and the building blocks of the BPM approach
(both, for the business and the IT perspective), and they also cover the important
topic of aligning BPM and SOA concepts. Here, readers get invaluable information
on modeling and composing tools, enterprise SOA, project milestones, and
monitoring approaches.

approx. 411 pp., 69,95 Euro / US$ 69.95
ISBN 978-1-59229-231-8, Nov 2008

>> www.sap-press.de/1849

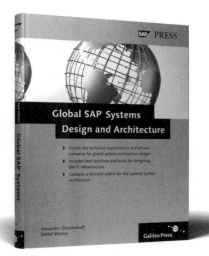

Covers the technical requirements and proven scenarios for global system architecture design

Includes best practices and tools for designing the IT infrastructure

Contains a decision matrix for the optimal system architecture

Alexander Davidenkoff, Detlef Werner

Global SAP Systems – Design and Architecture

When planning an international SAP system implementation, the central question is often whether one global SAP system or several distributed local systems will work best. To answer this question in the best possible way, project managers, IT managers, and other key decision makers can use this book as their comprehensive guide. The book provides the business-relevant facts and technical details necessary to design and bring to realization successful international SAP system implementation projects, and readers will learn about system requirements, the factors that influence the system architecture, and the available options for various different system architectures. And that's just for starters: the book also includes valuable tips, best practices, exclusive customer reports, and much more.

317 pp., 2008, 69,95 Euro / US$ 69.95
ISBN 978-1-59229-183-0

>> www.sap-press.de/1665